WITHDRAWN
UTSA LIBRARIES

Chekhov and his prose

Chekhov and his prose
by Thomas Winner

Holt, Rinehart and Winston
New York   Chicago   San Francisco

Copyright © 1966 by Thomas Winner. All rights reserved, including the right to reproduce this book or portions thereof in any form. Published simultaneously in Canada by Holt, Rinehart and Winston of Canada, Limited. Library of Congress Catalog Card Number: 66-10264
First Edition

Designer: Ernst Reichl
89475-0116
Printed in the United States of America

To Irene

Contents

Preface

Work on the present study was initiated in 1956—as part of a seminar I conducted as Fulbright lecturer at the École des Hautes Études of the Sorbonne in Paris—and was continued in seminars and research in the United States afer 1957. I wish to express my gratitude to the Duke University Research Council, the Horace Rackham Graduate School of the University of Michigan, the Social Science Research Council of the University of Michigan, and the Center for Russian Studies at the University of Michigan for grants in support of research and the writing of the present study. A number of my friends and colleagues have read the manuscript in its various stages and drafts. Special gratitude is due to Professors H. W. Dewey, James O. Ferrell, Ladislav Matejka, and John Mersereau for their careful reading of the manuscript and for their many excellent, stimulating suggestions. Professor Alan Gilbert and M. M. Gilbert read parts of the manuscript and offered valuable help. My colleagues, Professors Assya Humesky and Edith Iguatieff, kindly permitted me to consult them about the in-

ix

tricacies of the Russian language which are indispensable for
stylistic analysis. Needless to say, no one but myself is re-
sponsible for any inaccuracies in the manuscript or for any
of its shortcomings.

My main debt, however, is to my wife who collaborated
closely in the development of the manuscript. Her stimulating
thoughts, her insights into the literary problems, and her wide
knowledge have helped me immeasurably in my work, and it
is with great thankfulness that I dedicate this book to her.

The following publishers and journals have kindly permitted
me to use material which had originally appeared elsewhere:
*The Slavic and East European Journal, The University of
Nebraska Press, Brill and Company* (Leiden, Holland), and the
Indiana Slavic Studies.

Transliteration Table

Symbol	Approximate English Pronunciation	Russian Equivalent
C, c	*ts* as in tsar	Ц, ц
Č, č	*ch* as in church	Ч, ч
Š, š	*sh* as in ship	Ш, ш
Ž, ž	as in lei*s*ure, a*z*ure, French *journal*	Ж, ж
X, x	as in German *Buch*, Scottish Loch	Х, х
J, j	preceding vowel:	
ja	as *y* in English yacht	Я
ju	as *y* in English you	Ю
	(*e*, when initial or following a vowel, is always pronounced *ye*, as in yet, even though no *j* is written in transliteration)	e

	in final position or before a consonant:	-й
aj	as *i* in English high	
ej	as *ay* in English may	
oj	as *y* in English boy	
uj	approximately as *-ewey* in English dewey, but pronounced as one syllable	
ij	lengthens preceding vowel, as *-ee* in see; e.g. Dostoevskij	
'	softens the preceding consonant like *t* in the English pronunciation of tune as opposed to the American	-Ь
È, è	Non-palatalized *e*. Somewhat like French *è*, but shorter	Э, э

Russian names have been transcribed in a system familiar to English-speaking readers. Thus I have rendered Tolstoy, Chekhov, etc. However in all Russian titles as well as in Russian quotations, i.e. in material which is primarily meant for the reader with a knowledge of Russian, a system of exact transliteration has been employed in which each symbol stands for a Russian letter.

Introduction

Anton Pavlovich Chekhov was born on January 17, 1860 in the Russian town of Taganrog on the Sea of Azov and died in 1904. He is recognized today as perhaps the greatest of short-story writers whose innovations in form and technique as well as expressions of many hitherto untried themes have immeasurably altered our literary traditions. His plays, also revolutionary, were first produced in the Stanislavsky theater and have influenced world drama ever since.

Chekhov's father, Pavel Egorovich, was a severe and intensely religious man who insisted that Anton and his brothers take part in extended church services and work long hours in the small family shop. In his later life Chekhov was to say that he had no childhood at all. His studies began in a Greek school in Taganrog and later he enrolled in the *gimnaziya*, where he showed a marked interest in literature and wrote for the school newspaper. It was in the *gimnaziya* that Chekhov acquired the nickname Antosha Chekhonte, which he subsequently used to sign his humorous stories, and even some of his early serious works.

In 1876, the family store failed and Chekhov's parents were obliged to move to Moscow in order to escape debtor's prison. Anton remained in Taganrog for two years to complete his studies after which he enrolled in the medical school of the University of Moscow. (He became a Doctor of Medicine in 1884 and, although he did not intensively pursue the medical profession, his scientific interests are ever-present in his writings.)

Soon after he came to Moscow, Chekhov began to contribute to popular humor magazines. His quick facility enabled him to turn out quantities of jokes, anecdotes, and potboilers of all kinds which provided a necessary additional income for his impoverished family. At the same time Chekhov composed more complicated anecdotes as well as some parodies of current literary styles, notably of the cheap boulevard literature. A few of the works of this early period are, in fact, not comic at all, but serious in theme, and anticipate to some extent his later writings. Chekhov wrote for the humor magazines until 1887.

In 1884, his first collection of stories appeared entitled *Tales of Melpomene.* Two years later he contributed his first piece to a serious journal, *New Times (Novoe Vremja),* a conservative Russian daily paper whose editor was the writer A. S. Suvorin. In spite of their political differences, Chekhov and Suvorin became close friends, a friendship which continued until 1897, when Chekhov's defense of Dreyfus and support of Zola's contribution to this case brought him into opposition with Suvorin. It is in Chekhov's letters to Suvorin that we find many of his most interesting statements concerning his literary views and activities. The break with Suvorin marked Chekhov's increasing political liberalism and the beginning of his friend-

ship with several writers of the left, including Maxim
Gorky. When in 1902, the Russian Academy, under pres-
sure from the government, rescinded Gorky's membership,
Chekhov resigned in protest.

We can, somewhat arbitrarily, divide Chekhov's creative career into three main periods. During the first period,
1880 through 1887, Chekhov contributed primarily to
humor journals and wrote at a rapid pace. These early
rough works already indicate, however, Chekhov's wit and
irony which is to increase in subtlety and indirection in the
later serious writings.

After 1887 Chekhov wrote more carefully and abandoned
the humor journals. The second period continues until
1893. In 1888 Chekhov wrote the long story "The Steppe,"
which introduces his impressionistic style and experiments
with the actionless plot. The themes of sensitivity and
beauty contrasted to banality and ugliness, of life contrasted
to death and that of isolation dominate this work. During
these years other works, including "A Dreary Story" (1889),
reveal Chekhov's search for a coherent world view which
begins to absorb his thoughts and brings him to study
sympathetically some aspects of Tolstoy's philosophy, in
particular the doctrine of nonresistance to evil. Chekhov
undertook a trip to the penal colony of Sakhalin in 1889
to study Russian prison life which he described in a long
monograph, entitled *The Island of Sakhalin* (1891-1894).
This experience seemed to alter Chekhov's attitude to Tolstoyanism. In a number of short stories, especially in "Ward
No. 6" (1892), the Tolstoyan doctrine of nonresistance to
evil is satirically treated.

Other themes important in this period include the oppression of the peasants ("Peasant Wives," 1891), the hypocrisy of the upper classes ("The Wife," 1892), the *vie
manquée* ("The Teacher of Literature," 1889, 1894), and

the Narcissus theme ("The Princess," 1889 and "The Grass-hopper," 1892).

During the last period from 1883-1904, several stories continue to reflect Chekhov's concern with the Russian social scene, particularly with the peasant milieu ("In the Ravine," 1900, "My Life," 1896, and "The Peasants," 1897), as well as with the emergence of a new bourgeoisie ("A Woman's Kingdom," 1894, "Three Years," 1895, and "A Doctor's Visit," 1898). Other stories also voice earlier themes, now expressed with greater complexity. The problem of isolation, the *vie manquée,* and the conflict between beauty and banality are continued in "Rothschild's Fiddle" (1894), "The Teacher of Literature" (1894), "The Lady With the Pet Dog" (1899), and others. These three periods mark the evolution of Chekhov's style from that of the early humor stories to the complex forms and techniques we shall examine.

An important event in Chekhov's life was his association with Stanislavsky's Moscow Art Theater in 1898 which continued until his death. In May, 1901 Chekhov married one of Stanislavsky's best actresses, Olga Knipper.

Chekhov's brief life was marked by ill health. In the late Eighties there were the first warnings of tuberculosis of the lungs. From 1897 until his death in 1904, illness forced Chekhov to live either in the Crimea, or in German or French health resorts. Except for a few brief intervals he was no longer able to return to Moscow or to St. Petersburg, cities which he loved.

Chekhov's career comes at the end of the great age of Russian literature which gave the world the novels of Tolstoy and of Dostoyevsky. When Chekhov began to write for the humor journals in 1881, Tolstoy had completed his major novels, had rejected these works as frivolous, and was turning to didactic works, Dostoyevsky died in 1881. Chekhov's artistic life thus spans the end of the "golden age" of Russian literature and the threshold of what has been called the "silver age," associated with the Russian Symbolist movement.

Clearly Chekhov's works evolve from the Russian realistic prose tradition and most particularly from the lyrical and sometimes melancholy atmosphere of the short stories of Turgenev, who died in 1883. In the European tradition, his closest relationship is probably to Maupassant, from whom he learned the art of brevity and the striking conclusion of the story which he is to develop with such deftness.

The new literary form created by Chekhov indeed initiated the modern short story. Many Russian writers of the turn of the century, including Bunin, Kuprin, and even Gorky, are in part Chekhov's disciples. The actionless plot of so many of Chekhov's stories became the model for Bunin's prose poems. Today, there is hardly a more popular author in Russia. In addition to the many individual editions of Chekhov's writings, the Soviet Academy of Sciences is now preparing a new definitive and fully annotated edition of his works and letters which will comprise thirty volumes. A somewhat shorter collection of the complete works appeared between 1944 and 1951.

In Western literature Chekhov's influence has never abated.[1] Katherine Mansfield is perhaps the most strikingly indebted to Chekhov's art. Many relationships of Chekhov to the Existentialists and to other contemporary prose writers and dramatists needs further investigation. Thus Chekhovian themes, for example that of the senseless and absurdly wasted life of the little man, and that of isolation, lack of communication, and ineffectiveness of action are expressed in the works of Kafka, Camus, as well as in the contemporary works of writers of the French *nouveau roman,* and in the modern actionless drama of such writers as Becket and others. It is our task, however, to examine Chekhov's works themselves in this study.

As to the approach taken in this study, while I do not wish to ignore the contributions which extrinsic analysis can make in understanding Chekhov's writings, my own approach will be most commensurate with an immanent one. I shall consider the work of literature itself as a configuration encompassing its themes, its motifs, and its composition, as well as its devices and techniques, and its overall form and style.

Nevertheless, a work of art is always related to its environment. It is the *literary* environment which is of particular interest here and especially the literary traditions and conventions which Chekhov inherited and, in so many respects, changed. A basic assumption in this study is that each work of art is not only an independent whole but is also part of a tradition which the writer cannot ignore. Thus a certain tension exists in a literary work between the artistic heritage and the creative changes wrought by a great artist. The intellectual environment is also significant. Therefore Chekhov's evolving world view, which directly affected the totality of his works, will be explored within the context of the philosophical direction of some of the stories. Finally, one hopes to understand the development, the function and the role of all these elements within the configuration of Chekhov's art.

T. W.

Ann Arbor, Michigan
Fall, 1965

Chekhov and his prose

Chapter 1 / The Literary Beginnings
Chekhov the Humorist

At the age of nineteen the young medical student Anton Pavlovich Chekhov contributed his first short pieces to the Moscow humor magazines. Indeed, two years earlier, when Chekhov was still a student in Taganrog, he had submitted to his brother Alexander his earliest efforts in the vain hope that Alexander might find a publisher.[1]

On December 24, 1879, Chekhov sent a short parody, signed simply ". . . v" to the St. Petersburg journal, *The Dragonfly (Strekoza)*. Chekhov was to feel that this date marked the beginning of his literary career.[2] The acceptance of the story was announced through the *Dragonfly's* column "Mailbag" on January 13, 1880. The editor wrote:

To Mr. A. Ch-v. Drachevka Street. Not bad at all. We shall print it. Our blessings to your future struggle.[3]

The acceptance in 1883 of his story, "Two Romances," (*Dva romana*), by the significant St. Petersburg humor magazine, *Fragments (Oskolki)*, marked a turning point in Chekhov's career. The editor, N. A. Leykin, a writer of popular humor stories, met Chekhov in Moscow and, impressed by his talent, invited him to become a steady contributor, an important compliment. When Chekhov later gave Leykin a volume of his stories it was inscribed, "To my literary god-father."[4]

From 1883 to 1886, most of Chekhov's stories were published in *Fragments* and Chekhov's productivity began to increase prodigiously. In 1883 alone, he published over a hundred stories, although he later included only 20 of these in his collected works which appeared between the years 1899 to 1903. During the next three years, Chekhov continued to dash off stories at a rapid pace: 65 in 1884, 113 in 1885, and 109 in 1886.

In March 1886, the well-known novelist D. V. Grigorovich, who had read Chekhov's short story "The Huntsman" [*Eger*, 1885], wrote him praising his talent, but imploring him to write in a more leisurely fashion.[5] Chekhov replied gratefully, confessing to an early careless attitude toward literature and calling Grigorovich his "deeply beloved harbinger of glad tidings."[6] Chekhov resolved thereafter to work more slowly and escape from the creative confines in which he found himself. 1886 was, in fact, the last year in which Chekhov wrote predominantly humorous stories. In 1887, he still published 64 stories, but later their higher caliber led him to include 50 of them in his collective works. In 1888, only nine stories appeared in print, all of which were later included in the collective works. Many of these humor stories written during the first six years of Chekhov's creative career reveal a foretaste of interests and techniques which are found in his later art.

The earliest stories are largely the experiments of a student who is interested in form and who wishes to define his relationship to his literary predecessors. Chekhov's early writings were clearly influenced by Gogol, Lermontov and

Tolstoy, but the influence of Turgenev is particularly significant. Even in his earliest works, however, we find Chekhov rebelling against many conventions accepted by these writers. It was indeed almost inevitable therefore that Chekhov would take issue most importantly with Turgenev, from whom he had learned so much.

Traditional forms, typical of Turgenev's prose, such as lengthy introductions or elaborate prologues, digressions elucidating the hero's past, apostrophes to the reader, conventional denouements, and epilogues have little importance even in Chekhov's earliest works. Increasingly, he replaced them by terse introductions, impressionistic characterizations, internal rather than external action, and unexpected conclusions.

Two outstanding techniques lead to conclusions in Chekhov's early stories: the first, a resolution by means of a surprise ending, is well-known from Maupassant; but the second, a resolution by means of what has been called a zero ending,[7] is a Chekhovian innovation. In the first, more traditional method, the line of the story anticipates a predictable denouement; but instead the story turns in an unexpected direction, leading to a surprise ending. In the second form, however, the conflict leads to expectations of a dramatic conclusion, while in fact the story ends in a seemingly unmotivated relaxation of tensions, and without a climax. Both the surprise and the zero endings have in common the tension between the expected and the actual resolution which creates the aesthetic effect. The zero ending, which no longer relies so directly on outer action, has greatly influenced the short-story form ever since.

It is not surprising that the young Chekhov, who delighted in taking issue with existing styles and conventions, found parody an appealing medium. In parody, clichés, traditional styles or themes may be exaggerated and thus caricatured or, as Tynyanov[8] pointed out, they may be presented in a new and unaccustomed environment, which renders them absurd. Chekhov's parodies are not often satires of serious literature, but rather they generally caricature works at the periphery of literature, such as the comic sketches of the humor journals, popular ghost and melodramatic adventure stories, crime novels, and romantic fiction.

Chekhov's first published parody entitled "A Letter of the Don Landowner Stepan Vladimirovich N. to His Learned Neighbor Dr. Friedrich," appeared in *The Dragonfly* on March 9, 1880. The pompous manner and foolish thoughts of a poorly educated Russian landowner are parodied in a letter written in a baroque style which is interrupted by simple orthographic and stylistic mistakes, as well as lapses into popular usage. The landowner employs such redundancies as "mental ideas" (*umstvennye idei*) and "they think in their mind" (*mysljat v ume*).

Permit me, esteemed neighbor [*soseduška*], to introduce myself to you, though only through these ancient hieroglyphics; permit me mentally to shake your learned hand and to welcome you upon your arrival from St. Petersburg into our unworthy continent, inhabited by peasants and rural population, i.e. by a plebeian element.

High flown and colloquial comparisons are juxtaposed:

The Ruble, that sail of the nineteenth century, has no value for me; science has obscured it from my eyes by its wider reaching wings. Every discovery torments me like a little nail in my back [*kak gvozdik v spine*].

In this style, the landowner, who writes of his admiration for learning, observes foolishly that, "If we all derived from the monkeys, we should now be led from town to town to be shown by gypsies and we should pay money to show ourselves to each other . . ." He also asks if people can "exist on the moon if that body exists only at night and disappears during the day?" In answer to the question, "Why are the days short in winter and the nights long?" he replies, "because the days like all other objects—visible and invisible— contract in the cold . . ."

An early parody of romantic fiction was "One Thousand and One Passions, or A Terrible Night; A Novel in One Part with an Epilogue, (Dedicated to Victor Hugo)" [*Tysjača i odna strast', ili strašnaja noč; roman v odnoj časti s èpilogom (Posvjaščaetsja Viktoru Gjugo)*]. This work, again published by *The Dragonfly* (July 27, 1880), is a rather primitive piece which makes light of romantic clichés and of the highly metaphoric style and impatient pace of Hugo's prose. Comically inflated metaphors as, "What did I care about the burning house when in my breast 150 houses were aflame?" are frequent, as are clumsy pleonasms, such as "a bottomless pit without a bottom" (*bezdna bez dna*).*

Horror stories, common in the humor magazines in Chekhov's day, are parodied in several works written between 1883 and 1886. Among these are "The Crooked Mirror" (*Krivoe zerkalo*, 1883), the first of Chekhov's early stories to be included in his collected works; "A Terrible Night" (*Strašnaja noč'*, 1884) and "The Restless Guest" (*Bespokojnyj gost'*, 1886). In "The Crooked Mirror," the traditional magic mirror, in which all reflection is rendered beautiful, becomes a mirror whose crooked shape explains its miraculous qualities. A woman looking into the mirror suddenly finds herself beautiful and becomes enchanted by the mirror, the only object which has told her the truth. Her husband later discovers the secret of the mirror's success. Her ugliness is successfully distorted by the mirror's imperfections. Although his face is ruined by the mirror, he passionately loves the reflection of his wife which the mirror returns. Descriptions are in an exaggeratedly romantic style

* See Notes to Chapter I.

with hyperbolic images and systematic sound repetitions. Romantic clichés are made more grotesque by their association with realistic details.

My wife approached the mirror with hesitation and she also looked into it. Suddenly something terrible occurred. She paled, trembled all over and cried out. The candlestick dropped from her hands and rolled on the floor, extinguishing the flame. Darkness enveloped us. Then I heard something heavy falling to the floor: that was my wife who was fainting.

The wind moaned even more plaintively, rats ran about, mice rustled in the papers. My hair stood on end and moved when a shutter tore loose from a window and flew to the ground. The moon appeared in the window. I snatched up my wife . . . and carried her from the house of my ancestors. She did not awaken until the next evening.*

In two of Chekhov's best-known parodies, "The Swedish Match" (*Švedskaja spička*, 1883) and "The Shooting Party" (*Drama na oxote*, 1884), the subject of burlesque is the popular murder mystery. Surprise endings, preceded by elaborate complications including misleading clues and false evidence, caricature the traditional devices of the genre. In the denouement Chekhov ridicules the crime thriller conclusions. In "The Swedish Match," the apparent murder victim turns up in the end quite alive. He has simply been hiding with another man's wife. "The Shooting Party,"[9] relates a mysterious murder which is followed by a succession of dramatic events and misleading clues concerning the identity of the murderer. In the end, the trick is revealed: the murderer is the narrator himself.

Most of Chekhov's works published between 1880 and 1887 are not, however, parodies, but anecdotes or extended jokes, which achieve their effect by an element of surprise. A joke is characteristically a brief rendition of an incident

* See Notes to Chapter I.

or a conversation which leads to the expectation of a certain reply or solution which does not occur. Chekhov's anecdotes are distinguished from the jokes by their larger scope and action plot.

The earliest anecdotes usually conclude with a simple surprise ending which may be a consequence of a misunderstanding, a mistake, an ambiguous phrase, or an effort expended in vain. In some stories, however, it is the absence of the climax towards which the story builds, the apparently unmotivated fading of tension, or the zero ending, which creates the unexpected conclusion.

"The Decoration" [*Orden*, 1884] concludes with the more traditional surprise ending. A teacher, Pustyakov, has borrowed a government decoration which he wears to a dinner party only to find himself seated opposite a colleague who alone, among the assembled guests, knows that Pustyakov does not have the right to wear the decoration. Throughout the dinner the humiliated teacher eats and drinks using only one hand, covering his breast with the other in order to hide the decoration. A climax approaches as the teacher is asked to pass a glass of wine while he is standing, glass in hand, waiting for a toast to be pronounced. Now he must reveal the decoration which he has shielded. But the expected humiliation is converted into a farce when it becomes apparent that the colleague is also guilty. He, too, wears a borrowed decoration illegally. Two more surprises follow ironically: the other teacher's borrowed decoration is a higher one; Pustyakov, far from being chastened by this experience, only regrets that he did not secure a higher decoration. More subtle comedy is provided in the brief story "The Orator" (*Orator*, 1886). Zapoykin, the "orator" who can produce a speech for any occasion, is called upon to speak at the funeral of a high-placed bureaucrat. His speech is filled with rhetorical clichés and florid, well-turned phrases. In the end, it becomes clear however, that the orator has mistakenly described the wrong individual who is alive, present, and very angry.*

The most interesting of the early stories with a zero ending is "The Avenger" (*Mstitel'*, 1887). A man, who has surprised his wife with a lover, enters a gunsmith's shop bent on revenge. However, as the shopkeeper, with increasing enthusiasm, describes the murderous capacities of the various pistols, the husband's fury begins to give way to uneasy embarrassment. Sheepishly, he resorts to the purchase of a net to catch birds and escapes from the salesman with his ineffective acquisition. The expected melodramatic denouement fails to take place and, moreover, the general line of the story is inverted. Like an orchestral arrangement, the thoughts of the cuckolded husband express the deflation of tension as they are played in diminuendo against the rising fervor of the gunsmith's sales talk. The husband first reflects melodramatically: "I know what I must do . . . the foundations of the family have been assaulted, honor has been trampled underfoot, vice is triumphant. Therefore I, as a citizen, as an honest man, must take revenge. I shall kill first her and her lover and then myself. . . ." But gradually the frustrated husband loses heart and in the end he leaves the shop with the bird net, "feeling himself more insulted than before."

These early stories suggest the significance Chekhov gave to the finale in all his works. The surprise ending and the zero ending replaced the more traditional climax and conclusion of the formal story. In a letter to his brother Alexander about his first full-length play, *Ivanov*, Chekhov remarked, "I end every act like a story! I construct a quiet and peaceful action, but in the end I slap the audience in the face."[10] In the early stories, the relation of the conclusion to the body of the story sometimes appears contrived and the

* See Notes to Chapter I.

finale itself may lack subtlety. In Chekhov's later works, however, which rely almost entirely on internal action, the
conclusion becomes an organic part of the inner action, and
it often contributes to the lyrical meaning and structure of
the entire work.

Other formal characteristics of the early anecdotes which
suggest some of the innovations important in Chekhov's
later style include terse and abrupt introductions which
contrast with the slow and detailed introductions of Turgenev's works. Indeed, Chekhov's advice to young writers was
to "fold the story over and tear up the beginning."[11] While
in some anecdotes Chekhov continued to introduce his
heroes in a traditional manner, often the reader is ushered
in *medias res*. Thus "Examination for Advancement"
(*Èkzamen na cin*, 1884) opens abruptly with the remark:
"Galkin, the geography teacher, does not like me and I shall
fail his part of the examination today." The speaker is
identified only by the ensuing dialogue. Even more traditional introductions describing setting and protagonists are
generally limited to a few brief or even incomplete sentences, as the first lines of "Surgery" (*Xirurgija*, 1884) illustrate:

A provincial hospital. Because the doctor has left to get
married, the medical assistant, Kuryatin, is receiving patients.
He is corpulent, about forty years old, wears a worn silk jacket
and frayed knitted trousers. His face expresses a feeling of duty
and agreeableness. Between the middle and index finger of his
left hand he holds a cigar from which issues an evil smell.

Chekhov's increasingly compact style affects as well his
characterizations. Traditional leisurely revelations, often
including lengthy digressions familiar from Turgenev's
writings, are replaced by a few significant details of external
characteristics. This technique, on which is based Chekhov's
later impressionistic style, is suggested in a few remarks

Chekhov wrote to his brother in 1886 concerning the description of nature.

> In describing nature one must strengthen small details, grouping them in such a way that, after reading a passage, it is easy to see the picture with closed eyes . . . [Letter of May 10, 1886].

Significant details, in Chekhov's later works, often suggest general moods, atmosphere, and levels of meaning, whereas in the early works the use of such elements is more specific and obvious and may be limited to caricature. Thus there is the description of the English Governess in "The Daughter of Albion" (*Dočʹ Alʹbiona*, 1883):

> Near him stood a tall, thin English woman with crab-like protruding eyes and a large bird-like nose which looked more like a hook than a nose. She wore a white muslin dress through which thin yellowish shoulders were clearly visible. A gold watch hung from a gold belt.

Speech traits, as well as physical characteristics, may serve to demark Chekhov's protagonists. It is difficult to agree with Mirsky's assertion[12] that all of Chekhov's characters speak the same language—Chekhov's own. For in fact, characters in Chekhov's later stories and plays are often endowed with unique speech characteristics.[13] In the early stories the use of speech traits is generally limited to the obvious form of social language levels, as well professional jargons and foreign accents. The language of the lower bureaucracy, which had been so effectively parodied by Gogol and Dostoyevsky, characterizes the protagonists of many early anecdotes. Chekhov's reproduction of peasant speech already marks him as an expert in this technique. Thus a peasant, in "A Malefactor" (*Zloumyšlennik*, 1885), is tried for stealing nuts from railroad ties in order to use them as sinkers for his fishing line. The peasant's inability to understand the legal code is made vivid by the contrast between his speech, with its folk forms, and the bureaucratic style of the examining magistrate.

In some early stories,* however, speech patterns begin to suggest the more subtle and ideosyncratic language of the characters of the later works. Thus certain individualities of speech characterize the heroine of "The Long Tongue" (*Dlinnyj jazyk*, 1886) as flighty and affected. Her remarks are filled with affectations of folk expressions, endearments, and reduplications familiar in Russian spoken art and in the speech of the lower-middle class. *"Vysokie-vysokie gory"* (lit., high-high mountains) and *"černye-prečernye"* (lit., black-oh-so-black) are but two examples. Repetition of words, usually in groups of three, further characterize this heroine: *"tuman, tuman, tuman"* ("fog, fog, fog"), or *"kamni, kamni, kamni"* ("stones, stones, stones"). This device is frequent in Chekhov's later works. Comic use of Russianized foreignisms, as *bontonši* (from the French *bon ton* with a Russian plural ending), also convey the pretensions of the heroine.

Chekhov's later stories employ many shorthand signs which indicate banality and affectation on the part of the character. His protagonists often play nonsensically with language or pun, and in general perform verbal gymnastics. Perhaps the most famous example is the philistine Mr. Turkin in "Ionych" (1898), one of the last stories. He distorts the children's game of "conjugating" the phrase *ja idu po kovru* ("I am walking on the rug") by the use of the homonymic *ja idu poka vru,* thus changing the meaning to "I walk while speaking lies."*

Important themes in the early stories assault traditions and values of Chekhov's society just as his formal innovations assail the conventions of nineteenth-century literary art. Social satires, notably of bureaucracy and rank con-

* See Notes to Chapter I.

sciousness, are an example of early themes which continue
with different emphases in later works.

In the anecdote "Fat and Thin" (*Tolstyj i tonkij*, 1883), a
sudden awareness of rank distinction destroys the joyful reunion of two former schoolmates. Several stories published
in Leykin's *Fragments* are concerned with this theme, as
"Goose Conversation" (*Gusinnyj razgovor*, 1884) in which
a flock of geese address each other by titles and fly in forma-
tion according to rank. In the dramatic sketch "The Chame-
leon," a police officer, informed that a dog has bitten a man,
decides that the dog must be exterminated and its owner
punished. After learning that the owner of the dog is a
general, however, he finds reason to accuse the victim instead. Twice more the police officer must reverse himself.
When he is told that it is not the general's dog he changes
his mind and tone, and when he finally learns that the dog
belongs to the general's brother he again defends the dog.

The oppression of the Russian police state, a theme which
few Russian writers have ignored, found expression in Chekhov's early and also later works. A familiar character in the
early satire is the self-appointed supervisor of public morals,
exemplified by the hero of "Sergeant Prishibeev" (*Unter
Prišibeev*, 1885), who spies on and suspects everybody, and
who looks at the world with a disillusioned air because people have ceased to respect "law and order." He finally finds
himself in court, accused of having prevented religious pro-
cessions, wedding feasts, and the singing of songs. He has
even forbidden people to burn lights in their houses. When
questioned by the judge, Prishibeev freely admits his guilt.
"Where does the law say that people should be given freedom?" he asks. "If I don't take care of law and order who
will?" He boasts of his long experience in spying from the
time when he was a janitor in a school in Warsaw and de-
nounced students to the police. When the sergeant, who
believes he was saving the Empire, hears that he is con-

demned to prison for a month, he no longer undeistands anything. Nevertheless, upon seeing a group of peasants as he leaves the court, Prishibeev returns briefly to his former self. He straightens and shouts in an angry voice: "Disperse! No crowds! To your houses!"

"Sergeant Prishibeev," one of the last works Chekhov wrote for Leykin, though it was never published in *Fragments,* is the best known of Chekhov's early pieces. When Chekhov sent this work to Leykin, the censor forbade its publication. Leykin himself was surprised and wrote Chekhov that he did not understand what the censor found "liberal" in the tale (Letter to Chekhov, September 16, 1885). The censorship committee justified its refusal, saying:

This article is one of those which depict unpleasant social phenomena which have appeared because of the increase of police supervision. Because of the sharp exaggeration concerning the harm done by this supervision the article cannot be published.

Many of Chekhov's early works satirize the cheapness and vulgarity of much of the Russian press. In "Two Journalists (An Unlikely Story)" [*Dva gazetčika (nepravdopodobnyj rasskaz),* 1885], he depicts two reporters: Rybkin, who works for the paper "Sneeze-on-your-Head" (*Načixat' vam na golovu*), and Shleykin, whose paper is called "Judas-Traitor" (*Iuda predatel'*). Rybkin decides that he cannot continue writing generalities about murder, women's hats, the lowering of moral standards, mothers-in-law, and thievery. He has nothing more to say and ends by hanging himself. His more adaptable friend from the paper "Judas-Traitor," however, easily produces suitable articles for all occasions. When Rybkin hangs himself, Shleykin writes an obituary while sitting under the swinging body, and also composes other articles in which he examines such questions as the frequency of suicide and the right to punish those who attempt suicide.

Ignorance and mistrust of education have been subjects of satire in Russian literature since the days of Peter the Great. Chekhov, who was a scientist as well as an artist, also deplored the decline of education in his day, brought about in part by the suspicious attitude of the government towards intellectuals. Mistrust of free thinkers is a theme expressed in the satires "In the Bathhouse" (*V bane,* 1883) and "What Is Better?" (*Čto lučše?,* 1883). In the latter work the narrator, who bears the comic name Krokodilov, decides that taverns are more important than schools, but that it would be a grave mistake to forego education completely, for people must at least be able to read the sign "tavern."

Chapter 2 / The First Serious Stories
From Antosha Chekhonte to Anton Chekhov

The early Chekhov has been thought of only as a humorist. But some of the early works are serious in tone and begin to suggest the transition to be effected by the end of the 1880's, when Chekhov abandoned forever the role of Antosha Chekhonte for that of Anton Chekhov, the creator of the significant stories and plays on which his fame rests today. Although most of these early serious stories are still primitive and conventional, some of them begin to express elements of the new forms and styles of which Chekhov was to become master. In 1882, after only two years of writing, when Chekhov still signed his works Antosha Chekhonte, two serious stories appeared: "The Lady of the Manor" (*Barynja*) and "Late Blooming Flowers" (*Cvety zapozdalye*). Although neither of these stories are included in the collected works, they provide considerable insight into Chekhov's emerging style.

As early as 1883, the first year of his association with Ley-

kin's *Fragments,* Chekhov complained of the constrictive
narrowness of the humor reviews. Replying to Leykin, who
had criticized two of Chekhov's stories as too serious, Chekhov wrote:

> It seems to me that a serious piece, a brief one of approxi-
> mately one hundred lines, will not be too disturbing, especially
> since the masthead of *Fragments* does not carry the words "hu-
> morous satirical journal." . . . To tell you the truth, this ever-
> lasting chasing after the funny is very often difficult. Sometimes
> one hunts for humor and then blunders into a work that nause-
> ates one. And willy-nilly one seeks out something serious. (Letter
> to Leykin dated "after April 17, 1883.")

During the ensuing three years only a few serious stories appeared, notably "In Fall" (*Osen'ju,* 1883), a story about an
alcoholic; "Oysters" (*Ustricy,* 1884); "The Huntsman"
(*Eger,* 1885); and "Sorrow" (*Gore,* 1885). By 1886 and 1887,
Chekhov's dissatisfaction with his role as a humorist was fast
becoming irrevocable and there is a sudden increase of serious stories in this period, 35 in all.

The first serious work, "The Lady of the Manor," which
appeared in installments in the July and August issues of the
review *Moskva* in 1882, initiated a series of stories about
peasant life which was to culminate in the famous story
"The Peasants" (*Mužiki,* 1897). "The Lady of the Manor" is
primarily a traditional treatment of the problem of the conflict between peasant values and those of the decadent aristocracy, and the resulting disintegration of the way of life of
a peasant family. The naïve young peasant Stepan Zhurkin
is compelled by his family to betray his wife and become the
lover of the lady of the manor in order to improve the
family's material position. Night after night the unhappy
Stepan, now dressed in an elegant coachman's uniform,
drives his mistress into the steppe for a night of love. His

inner conflicts drive him to despair and in the end he beats his wife to death.

Demoralization of the peasants was a common theme in the Russian literature of the late nineteenth century, when the question of the peasants' position in the country was becoming acute. The Emancipation Decree of 1861, which was preceded by intense discussions and menacing disorders, freed the peasants from serfdom. But since only limited land was left to the peasant which had to be redeemed by payments to the state, the peasants began to lease from the gentry and were left, therefore, at the mercy of this class. The situation of the peasants was worsened by a number of crop failures in 1867, 1870, and 1873 and many peasant households had to work their land without a horse.[1]

Aleksey Pisemski had treated the subject of the peasant brutalized by his sufferings in the tragedy *A Bitter Fate* (*Gor'kaja sud'bina*, 1859), which may have been Chekhov's model for "The Lady of the Manor." In Pisemski's work a married peasant woman is seduced by a landowner. Her husband seeks revenge by killing the illegitimate child his wife bears and then surrenders himself to the justice of society. There are also parallels to Tolstoy's later morality play, *The Power of Darkness* (*Vlast' t'my*, 1887), in which greed and sensuality among peasants lead to murder. In all three treatments a consequence of the collapse of peasant values is violence, murder, and final surrender to the law. The didactic tone of Pisemski and the moralistic one of Tolstoy's tragedy, are absent from Chekhov's story, however, which does not end in a moral awakening; instead Chekhov's unhappy murderer sits by the body of his wife, stupefied by his deed, while the peasants surround him in silent horror and the aristocratic seductress decries hypocritically the lack of morality of the lower classes.

This work foreshadows many of the story-telling devices of the later Chekhov. "The Lady of the Manor" is tersely written, and lacks a traditional prologue, exposition, or epilogue. The concentrated action and the essentially dramatic form rely upon dialogue far more than on narrative elements. Characters are delineated by a few details, primarily by speech traits. Thus the lady of the manor is revealed by her affected use of French and her condescension when addressing the peasants. Peasant speech is marked by folk idiom orthographically indicated, such as *rup'* instead of *rubl'* (ruble), etc. Popular maxims also characterize the peasants' speech, such as *Blago slez ne pokupat', darom dadeny* (Tears are free, you can't buy them). Stepan's wife laments her abandonment in a formula of the folk lament for the dead, *Na kogo že ty menja, sirotu, ostavil* (For whom have you forsaken me, orphan that I am).

In "The Lady of the Manor" there are some early examples of Chekhov's impressionistic nature paintings as well as his personification and symbolic treatment of nature. In the later stories and plays such nature depictions often reveal the inner life of the protagonists as well as provide many-leveled commentaries on the action and mood of the story. In one important scene from "The Lady of the Manor," a personified nature—although too obviously and schematically—acts as a contrast to the world of greed. The action is initiated when Stepan escapes from the pressures of his family. He departs from his hut at night in order to sleep outside, while his wife cries and his brother speaks crudely. There follows an overly romantic nature painting which contrasts to and comments on the scene which follows when Stepan is taunted by his brother and beaten by his father:

It was quiet outside and gently a Russian summer night was falling. The moon rose from behind the distant hills. Tousled little silver-edged clouds floated to meet it. The horizon grew paler and its entire width was bathed in a pale pleasant green color. The stars twinkled more weakly and, as though they were afraid of the moon, pulled in their little rays. The damp night air rose from the river and, covering everything, caressed one's cheeks.[2]

The next few discordant lines suggest the ensuing dispute:

The clock in Father Grigori's hut jangled out nine o'clock and could be heard all over the village. The Jewish tavern keeper shut his windows noisily and hung a greasy lantern over the door. The streets and yards were deserted and silent.

Stepan lies down in the grass to rest but is immediately joined by his brother, who taunts him, urging him to overcome his scruples and join the lady of the manor. After the brother leaves, Stepan's pregnant wife comes out of the hut and begs Stepan not to abandon her. But she is soon called back and Stepan's father, using his patriarchal prerogative, beats Stepan and forces him to promise acquiescence to the lady's demands. As the father returns to the hut, it appears to Stepan that he hears him saying "I gave him a good thrashing." Now the three encounters are terminated by discordant sounds, in a scene which makes its own comment.

. . . The pitiful notes of an untuned piano could be heard in Father Grigori's hut. At nine the priest's wife usually began her music. Muted, strange sounds floated over all the village. Stepan rose, climbed over the fence and set off down the street. He went down to the river. The river gleamed like quick-silver and the sky with the moon and stars was reflected in it. All was silent as the grave. Nothing moved. Only rarely a cricket chirped. . . . Stepan sat down by the river's edge, directly by the water, and supported his head with his fist. One dark thought after the other filled his head.

While "The Lady of the Manor" embodies many incipient innovations, in other respects it testifies to its author's still developing artistic maturity. Many aspects of the construction of the story remains conventional. External action is still the key to the structure, and the tragic conflict is traditionally solved by a violent act, the murder of Stepan's wife.

In contrast to "The Lady of the Manor," which suggests Chekhov's later naturalistic peasant stories, the second serious work, "Late Blooming Flowers," anticipates the lyrical stories which frequently express the theme of the *vie manquée*. The many later Chekhovian characters who fail to act in time to attain their goals are foretold by the two main protagonists in this story of a love affair of a lonely aristocratic provincial girl, Marusya, and Dr. Toporkov, a calculating physician, who had saved both her brother's life and her own when they were dangerously ill. When the matchmaker, sent by the doctor, indicates the doctor's interest in Marusya, Marusya is happy even though she suspects the doctor's materialistic motive. But while she waits for the doctor to come she learns that his choice has shifted to the daughter of a rich merchant. As the story draws to a close Marusya, ill with tuberculosis, visits the doctor, who behaves without feeling. The doctor relents, however, when Marusya confesses her love for him, and takes her to France, hoping that through a miracle she will recover. She, however, dies in France and the doctor returns home. Marusya's early hesitation and the doctor's crassness, repented too late, destroyed their chance for happiness in this early treatment of Chekhov's theme of the missed opportunity.

The construction of the story is thoroughly traditional. In the first of the three chapters the situation of the heroine is indicated and the other protagonists are characterized: the weak mother, the decadent brother, who drinks, and the businesslike doctor, who is capable of more feeling than first appearance would indicate, are also types succeeded by more subtle versions in Chekhov's later works. The second chapter contains the development of the action: the fruitless proposal. The final chapter, in which Marusya declares her love, is followed by the tragic climax and a traditional epilogue. In spite of its obvious construction, it indicates some of the direction of Chekhov's talent. Lyrical personifications of nature, though still constructed and employed somewhat artificially, are worthy of notice.

Yellow leaves which had fallen to the ground a long time ago patiently awaiting the first snow. . . . Nature is falling asleep quietly and peacefully. . . . As though tired by spring and summer, it lies quietly and silently, basking in the warming, caressing rays of the sun.

Reflecting a sadder mood, nature sets the melancholy tone in a passage somewhat marked by clichés:

Fall came, as raw and muddy as last year's.
Outside the morning was grey and tearful. Dark grey clouds, which looked as though they were smeared with mud, completely covered the sky and invited gloom by their stillness. The sun seemed not to exist. Not once, in the course of an entire week, had it looked upon the earth, as though afraid to dirty its rays in the liquid mud.
Rain drops drummed against the windows with special force; the wind wept in the chimneys and howled like a dog which had lost its master. . . .

The poetic mood is underscored by euphonic techniques, especially systematic sound repetition which becomes so important a device in the later works:

davno opavšie želtye list'ja, terpelivo ožidajuščie pervogo snega.
. . . (. . . yellow leaves which had long fallen to the ground a long time ago patiently awaiting the first snow. . . .)

Ona . . . nežitsja pod grejuščimi, laskajuščimi lučami solnca. . . .
(It [nature] . . . is basking in the warming caressing rays of the sun. . . .)

. . . na dvore stojalo seroe slezlivoe utro.
(. . . outside the morning was grey and tearful.)

The compositional relationship of these nature scenes to the rest of the story material is still mechanical. Each chapter is introduced by a nature picture which almost allegorically predicts the mood of the action of the chapter. Thus the themes of illness and isolation in the first chapter are introduced by the observation that the weather is "dark and autumnal." Momentary hope in the second chapter is suggested by the description of a clear frosty day in late autumn; and the last chapter, which ends tragically, begins again with the description of a gray, cold day.

The delineation of the protagonists foretells little of Chekhov's later method of subtle characterization. Thus we are not able to understand the motivation for the change in the doctor after Marusya declares her love. Such oversimplifications are rare in Chekhov's later psychological portraits. Participants in this story are often portrayed by obvious self-revelatory actions, external characteristics, and description. Yet some hints of Chekhov's technique of depiction of characters by significant details can be noted even in this early work, as the following passage illustrates:

Toporkov announced his arrival by a cough and, without greeting anyone, went directly to the patient's room. He passed through the hall, the living room and the dining room without looking at anyone, with a serious air of a general, as the squeak of his gleaming boots resounded throughout the house. His enormous figure commanded respect. He was stately, serious, impressive and had devilishly correct features, as though carved from ivory. Gold-rimmed glasses and his extremely serious and immobile face completed his haughty bearing. He was a plebeian by origin, but, except for his strong muscles, there was almost nothing plebeian in his appearance. Everything was aristocratic, even gentlemanly. His face was pink and handsome, even very handsome if one were to believe his female patients. His neck was as white as a woman's. His hair was soft as silk and beautiful, but unfortunately close cut. If Toporkov had been interested in his appearance he would not have cut his hair, but would have allowed it to fall in waves to his collar. His face was handsome, but too dry and serious to be agreeable. Dry, serious and immobile, it expressed nothing but the great fatigue of a hard full day's work.

In the later stories only a few strokes would be needed to convey the picture of Toporkov and the frequent shifts to the author's voice would not be required. ("If Toporkov were interested in his appearance he would . . .") Apostrophes to the reader, which never appear in the later works, also encumber the narrative. ["And Marusya (forgive her, dear reader) remembered Turgenev's Rudin. . . ."] Even a number of direct comments on the action by the author are still included in this story:

At the same time he was tortured by a small (probably a very small) nagging of his conscience.

This news affected my heroine too cruelly.

A cycle of children's stories, which begins in 1883 with "A Naughty Boy" (Zloj mal'čik), represents a group of serious works which are written from a child's point of view; a technique used earlier by Tolstoy in his *Childhood*. In the first story of this group, "A Naughty Boy," a little boy tries to blackmail his sister, whom he has surprised with her lover; and in "Oysters" a story about which Chekhov later wrote jokingly that he had "tried himself out as a medicus,"[3] the phantasies of a child are realistically depicted as he begs before a restaurant advertising oysters, and dreams of oysters which he has never tasted. When he learns that oysters are eaten alive, he imagines them as frogs which try to bite his tongue as he is about to swallow them.

Many of the children's stories are satires of the adult world, implied by childish misunderstandings. In "The Cook's Marriage" (Kuxarka ženitsja, 1885), little Grisha

watches through a peephole as Pelageya the cook is being
married to a coachman. The child wonders why Pelageya
must suddenly hand over her pay to her new husband and
why she is no longer free. The title itself *Kuxarka ženitsja,*
which uses the Russian word for "to marry" that is reserved
for men, instead of the woman's *vyxodit zamuž,* marks the
naïve child's view. This is also expressed by details, such as
the drop of sweat which hangs from the bridegroom's nose
and the noisy manner in which he chews sugar, "which made
a shudder run down Grisha's spine." Russian folk tradition
suggests children's phantasy as Grisha's dreams of Pelageya's
abduction by a sorcerer (*Černomor*) and a witch.

In "Grisha" (1886) a two-year-old child observes the
clandestine rendezvous of his nursemaid and her lover, and
consequently is given castor oil by his mother to cure him of
his excitement and apparent illness. The child's impression
is imaginatively developed in this story by skillful use of a
device called by the Russian formalist critics "making it
strange" (*ostranenie*), a peculiar semantic shift which transfers a depicted object to a different plane of reality. The
habitual is "made strange" by a distortion causing the per-
ceiver to see the object in a fresh light, as though for the first
time. In this formalist view, such a counteracting of automatic responses and restoration of a fresh vision of the world
is the fundamental function of art.[4]

Up to now Grisha has known only a four-cornered world: his
bed stands in one corner, the nurse's trunk in the second, a chair
in the third, and the icon lamp burns in the fourth. If one looks
under the bed one can see a doll, its arm torn off, and a drum.
Behind the nurse's trunk there are many different things: empty
spools of thread, papers, a lidless box and a broken clown. This
world includes not only Grisha and the nurse, but often also
mamma and the cat. Mamma resembles the doll and the cat
papa's fur coat, only the fur coat has no tails and eyes. From the
world which is called the nursery a door leads into a space in

which one eats and drinks tea. Here stands Grisha's chair on its high legs and here hangs the clock which exists only to swing its pendulum back and forth and to strike.

When Grisha enters the apartment of the nurse's lover he "sees a dark ceiling, an oven fork with two horns and a stove which looks like a big dark bird."

Thus the familiar world of the nursery is replaced by the new, strange, and frightening world of the apartment.

The most significant of the children's stories are "Vanka" (1886) and "Sleepy" (*Spat' xočetsja,* 1888).[5] Vanka, an eight-year-old village orphan who is apprenticed to a cobbler in Moscow, writes a letter to his grandfather in his village complaining of mistreatment and asking that he be taken home. The boy adresses the letter to "grandfather Konstantin Makarych in the village," drops it in the mailbox and dreams happily of the arrival of his rescuer. There are two components of the narration. The direct discourse of the boy alternates with the narrative sections which comment upon the boy's behavior. The opening paragraph introduces Vanka and the setting, and describes the boy's preparations for writing the letter (he often looks fearfully at the door and window lest he be surprised). Then follow a few lines of the letter, after which the narration returns to a description of Vanka's gestures and the setting. The grandfather is then presented in a narrative passage which gradually shifts to the boy's view, and which is supported by nature descriptions. Tersely impressionistic, the view of nature reveals both the boy's reminiscences and his longing.

The air is calm, transparent and fresh. The night is dark, but one can see the entire village, with its white rooftops and the spirals of smoke emerging from its chimneys, as well as the trees white with hoarfrost, and the snowdrifts.

Nature is personified in childish images:

The entire sky was strewn with gaily winking stars and the Milky Way was so clear that it seemed to have been washed and rubbed down with snow before the holidays.

Next there follows a quotation of most of the letter in which Vanka describes Moscow and begs to be fetched home to the village. In Vanka's thoughts, which continue the story, he remembers Christmas time at home in the village. We return to the conclusion of the letter and a final narrative passage: Vanka mails the letter with the incomplete address and goes home to dream of his rescue.

"Vanka" anticipates "Sleepy" (*Spat' xočetsja*), the most serious of the children's stories. In "Sleepy" a child is again exploited by an employer, but the consequences are tragic. The tired child watches nightly over her employer's baby, becoming ever more exhausted, and in a moment of despair she strangles the infant. Relieved by her action, even as Vanka was relieved by his call for help, she falls asleep, her torment gone. This story contains a masterful treatment of the child's dreams, subtle use of recurrent images, and impressionistic description. Its musical construction anticipates many of Chekhov's mature works.

A group of Chekhov's early serious stories, set in a peasant and village milieu, bears resemblance to Turgenev's cycle, *The Sportsman's Sketches* (*Zapiski oxotnika*). In these sketches an aristocratic narrator tells of the peasant types he meets on his hunting trips.[6] The debt to Turgenev is evident in the poetic depiction of the simple Russian peasant, who is contrasted to the prose of everyday life, as well as in the lyrical and poetic nature settings frequently with symbolic overtones. But in Chekhov's stories themes of isolation and of the *vie manquée* replace the Turgenevian ones which lead to the more traditional dramatic conflict.

The first story of this group, "The Huntsman," is one of the few early stories Chekhov included in his collected works. It appeared in the Petersburg *Gazette* on July 18,

1885 and quickly attracted attention. In a brief dramatic scene the story presents two contrasting characters: a freedom-loving huntsman and his stolid peasant wife, whom the hunter had married while drunk. The tragedy of these two who cannot understand each other and their consequent isolation is the focus of this work. The story is limited to a brief description of their meeting and conversation in an open field, and their parting which follows—their differences still unresolved. This lack of resolution, or "studied unfinishedness," becomes ever more frequently the note which concludes Chekhov's stories.

"The Huntsman" is tersely presented by a direct and objective view. A few brief lines describing the natural setting compose the opening, after which there follows the drama between the huntsman and his wife.

It is a hot, sultry noon. There is no cloud in the sky. The grass, burned by the sun, looks cheerless and hopeless: even rain will not revive its green color. . . . The forest stands silent and motionless, as though looking somewhere over its treetops or waiting for something.

These few impressionistic details set the mood for the scenes which follow. The role of nature is not limited, however, as it is in "Late Blooming Flowers," to a schematic accompaniment of the action. Rather, it is part of the total instrumentation of the story, in which nature scenes, much like musical motifs, are woven throughout the action and characterizations. The following paragraph is the first description of Egor Vlasych, the huntsman:

At the edge of the clearing a tall narrow-shouldered man of about forty joggs along lazily with a waddling gait. He is dressed in a red shirt, patched pants not of peasant cut, and high boots. He trudges along the road. On the right is the green meadow, on the left a sea of golden ripe rye stretches all the way to the horizon. He is red and hot. A white cap with a straight peak like a jockey's, obviously a present from a generous master, sits boldly on his fine blond head. A hunting bag with a crumpled black-cock hangs over his shoulder. The man holds a two-barrelled rifle in his hands . . . and squints at his old, thin dog who is running ahead and sniffing at the bushes. It is quiet all around, not a sound. . . . All living beings have hidden from the heat.

Towards the end of the fruitless conversation between husband and wife, nature again appears in a musical, and this time symbolic, role:

They are silent. Three wild ducks fly over the clearing. Egor's eyes follow until the ducks become three barely visible dots which disappear over the forest.
"How are you earning your living?" he asks, glancing from the ducks to Pelageya.
"Now I go out to work and in winter I take a baby from the children's home and feed it with a bottle. That brings a ruble and a half a month."
"Hm. . . ."
Again silence. From the harvested field a quiet song rises only to be broken off at the very beginning. It is too hot to sing. . . .
"I hear that you have built a new hut for Akulina," said Pelageya.

Here the musical quality of the nature picture is even more pronounced than in the earlier passage. Nature is a part of the conversation in which it participates. The suggestion of the symbolism of the disappearing ducks and the delicate use of sounds foreshadows Chekhov's later sophisticated use of audial and visual elements and of nature symbolism. The interrupted song heard in the distance, portending something mysterious, foreshadows the use of sound symbolism in Chekhov's later works.

The conversation between husband and wife has led nowhere. The story concludes as the huntsman walks away from his wife, in a coda painted in impressionistic colors:

He walks down the long road, straight as a stretched belt. She, pale and motionless as a statue, stands and watches his every step. But now the red color of his shirt begins to fade into the dark color of his trousers; his steps are no longer visible, his dog can no longer be distinguished from his boots. Only his cap remains visible, but . . . suddenly Egor turns sharply to the right . . . and the cap disappears in the green.

"Good-bye Egor Vlasych," whispers Pelageya, standing on tip toes in order to see the white cap just once more.

In March 1886, eight months after he wrote "The Huntsman," Chekhov's "Agafya," a second peasant story reminiscent of Turgenev, was published in Suvorin's *New Times*. A narrator-observer describes a nocturnal rendezvous between the village Don Juan, Savka, and the wife of the railroad switchman, Agafya. Savka, a variant of the Egor type in "The Huntsman," is again an antithesis to the submissive type, Agafya, who offers him her love. Savka is not a villain, nor is he brutal; nevertheless he treats Agafya unkindly. Like the huntsman, he is a rebel and a nonconformist who is sometimes gentle and sensitive to nature. The emptiness of Agafya's life has led her hopelessly to Savka, but at the close of the story we see her walking slowly, though steadfastly, towards the threatening figure of her husband, in a denouement which suggests again the theme of a *vie manquée*.

The aristocratic narrator in "Agafya," a counterpart to Turgenev's aristocratic observers of peasant types, is a rare figure in Chekhov's stories. In this work the view of nature is limited to the perspective of the narrator and consequently the role of nature is unusually constricted.

"Agafya" concludes, as did "The Huntsman," without resolution. Savka and the narrator watch Agafya from the distance; the latter comments on Savka, while Savka comments on Agafya:

I looked at Savka's face. It was pale and tensely drawn in an expression of squeamish pity like that seen on the faces of people watching animals being tortured.

"When the cat laughs the mice cry," he sighed.

Suddenly Agafya jumped up, shook her head and walked towards her husband with bold steps. She had apparently found her strength and made her decision.

Chekhov's friend and fellow writer, the poet Palmin, wrote to the author about "Sorrow" : "This is the best thing you have written so far. It conveys a feeling of a mixture of laughter and sadness" (Letter of 27 November 1885). In this story, the Turgenevian theme of the talented man from the lower rungs of life has been broadened to the more general one of isolation and of the frustration of the misspent life.[7]

The turner, Grigori Petrov, is driving through a snowstorm to deliver his wife to the district hospital, but she dies on the way. He in turn loses consciousness from the cold and awakens in the hospital as he is dying. As Grigori walks through the snowstorm alongside the sleigh, he tries to communicate with his wife, whom he has always mistreated. He addresses her, but the remarks are a monologue, for she is dead. Grigori is a gifted craftsman, yet his life has been disorderly. A crucial event now forces Grigori to re-evaluate his life, a pattern which is repeated in many of Chekhov's stories. Pictures from the past come to Grigori's mind as he walks beside his dying wife and he unhappily realizes his misspent life. The internal monologue is punctuated by the phrase which becomes the Leitmotif of the story—"to live anew" (*žit' by syznova*)—ironic because of Grigori's impending death. The story is presented by means of Grigori's internal speech, a few authorial comments and several nature pictures. A brief statement describes Grigori struggling through the snowstorm.

Wherever you look whole clouds of snowflakes are circling about, so that you can not tell whether the snow comes from the sky or from earth.

As he rehearses his speech to the doctor he imagines the doctor's contemptuous remarks concerning the shiftless Grigori. He will promise the doctor a cigar case and a croquet gate for curing his wife. The storm accompanying his thoughts hints at the irony of Grigori's fate. He will only briefly awaken from his frozen slumber, just as he only briefly awakens to a realization of his life before his death. Interrupting Grigori's thoughts, the author's voice reveals the events which preceded the story's action.

The turner remembers that the sorrow began last night. When he returned home last night, drunk as usual, and began—as was his custom—to swear and shake his fists, the old woman looked at her ruffian as she had never looked at him before. Usually the expression in the old woman's eyes was martyred and meek, like that of an underfed, beaten dog. But now her gaze was stern and immobile, like the look on ikons or on dying people. It was with this strange look, which boded evil, that all the sorrow had begun.

This passage is followed by Grigori's guilty reflections, and his promise of greater kindness to his wife when she recovers. Her death is conveyed by two details, which are underscored by anaphora:

It seems strange to him that the snow does not melt on the old woman's face; *it seems* strange that her face itself has somehow become elongated and taken on a pale-gray, dirty-waxy color and has become severe and serious. [Italics supplied]

(*Stranno* emu kažetsja, čto na lice u staruxi ne taet sneg, *stranno*, čto samo lico kak-to osobenno vytjanulos', prinjalo bledno-seryj, grjazno—voskovoj cvet i stalo strogim, ser'eznym.) [Italics supplied]

Grigori's internal speech is disjointed and filled with meaningless phrases, as "be so kind as to see" (*sami izvolite videt'*), as well as with stumbling fillers (As soon as my Matrena, sort of, gets well. . . . And you, Matrena, kind of . . . ; and you kind of . . .). In situations of great agitation he uses a "big word," *komissija* (commission), the meaning of which he does not understand.*

She must have died. Komissija! (*Pomerla, stalo-byt'. Komissija!*) . . . and I myself sent her to beg for her bread, komissija! (*Sam ja posylal ee xleba u ljudej prosit', komissija!*)

In many respects the year 1886, which saw the publication of several children's stories discussed earlier, as well as of *Agafya*, was significant for Chekhov. It was in this year that Chekhov made his first contribution to A. S. Suvorin's influential daily newspaper *New Times*. "A Requiem" (*Panixida*) appeared on February 15, 1886. Not only did Chekhov receive a larger sum from Suvorin than he had from Leykin, but he was free from the restrictions on length and subject imposed by the humor journals.

From this time on Chekhov contributed growing numbers of serious stories to *New Times,* which he signed with his own name rather than the former *nom de plume* Antosha Chekhonte. Of the 109 stories by Chekhov published in 1886, 16 were printed in *New Times*. Other serious stories were published in another daily, The Petersburg *Gazette* (*Peterburskaja gazeta*), to which Chekhov was a steady contributor from May, 1885 to the end of 1888. Of the 64 stories published in 1887, 20 were of a decidedly serious vein and half of these were published in *New Times*. In 1888, only nine stories were published and all of them were

* There is the hint of a double meaning in the use of this word, which the literate reader of Chekhov's day would not have failed to note; *komissija* in the early nineteenth century could also mean "troubles" as the word is used in Griboedov's comedy *Woe from Wit* (*Gore ot uma*, 1822-1823).

serious works, signed, with one exception ("Sleepy") with Chekhov's own name.

In the serious stories which appeared between the years 1886 and 1888 we find some earlier themes as well as the introduction of some new ones.

A more subtle treatment of the theme of the lost life occurs in the story "Daydreams" (*Mečty*), which appeared in *New Times* on November 15, 1886. A tramp, arrested for refusing to reveal his name, tells his story to the convoy guards who are conducting him to the district center. He had escaped from forced labor to which he was sentenced as a child accomplice to a murder, and therefore he had been forced to conceal his identity. His servant mother had been mistress to her master, whom she had poisoned when he took another mistress. The theme of the master-servant liaison, which parallels that of "The Lady of the Manor," is limited in this story to that of a background. The tramp tells the guards that he would prefer a sentence to Siberia as a vagrant than forced labor, and he paints an idyllic picture of the free life in Siberia. The guards are momentarily swayed by the depiction. However, one of the two guards catches himself and rudely tells the prisoner he will never make it to Siberia but will die from weakness on the road. For a moment the gray existence of the two convoy soldiers and their prisoner was lightened by the romantic dream of Siberia, but the remark of the soldier returns the mood to reality, and the prisoner is left even more pathetic and timid.

Certain new themes, those of social injustice, of the little man helpless before the law, and the illusion of man's dreams are expressed in this work. The conflict of the routine, and constricted with the dream of freedom is supported by symbolic nature pictures. Fog suggests their prisonlike world:

The travellers have been walking long, but they are unable
to break out from the small piece of earth which surrounds
them. In front there are some ten yards of the dirty, dark-brown
earth of the road, and behind them the same. And beyond, as
far as the eye can see, there is an impenetrable wall of white
fog. They walk and walk, but the ground is always the same, the
wall is no closer and the patch of earth remains unchanged.

In this setting the tramp recounts his tale of injustice
and depicts the broad spaces of Siberia.

In the autumn stillness, when cold, raw fog covering the
earth penetrates the soul and seems to be a prison wall before
your eyes, demonstrating the limitedness of man's will, it is
sweet to dream about broad, quick rivers with wide, craggy
banks, impenetrable forests, limitless steppes. Slowly and calmly
the imagination pictures early morning, when the flush of dawn
has not yet disappeared from the sky; a man, looking like a
small dot, walks along the deserted banks; age-old fir trees, high
as masts . . . , look sternly at the free man; roots, huge rocks and
prickly brush block his way; but he is strong in body and bold
in spirit, he does not fear the firs, the rocks, his solitude, nor
the rolling echo which resounds at each step he takes.

The optimistic dream of a free man is followed by the
soldier's remarks:

". . . You won't get to those free places. How could you? You'll
walk some three hundred versts and give up your soul."

These deflating words, addressed to the prisoner, clearly
can be applied more generally to the state of man.
    Stylistic accomplishments in this work demonstrate Che-
khov's increasing skill. Highly concentrated poetic images
support the personifications of nature.

Dark hostile tears are on the grass. These are not the tears of
quiet joy which the earth sheds when it meets and accompanies
the summer sun. . . .

. . . a pitiful birch tree, wet, naked as a street beggar.

The three protagonists are impressionistically drawn. The tramp's insignificance is underscored by a few details: he is

. . . a small, infirm man, weak and sickly, with small, colorless and very indistinct features. His eyebrows are thin [*židen'kie*] . . . his moustache is barely visible.

His nose (*nosik*), his forehead (*lobik*), his mouth (*malen'kij rotik*), and his voice, a saccharine tenor (*slaščavyj tenorok*), are all described in diminutives.

The theme of individual isolation is suggested in many of Chekhov's early stories, including the children's stories and "The Lady of the Manor," but it is first fully developed in the brief sketch "Misery" (*Toska*, 1886), the tale of the cab driver, Iona Potapov, whose son has just died and who has no one to tell of his sorrow.

Details in the opening scene depicting the isolated figure of Iona Potapov summon a complex of moods and attitudes.[8] Wet snow falls on the shoulders of the cab driver and on his horse as Iona sits still, hunched over. As in "Sorrow" and "Daydreams," snow and fog seem to enclose the cab driver in a shell. Such symbols of isolation in Chekhov's works frequently take the form of a protective substance, separating the individual from his surroundings.

The static picture of the cab driver passes to one of motion as the first passenger forces the cab driver into action. Iona sits up and the snow falls off his shoulders and off the back of his horse. He tries to drive through the heavy snow, and through the invisible traffic around him, evidenced only by abrupt curses and shouts at the cab driver which echo through the snow and fog. Iona tells his passengers of his grief, but their only response is rude answers or fragments of conversation. The use of such metonymic devices as visual and audial details (snow, fog, noises) and seemingly disconnected discourse convey the lonely isolation of the individual and anticipates Chekhov's mature style.[9]

Many of the serious themes we have considered express some aspects of the pathos of the individual lost in a cold society. All these characters, those who try too late to find happiness, children misunderstood by the adult world, a rebellious youth, a peasant woman who cannot find love, a prisoner and his guards who secretly yearn for freedom, or the lonely cabman, suggest the attempts of people to break out of their isolation.

Another more intuitive and philosophical theme which only fleetingly appears in the early stories, but which becomes very significant in the later works, is concerned with the problem of the hidden personality which reveals itself.[10] A chance remark or gesture may betray the inner ego and destroy in a moment the façade which the individual has carefully constructed. "The Father" (*Otec*, 1887) presents this theme in primitive and grotesque form. A man addicted to drinking comes to his son to borrow money. Clowning all the time, he talks briskly and casually about the loan, but at moments his casual talk is interrupted by characterizing remarks which compose a kind of confession:

I planned to visit you five times, but never seem to find the time. It's always one thing or another . . . just terrible! Actually, that's a lie. . . . I always lie. You mustn't believe me.

The story portrays compulsive confessions, but other stories present subtler self-revelations. In one of the most successful early stories, "The Letter" (*Pis'mo*, 1887), a deacon reports the facts of his son's sinful life to the archdeacon. His son keeps a mistress and eats forbidden food on fast days. The archdeacon dictates a pompous and harsh letter to the wayward son which delights the deacon. But an acquaintance, Father Anastazi, an unfrocked priest, asks the deacon to forgive his son rather than to send the letter. The deacon refuses to comply, explaining that it is his paternal duty to instruct his son in the right ways of living. Just before he posts the letter, however, the deacon hurriedly adds a postscript of local gossip, the style and content of which alters the censorious tone of the original letter dictated by the archdeacon and reveals the simple personality of the naïve deacon.

Perhaps the most important protagonist of the story is Father Anastazi, the defrocked priest whose comments on the action act as a chorus to the story. This is one of Chekhov's earliest works about the clergy[11] and is to be followed by many others in which the Russian priest is shown with affection. Father Anastazi is himself a drunkard; he has been punished by the church for selling illegal marriages. But he is sympathetically contrasted to the unforgiving archdeacon.

In techniques which look toward Chekhov's later stories, oblique devices provide characterization: a brief, almost incidental gesture, a distinctive manner of speaking, a certain timbre of the voice or a recurrent detail which becomes a leitmotif. Father Anastazi is associated with a light cough. The story also exemplifies a stylistic idiosyncracy, noted in "The Long Tongue," which increasingly permeates Chekhov's stories. Chekhov delighted in employing ternary rhythmic repetitions based on reiterations of a word, or phrase, or composed of syntactical parallels. Sometimes three epithets or nouns are used in succession:

Èto byl starik 65-ti let, *drjaxlyj* ne po letam, *kostljavyj* i *sutulovatyj* . . . (This was an old man of 65, prematurely decrepit, rawboned and round-shouldered . . .)

Starik kazalsja uže o. Fedorovu ne vinovnym i ne poročnym, a *unižennym, oskorblennym, nesčastnym*. . . . (The old man appeared to Fr. Fedor no longer guilty and sinful, but insulted, injured and unhappy.)

Na lice ego zaigraly *styd, robost'* i žal'kij prinuždennyj *smex*.
(Shame, timidity and a pitiful forced smile played on his face.)

A pervasive Chekhovian theme, already implied in many
of the stories discussed, is that of the conflict between beauty
and the elusive quality expressed by the Russian term
pošlost'. This untranslatable term connotes vulgarity, banality, poor taste, superficial values, conceit, and dilettantism.
(Akin to this term is the German word *Kitsch* with its
further connotations of the shoddy and second-rate.)[12] The
underlying theme of many of Chekhov's later stories and
plays is the antagonism between two worlds: that of beauty,
spontaneity, and innocence on the one hand and the mer-
ciless environment of hypocrisy, vulgarity, and banality
which make up the world of *pošlost'* on the other. Many of
Chekhov's sensitive souls suffocate in the surrounding of
pošlost'.

This is first well developed in "A Requiem" (*Panixida*,
1886). (See p. 34). The chief protagonist, the shopkeeper
Andrey, has come to church to hear a Requiem Mass for his
daughter. Because she was an actress, Andrey insists on
calling her "the harlot Maria" (*bludnica Marija*), in spite
of the remonstrations of the priest. The term is appropriate
to her, he insists, just because she was an actress. Andrey's
crudity is implied by the antiphonal technique of the story.
As the choir sings the Requiem Mass, the stolid shopkeeper
with his heavy galoshes begins to reminisce about his daughter's childhood. He remembers a walk she took with him.
She was enthralled by the beauty of the landscape. But
Andrey, embarrassed that his daughter was an actress, could
not share her enthusiasm and complained that all this nature was only taking up space and gave "as much profit as a
billy-goat's milk."

Andrey's feelings about his daughter are momentarily
softened as he listens to the Requiem choir. But the for-

bidden word *bludnica,* slipping unconsciously into his silent prayer, reminds us that his feeling of kindness is only a superficial sentimentality. The conclusion is a typically Chekhovian lyrical coda leaving the story unresolved.

. . . Little streams of bluish smoke which came from the censer were bathed in a broad, slanting ray of light cutting across the gloomy, lifeless emptiness of the church. And it seemed that with the smoke the soul of the departed was floating in the light. Streams of smoke, like a child's curls, were swirling and floating up to the window, as though shunning the gloom and sadness which fills this poor soul.

The theme of the *vie manquée,* in which an individual seeking happiness is paralyzed in the decisive moment by weakness and indecision, becomes more important in the serious stories of 1886 and 1887. Stories centered around this theme are among Chekhov's most intensely lyrical narrations.

Perhaps the most significant work of this period expressing this subject is "Verochka" (1887), in which a failure of communuication leads to the missed opportunity. As the story opens Ivan Alekseevich Ognev leaves the house of a local family in a provincial town, where he has been carrying out a statistical survey. Vera, the young daughter of the house, follows him and suddenly declares her love. He does not know how to reply and his clumsy answers cause Vera to return home unhappily. Ognev, regretting his coldness, goes back once more to Vera's house, but he succeeds only in standing helplessly and impotently under her window. He walks away, deeply disturbed, and when he returns to his rooms he gazes for a long time in frustration at the light.

External details and nature pictures convey Vera's defeat. Earlier a carefree Vera wore a blouse which was so loose-fitting that it did not touch her figure. She was casually dressed and her hair emerged from under her headscarf.

Later nature appears to prophesy the outcome of the conversation between Ognev and Vera. As they walk nature seems to be "covered by a veil; all nature hid behind the opaque lusterless puffs of mist." After the fruitless conversation Vera seems smaller, hunched over, wrapped closely in her cloak in an image echoing that of veiled nature. Impressionistic nature pictures provide mood and a rythmic pattern. They interrupt dialogue and internal speech throughout the story and form a transition between direct speech and internal monologue.

The story is presented in understatement. Even the most intense scene, the point of the highest tension before Vera's declaration, is conveyed simply by the observation that Vera trembled and "not one curl, as usual, but two were falling on her forehead." The anticipated climax does not appear. Ognev notices nothing and tactlessly asks Vera if she is feeling unwell as she struggles in vain to express her feelings. Vera's simple statement "I love you," only disagreeably surprises and shocks Ognev. Only later he regrets his missed opportunity.

The last of the early serious stories to be discussed is "The Kiss" (*Poceluj*, 1887), which is a somewhat lighter treatment of Chekhov's themes of isolation, lack of communication, and missed opportunities. The renaissance plot device of mistaken identity[13] is wittily and ironically employed in this funny and yet sad story of fate's tricks on the timid Second Captain Ryabovich, who is invited with his fellow officers to a party at a local landowner's. In the brilliance of the party he thinks, "I am the most shy, the most modest and the most colorless officer in the whole brigade." But an adventure changes this view. In a dark room, through which he inadvertently passes, he is suddenly embraced by a young girl whom he cannot see. The officer is thereby introduced to a new world of dreams. He cannot imagine who the girl is and forms an image of her, "the image he desired but which was nowhere to be seen at the table." He forgets that he is colorless and shy. He is now an ordinary man with an ordinary life. He smiles on everyone. As he leaves the house a nightingale sings in spite of the jostling her bush was given by the officers.

No one pays credence to Ryabovich's story, but he waits, nevertheless, for his regiment's maneuvers to carry him back to the manor. He does return. But this time loud voices of peasants picking cabbage ominously disturb the scene and the nightingale no longer sings. The general's sheets are hanging near the bridge and feel cold and rough to his touch. The reflection of the bathhouse is broken up by the ripples of the river—and just as suddenly Ryabovich's dream breaks into pieces. Life, like the river, wanders aimlessly, he reflects, like an incomprehensible jest. The nightingale, the voices of the peasants, the feel of the general's sheets, and the river all form comments on the changing moods of the story and provide a subtext. Subtexts become very important in the structure of Chekhov's mature stories and plays and this technique is suggested in "The Kiss." A subtext may be defined as an undercurrent of themes and motives, usually expressed by seemingly trivial and irrelevant details and remarks, which comment, in various subtle and indirect ways, frequently ironically, on the action and inner meaning of the story. Ryabovich goes back to his quarters only to find that his comrades have received the long-awaited invitation from the landowner. His momentary joy is quickly stilled and he goes to bed in anger. The individual who cannot communicate with his fellow man is here lightly treated in the conception of the absurd and ineffective, but pathetic, soldier whose only friend is the invisible woman of the chance encounter in the dark.

Certain stylistic advances as well as general themes mark the early serious stories. They form a significant evolutionary chapter in the development of Chekhov's art. After this

period we find far fewer traces of conventional devices and
plot structures which we have noted were often parodied
in the humor stories and sometimes employed in the early
serious stories. By the late 1880's there has clearly been
initiated, though often still in primitive form, the compact
impressionistic story which focuses on the themes which will
so intensely occupy Chekhov in his later works.

Chapter 3 / "The Steppe"
An Allegory of Life and Death

In the year 1887, Chekhov was invited to contribute to one of the principal intellectual journals, the *Northern Messenger (Severnyj Vestnik)*. In February, 1888, he submitted "The Steppe" (*Step'*), one of his longest works, the objectives of which he outlined in a letter to his literary mentor, D. V. Grigorovich.[1]

I have started a long work. For my debut in the big journals I have taken the steppe, which has not been described for a long time. I am depicting a plain, purple distances, shepherds, Jews, priests, thunder storms at night, wagon trains, steppe birds, and so on. Each chapter constitutes a separate narrative, and all chapters are connected by their close relationship, like the five figures of a quadrille. I am trying to give them a common smell, a common tone . . . perhaps it will open the eyes of my contemporaries and will show them what riches, what treasures of beauty, have yet remained untouched and how much space there still is for the Russian artist.

Chekhov wrote to his friends that he lacked confidence in his undertaking,[2] but he gained courage after he began work, and when the story was completed he told his friend, A. Lazarev-Gruzinski, "I do not know whether I have succeeded in it or not, but it is my chef-d'oeuvre."[3] He informed Pleshcheev, the editor of the *Northern Messenger,* and Grigorovich of plans to continue "The Steppe" if it were well received,[4] but this plan never materialized.

Superficially, "The Steppe" is constructed as a traditional tale of the adventures and observations of a traveling hero. There is not, however, a dramatic conflict, nor is there the traditional action plot. Rather, there is an inner, symbolic action expressed by the subtextual play and dialogue of themes and counter-themes, motifs and counter-motifs, as in a musical work.

A young boy, Egor, travels through the steppe country of southern Russia with his uncle and the village priest. The destination is a distant district town where Egor is to attend boarding school and his companions are to sell wool. The eight chapters of "The Steppe" compose three parts. In the first, Egor, his uncle, Kuzmichov, and the village priest, Father Khristofor, ride together; in the second, Egor moves to a wagon caravan transporting wool; the concluding section forms a kind of epilogue, as the wagon train with Egor, the uncle, and the priest meet at their destination. But while in traditional tales of the traveling hero, such as *Don Quixote, Gulliver's Travels,* or Diderot's *Jacques le fataliste,* the heroes are active participants in adventures, even though in the case of *Don Quixote* the reality of these adventures is left in doubt, Egor's role is a passive one. The dramatic tension, insofar as it exists, consists more in Egor's withdrawal from the activity of his surroundings. In the end the journey itself seems to be of little use and Egor, who has witnessed so many adventures, seems more alone than ever.

From its first publication the significance of "The Steppe" has been the subject of discussion. Pleshcheev[5] praised the story for its poetic description of Russian landscape, while others, and notably the critic, N. K. Mikhailovski,[6] found that Chekhov was not master of the long form and that the work was shapeless. There are few pages in Russian literature in which the Russian landscape is painted so poetically and the poetic qualities of "The Steppe" may be its most significant ones. Nevertheless, there are other important dimensions of the work.

Inner meanings in "The Steppe" are connected thematically and stylistically to Chekhov's later works. A subtext, which echoes throughout the story, states and restates the Chekhovian contrast of the world of art, sensitivity, and beauty to that of *pošlost'*, ugliness, and vulgarity. Philosophically, this contrast is also expressed as the struggle of life and death forces on the steppe. There is the melancholy song heard during the noonday rest of the travelers in which nature appears to brood over the realization that it will soon have to die unsung and unnoticed. In another passage, nature utters one last desperate cry: "A singer! A singer!" No one hears nature's forlorn cry except the boy Egor. It is through his poetic perception that nature is reflected. Egor is as lonely, as deserted, and as misunderstood as is nature, with which he is identified, and no one has the time to heed him. His uncle and Father Khristofor are single-mindedly concerned with the business of selling wool at a good profit. Nor can Deniska, the driver, understand Egor. Egor suggests the many other sensitive protagonists of Chekhov's stories and plays who are isolated by the vulgarity surrounding them. The people who are part of *pošlost'* in a Chekhovian milieu are indifferent to beauty and likely to destroy it, just as those who surround Egor are indifferent to him and to the nature through which they are passing.

As the story opens the themes of emptiness and death,

joined to the ugliness of the town, are introduced. Egor and
the other passengers, beginning their journey, drive by the
village jail, the smoky forge, the graveyard, and the brick
kilns which issue black smoke and red dust. But Egor first
sees the graveyard as pleasant and gay:

... the cozy, green graveyard surrounded by a stone fence; from
behind the fence white crosses and monuments, which were
hiding in the green of the cherry trees, peeked out gayly and
looked from afar like white dots.

Egor's mood changes as he thinks of his grandparents who
lie buried there. He remembers how much his grandmother
had wanted to live and how even in death her eyes had refused to remain closed.

As the carriage leaves the town, the vastness of the steppe
to be traversed suggests the hopelessness and absurdity of
the journey: "You travel on and on, never knowing where it
[the steppe] begins and where it ends."

The superficial and pompously worded remarks of the
priest, phrasing the goal of the trip for little Egor—education—accentuates Egor's sudden feeling of desperation and
loneliness as he loses sight of the familiar town.

". . . Never mind, my boy Egor . . . say a prayer to God. You
are not going towards evil, but towards good. Learning, they
say, is light and ignorance is darkness . . . that's surely so. . . .
Learning together with faith gives fruits pleasing to God."

The first picture of the steppe, one of the many impressionistic paintings, conjures an illusion of life. The rising
sun, which is nevertheless associated with the distant funeral
mounds and with an absurd windmill, momentarily warms
and rejuvenates the earth.

At first, a long way ahead where the sky joins the earth, near
the funeral mounds and the windmill—which from afar looked

like a little man waving his arms—a broad bright yellow streak of light crept across the earth. A minute later another streak like the first one shimmered somewhat closer; it crept to the right and embraced the hills. Something warm touched Egor's back, the streak of light, which had stolen up from behind, slipped over the carriage and the horses, ran to meet other streaks, and suddenly the whole wide steppe threw off the penumbra of dawn, smiled and began to glitter with dew.

Yet soon the sun's heat attacks and destroys the hope and freshness of the morning steppe life, and the "deceived steppe" takes on its usual desiccated summer appearance.

Succeeding passages present a series of impressionistic pictures playing upon the themes of futility and death which have been introduced: a kite flies aimlessly overhead "and suddenly stops in mid-air, as though reflecting on the dullness of life"; a girl lies on top of a passing wagon laden with grain, "sleepy and exhausted by the heat"; a lonely poplar appears on the horizon, but "who planted it there and why it is there, no one knows"; the carriage passes a group of reapers whom the heat seems to be suffocating; wild dogs hurl themselves against the carriage and Egor fears that he will be torn apart by their teeth. In these and subsequent scenes the figure of Egor is identified by his bright red shirt which is blown by the steppe winds. Its vitality attracts and fascinates the passers-by as the boy travels across the steppe.

The interplay of the themes of life and death continues as the travelers rest at noon. Nature is again friendly and happy, but only fleetingly so: the air appears fresher and a spring of clear water seems to give new vitality. Everyone sleeps, felled by the heat; only Egor is awake. He thirstily drinks the cool spring water. But then a sad song ("like weeping") is heard and a birdlike child appears from nowhere, its belly swollen from malnutrition. The child looks with fascination ("as though he saw a spirit from the other world") at Egor's red shirt. "The red shirt tempted and caressed him." When the child runs away in fear, Egor, abandoned and lonely, falls asleep at last. After Deniska awakens, Egor joins him in playing with a grasshopper and a fly in a scene which is a grotesque variation on the themes of life and death. The grasshopper bites off the fly's belly but the fly, unaware of its impending death, goes off to feed on the horses' blood. As the scene ends there is a brief respite and the steppe is again betrayed into a moment of hope. A thunderstorm interrupts the deathlike stillness. But the longed-for reviving rain does not come to awaken the steppe:

Beyond the hillocks came a distant rumble of thunder; a little breath of fresh air followed. Deniska gave a cheerful whistle and whipped up the horses. Father Khristophor and Kuzmichov held on to their hats, and strained their eyes as they looked in the direction of the hillocks. . . . How nice if there were to be a drop of rain!

Just one more small effort, it seemed, one spurt, and the steppe would have the upper hand. But an invisible tyrannical power little by little fettered the wind and the air, settled the dust, and once more, as if nothing had happened, silence reigned.

The first section ends with a scene at a Jewish inn where the travelers rest.

In the second part of the story Egor is transferred to the wagon caravan and continues the journey with the rough wagon drivers. Their depiction expresses the conflicting life and death themes in a more fantastic and stylized manner. Unlike the priest and the uncle, the carters are not entirely indifferent and hostile. Most are friendly to Egor and some feel simple compassion. The futile attempts of the carter Emelyan to sing echo again nature's vain efforts to shake off torpor. On the other hand, some of the carters suggest death: in spite of the heat old Panteley is forever cold, beats his arms against his chest, and speaks "as though

his lips were frozen." Another carter, Vasya, has a tumor
on his chin, his face is bandaged, and he marches stiffly, like
a wooden puppet. Emelyan's singing voice has been destroyed by illness. The main death figure among the carters
is Dymov who is death's agent as he kills a harmless grass
snake; he tries to push Egor under the water as they swim
and Egor fears he will be drowned. Death themes are expressed with even more violence in the murder tales with
which the carters entertain each other and frighten Egor,
as they sit by the campfire.

A storm, which provides yet another moment of hope
to the thirsty steppe, concludes the second section of the
story as it did the first part. But the rain that follows is de-
structive and Egor falls ill with a fever. Again, the final
scene takes Egor out of the steppe as the carters, halted by
the storm, seek shelter at a peasant's hut. Egor is comforted
by the peasant's wife, as he had been by the innkeeper's
wife in the earlier scene.

In the concluding part of "The Steppe," the caravan with
Egor meets with Kuzmichov and the priest as Egor is given
over to the keeping of yet another motherly, but prosaic,
figure. The story ends inconclusively with the melancholy
question, "what will this life be like?" The steppe has been
crossed, but nothing seems very different except that Egor
is sad.

While "The Steppe" is a departure for Chekhov, it bears
certain connections to earlier Russian works. Critics have
noted its analogy to Gogol's *Dead Souls*,[7] and Chekhov himself acknowledged this when he wrote to his friend, D. V.
Grigorovich:

I know that Gogol will be angry with me from the other
world. In our literature it is he who is the king of the steppes.
I stole into his domain with good intentions, but have said a
lot of nonsense.[8]

The beginning of "The Steppe," as the Russian critic Shklovski has noted,[9] is indeed an inversion of the initial passage of *Dead Souls:*

. . . Into the gates of the inn of the provincial town of NN there drove a rather pretty little chaise on springs, of the type customarily used by bachelors, such as retired lieutenant colonels, staff captains, landowners with about one-hundred serfs,—in short by all those who are called "gentlemen of a middling sort."

In "The Steppe" the chaise is of a different character:

From N., the district town of the Z. *gubernija,* an unsprung chaise drove thunderingly over the post road. It was one of those antediluvian chaises in which in today's Russia only salesmen, drovers and poor priests ride.

In Gogol's carriage sits Chichikov who, as the novel unfolds, drives through Russia in search of a fantastic and insubstantial treasure. In Chekhov's carriage the two adult occupants, Kuzmichov and Father Khristofor, are also bent on a journey for profit. In both works the quest leads the participants through the Russian countryside to whose beauties they remain oblivious. The analogy to Gogol's novel is also expressed in the contrast of the poetic painting of the vastness of the Russian land to the shallowness of man's materialistic goals. The relationship of the two works, however, is limited to these external similarities, for Gogol's exuberant, biting satire differs profoundly from Chekhov's reflective and poetic tale.

The common criticism that "The Steppe" is formless,[10] which echoes Chekhov's own misgivings,[11] has perhaps only partial justification. The eight chapters are united by an inner action and a common atmosphere to which Egor reacts, and it is this which provides the essential unity of the story. There are, however, passages in "The Steppe" which betray Chekhov's inexperience with the long form of narration. Faults which are present in "The Steppe" occur infrequently in the shorter stories of this period. There are unnecessary authorial explanations, apostrophes to the reader ("Who is Varlamov?"), even the use of clichés and sometimes an uncharacteristic lack of restraint as in the description of the storm ("The black sky opened its mouth and breathed white fire."). These defects are, however, rarer in the early part of the story where a greater lyrical beauty and simplicity was achieved than in the other two sections. The ending of the story does not attain the understatement and conciseness of the conclusions of Chekhov's other works written at this time. Its inconclusiveness alone unites it with the usual Chekhovian resolutions.

In Chekhov's later works the theme of the effect of vulgarity and emptiness on certain individuals is differently handled. Such individuals are usually transformed, or even destroyed, by unfriendly environments. This problem appears in "The Steppe" in many poetic variations, but Egor remains unchanged by his environment. We know, however, that Chekhov wrote to Grigorovich[12] of plans to continue the adventures of Egor, who was to commit suicide in St. Petersburg. What would drive people to suicide, Chekhov asked? In his answer are suggested many of the problems posed in his later works:

. . . On the one hand physical weakness, nervousness, early sexual maturity, passionate thirst for life and truth, dreams about activity as broad as the steppe, nervous self-analysis, lack of knowledge and broad sweep of ideas; on the other hand—a limitless plain, a cruel climate, a gray crude people with a heavy and cold history, Tatar conditions, bureaucracy, poverty, ignorance, coldness of the capitals, etc. Russian life ties the Russian . . . like a stone weighing a thousand *puds*. In Western Europe people die because they live closely and suffocatingly, but here, because there is space . . . so much space that man in his smallness cannot orient himself.

While "The Steppe" is not free from defects, most of which were later overcome by Chekhov, it suggests, both thematically and stylistically, important concerns and methods of Chekhov's artistic maturity. Nature is often to be a participant in the inner world of Chekhov's characters. A technique which becomes more important in the later stories and particularly in the plays is the use of recurrent sound motifs whose meaning is symbolic. In this story, there are such examples as the song which echoes on the steppe in the first part, the creaking swinging door in the scene in the inn, and the shouts of the driver Dymov in the storm scene. There are also the shorthand devices for characterization by the use of brief external descriptions. Thus Egor's uncle has no beard, wears glasses, and "looks more like a bureaucrat than a merchant." The uncle Kuzmichov is metonymically identified by his "businesslike dryness." Other characters are also drawn by a few strokes. The superficial Father Khristofor has a broad top hat, moist eyes, and an ever-present smile. The caravan drivers, who are almost "humors," are defined by their marionette-like appearance. Varlamov, the business agent, is similarly presented. He appears only fleetingly toward the end of the narrative, but he is frequently mentioned and his presence is felt. He is described as "whirling around" (*kružitsja*) the steppe and when he finally appears, as seen by Egor, he is sitting on an ugly horse, shouting crassly at his subordinates. When Varlamov becomes angry the horse, with which Egor sympathizes, appears to feel his burden increase in weight.

Many characters are identified by distinctive speech traits. The priest speaks rapidly, mumbling as though he were reciting a litany; his remarks are filled with clichés. His self-conscious tone is indicated by his use of Latin phrases remembered from boyhood and his bookish Russian. Puns and plays with words further denote his superficiality. The dry personality of uncle Kuzmichov is reflected in his brief, matter-of-fact phrases. The drivers and the Jewish inn-keepers are also characterized by their idiom and their sub-standard Russian.

Various devices are employed to create the poetic effects of "The Steppe." For example, moods are conveyed through sound patterns. We may mention first the more obvious uses of onomatopoeia: in the sound of the carriage—*ona tarax-tela i vzvizgivala* (it rattled and screeched); in the sound made by the reapers—*vžži, vžži;* in bird sounds—*splju, splju;* and in the sound of thunder—*trrax! tax! tax! tax!* ... *Rrra!* There are other euphonic devices as systematic sound repetition in the opening paragraph which combines as-sonance and alliteration.[13]

Iz N., uezdnogo goroda Z-oj gubernii . . . vyexala i s gromom pokatilas' po počtovomu traktu bezressornaja, ošarapannaja brička. . . .
From N., the district town of the Z. *gubernija,* an unsprung chaise drove thundering over the post road.

The stress in this passage is on *p* and *b* (*pokatilas' po počtovomu . . . bezressornaja ošarapannaja brička*) and on *r* (*traktu, bezressornaja, ošarapannaja brička*). In another passage, front and back variants of the vowel *i* are empha-sized, as well as *l* and palatalized *l'*.[14]

. . . dym bol'šimi klubami šel iz-pod dlinnyx kamyšovyx kryš.
. . . smoke in thick clouds rose from the long thatched roofs.

The lyrical qualities of the work also depend upon seman-tic deformations which, we have noted, contribute to a fresh perception, or "making it strange." When the wagon train stops by a silent grave it seems to Egor "audibly" silent (*slyšno kak ona [mogila] molčit.*) Later the rising moon appears to Egor "blood-red and gloomy, as though it were ill" (*točno bol'naja*). When thunder sounds, Egor thinks of "someone walking on a metal roof. Probably the person who was walking was barefoot, because the metal grumbled dully" (*železo provorčalo gluxo*).

With the completion of "The Steppe," Chekhov reached a turning point in his work. From that time on he abandoned forever the short, hurried humor stories and devoted himself to the serious and ambitious themes which were interesting him increasingly. "The Steppe" is distinguished from the body of Chekhov's work, however, by its length (there is only one other story of similar size, "The Duel" [1891]) and by its strong allegorical implications. In later works the themes of death and futility are suggested and implied by many poetic devices and moods, but they do not compose a clear allegorical theme which can be said to dominate the whole as it does in this, one of the most pessimistic of Chekhov's works.

Chapter 4 / Chekhov and Tolstoy
An Ideological Relationship

> . . . Tolstoy's philosophy touched me
> strongly . . . for some six to seven years.
>
> —from a letter by Chekhov to
> Suvorin (March 27, 1894)

Scholars have frequently noted that during a period of his
life Chekhov was strongly influenced by Tolstoy's moral
teachings.[1] Yet little attempt has been made to determine
the limits of Tolstoy's influence. Even the English critic,
Ronald Hingley, who has treated this problem more fully,
falls short of a clear statement concerning the question.
There is, however, general agreement that Chekhov's writing during the period of the 1880's shows the influence of
Tolstoy's precepts. I should prefer to narrow such a period
to the years when Chekhov's interest in serious stories became dominant, from 1885 to 1890 the year in which Chekhov undertook his trip to the penal colony of Sakhalin after
which he became increasingly critical of "Tolstoyanism."

The ethical system formulated by Tolstoy in his later
years after his so-called "conversion" in the late 1870's, had

57

a widespread effect not only in Russia, but throughout the world. Tolstoy's five "commandments" or rather prohibitions, were for him central to the teachings of Christ: 1. Do not resist evil. 2. Do not be angry. 3. Remain true to one woman, and avoid sexual desire as far as possible. 4. Do not take oaths. 5. Love your neighbor and do not judge your fellow man. In addition, the Tolstoyan outlook included the romantic view of the superiority of the peasant way of life and of physical labor. The artistic influence of Tolstoy on Chekhov was of course extensive but this subject, treated elsewhere in various parts of this study, can be separated from that of the effect of Tolstoy's moral teachings.

One searches in vain through Chekhov's letters, his notebooks, and personal papers of the 1880's for suggestions of a positive attitude toward the moral system of Tolstoy. But examples of the influence of Tolstoyanism can be found in some of Chekhov's short stories written in the latter half of this decade. Chekhov's earliest remarks about Tolstoy in his correspondence refer to two of his own works of the 1880's, "Slime" (*Tina*, 1886), which is a naturalistic depiction of a nymphomaniac, and "Good People" (*Xorošie ljudi*, 1886). In a letter to his friend, the writer Maria Kiseleva, written in January 1887,[2] Chekhov defines some of the limits of Tolstoy's moral influence as he defends himself against Madame Kiseleva's accusation concerning his treatment of sex in "Slime." He mentions, as if to lessen the sharpness of his reply, that he has written a work ("Good People") about Tolstoy's gospel of non-resistance to evil which, he states somewhat facetiously, "has amazed the public."

First of all, like you, I also dislike the kind of literature about which you write [i.e. literature treating sex realistically]. . . . But if you ask my honest and sincere opinion, then I must say that the question of the right of this literature is still an open

one and has not been solved by anyone. Neither I, nor you, nor
the critics of the world have any exact data which would give
us the right to deny this kind of literature. I do not know who
is right, Homer, Shakespeare, Lope-de-Vega, the ancients in
general, who were not afraid to dig in "the dung heap" but who
were much more insistent than we are in questions of morality,
or the modern writers who are fussy on paper but cold and
cynical in their soul and in life? I do not know who has bad
taste: the Greeks who were not ashamed to sing about love as
it is in reality, or the readers of . . . Boborykin. Like the question
of non-resistance to evil, freedom and will, etc., this question
can be solved only in the future. . . . References to Tolstoy and
Turgenev who avoid the "dung heap" do not clarify this question. Their squeamishness proves nothing. . . . A writer must
be as objective as a chemist. He must . . . know that dung heaps
play a very honorable role in pictures of the countryside and
that evil passions are as much part of life as good ones.

  Chekhov's attitude to Tolstoy's puritanical views on love
and sex is, as these remarks indicate, somewhat ambivalent.
While Chekhov sympathized with some of Tolstoy's views,
he never shared Tolstoy's ideal of sexual abstinence, a part
of Tolstoy's mystique of asceticism. Chekhov's censure of
sexuality is directed primarily to its vulgarized aspects, particularly prostitution, and hence to Chekhov it is more the
problem of human dignity in the midst of vulgarity than a
question of morality and ethics.
  The work which is frequently, although mistakenly,
identified with the Tolstoyan outlook concerning chastity
is "Misfortune" (*Nesčast'e,* 1886), a story of a young married
woman who resists her suitor's advances only to succumb
to them in the end. While Chekhov first mentioned reading
Anna Karenina only in 1887,[3] there can be little doubt that
he was acquainted with this work when writing "Misfortune," for the influence of Tolstoy's novel is unmistakable
in Chekhov's story. Chekhov's treatment of the theme of

the adulterous woman, however, is ironic and not moral. The heroine's brief struggle for marital fidelity is motivated by sentimentality, and she hypocritically enjoys her short-lived moral position. The many parallels with Tolstoy's novel emphasize the ironic meaning of Chekhov's story. In fact the flippant treatment of the problem of adultery in "Misfortune" is almost a light parody of *Anna Karenina,* as are many later stories by Chekhov.

In several other stories of the 1880's, in which there is a sexual theme, a distinction is made between romantic and purely physical love. Even in these stories, however, which include "Volodya" (1887) and "A Nervous Breakdown" (*Pripadok,* 1888), the problem of vulgarization of sexual relationships overshadows the moral issue. In "Volodya" a student is tortured by the banal environment into which his selfish mother places him. When he finds himself attracted to a young, sensuous married woman, he tries to escape to her world. He embraces her, but the conflicts are not to be overcome, and he finally commits suicide.

In "A Nervous Breakdown" a young student is taken by his friends on a tour of Moscow brothels and is horrified by the debasement he sees in the faces of the prostitutes and their customers. He runs home and dreams of saving the prostitutes, in a scene reminiscent of Gogol's *Nevski Prospekt.* He realizes that he is helpless and incapable of living as "the others do," and he feels himself an outcast because he cannot behave like his friends. Assuming his moral suffering to be a psychotic symptom, his friends take him to a doctor.

"Maybe you are right [the student tells them]. Perhaps, but it seems strange to me! . . . I am praised to the skies for having written works which will be abandoned and forgotten within three years but, because I cannot speak about fallen women as cold-bloodedly as about these chairs, I am . . . called insane. . . ."

In 1888, Chekhov reported that he was reading Tolstoy's *The Power of Darkness*,[4] but did not comment on it. It must have been in 1890, shortly before his trip to the penal colony of Sakhalin, that Chekhov became acquainted with Tolstoy's *Kreutzer Sonata*, which he praised in a letter to the poet Pleshcheev[5] as being aesthetically gratifying, but he criticized the ascetic views expressed in it concerning sex. He writes:

I am not saying that it is a brilliant work, I cannot judge this. But in my opinion it will be hard to find something equal to it in the seriousness of its intent and the beauty of its execution. . . . It is true, the story has its shortcomings which are very annoying. . . . One matter which one cannot forgive its author is the boldness with which he treats things about which he knows nothing, or which he does not want to understand out of stubbornness. Such are his statements on syphilis, educational institutions, about women's abhorrence of the sexual act, etc. These not only can be disputed but they show a man who is ignorant and who has not taken the trouble in his long life to read one or two books written by specialists.

After Chekhov's visit to Sakhalin, however, he wrote to his publisher Suvorin:[6] "Before my trip the *Kreutzer Sonata* was a great event for me, but now it seems to me to be a ridiculous and senseless work."

There is no evidence that Chekhov ever shared Tolstoy's religious outlook, his equation of God with love, which is expressed by Prince Andrew in *War and Peace*. Chekhov was certainly not a seeker after God, but instead an agnostic, a positivist and an admirer of Darwin. Tolstoy realized his distance from Chekhov's outlook and spoke of Chekhov as "a complete atheist."[7] When in 1897 Tolstoy visited Chekhov, who lay critically ill in a Moscow hospital after a lung hemorrhage, Tolstoy expressed his views about immortality, a conception which, Chekhov wrote, was incomprehensible to him.[8] As Chekhov had stated much earlier in a letter to Pleshcheev,[9] his only belief was in "the human body . . . and the most absolute freedom."

Tolstoy's romantic view that self-perfection can best be realized in a life of simplification, a return to nature and to the humble labor of the peasant is an outlook fleetingly reflected, but often considered, in Chekhov's works. We find this idea expressed, although without the religious, mystical coloration which Tolstoy gives this theme, in a short story, which in other respects also shows the influence of Tolstoy. In "Good People" (*Xorošie ljudi*, 1886), the heroine, a physician, who is to some extent a Tolstoyan figure, begins to be attracted to an ascetic life and takes upon herself some of the servants' functions in the household. It must be noted, however, that later in his long work "The Duel" (*Duèl'*, 1891), as well as in the story "My Life" (*Moja žizn'*, 1896), Chekhov treats the same kind of theme more critically and satirically.

A certain rapprochement between the views of Chekhov and Tolstoy is most evident in Chekhov's brief acceptance of the tenets of Tolstoy's doctrine of non-resistance to evil, as evidenced by a few of Chekhov's stories, although Chekhov says little about this problem in his correspondence. Probably the only work consciously and intimately concerned with this tenet is the previously mentioned "Good People." A detailed argument takes place between the doctor, who defends Tolstoy's doctrine and her brother, who denies it. We sympathize with the Tolstoyan sister, rather than with the cynical brother, an ineffectual art critic who expresses some of the decadent qualities later found in the character of Prof. Serebryakov in *Uncle Vanya* and in *The Wood Demon*. This moralistic story, which praises in Tolstoyan terms non-resistance to evil and humble labor, differs in tone from Chekhov's later work. Fifteen years after its first publication, when Chekhov revised it for inclusion in his *Collected Works*, he eliminated part of the debate over

Tolstoyan views and weakened the Tolstoyan emphases of
the story.

In the three years after "Good People" appeared, there
followed a number of stories concerned, in varying measure,
with non-resistance to evil, as well as the play *The Wood
Demon (Lešij)*, which has justly been termed a morality
play on Tolstoyan lines.[10] We know, however, that Chekhov
soon rejected this play and even questioned it as he finished
it.[11] In the short story "The Meeting" (*Vstreča*, 1887),
which Chekhov excluded from his *Collected Works* in 1901,
as well as in "The Beggar" (*Niščij*, 1887) and *The Wood
Demon* (1889-90), Chekhov considers the Tolstoyan view
that vice can be conquered by kindness, humbleness and
non-resistance. In "The Meeting" a thief is regenerated
when his victim refuses to report him. In "The Beggar" the
the Tolstoyan view is lightly and somewhat facetiously
treated when a tramp is saved by the kindness of a cook who
chops wood for him.

Two other works of this period are sympathetic to the
related Tolstoyan injunction against giving vent to anger.
"An Unpleasantness" (*Neprijatnost'*, 1888) is the story of a
country doctor who slaps his medical assistant for appearing
at the clinic drunk, and then tortures himself with the
thought that by his lack of control he has lost his innocence.
The doctor realizes that nothing has been solved and life
goes on as usual, though he has begun to see more intensely
the stupidity of the life he leads.

In the notable story "Enemies" (*Vragi*, 1887) a doctor,
whose child has just died, is called to the home of a rich
neighbor whose wife, he is told, is dying—only to realize
that she has merely pretended illness in order to facilitate
an elopement with her lover. The doctor becomes enraged,
as does the cuckolded husband, and there follows a verbal
battle between the two unhappy men. The story ends with

a Tolstoyan note concerning the immorality and futility of violent thoughts and actions.

The influence of another Tolstoyan moral tenet, the vanity attached to all earthly goods, is felt in two works of these years.[12] "The Cossak" (*Kazak*, 1887) is a story with mystical overtones and "The Shoemaker and the Devil" (*Sapožnik i nečistaja sila*, 1888) is a kind of moralistic parable about a shoemaker who envies the rich but realizes that they are not better off than the poor, because they will burn in the same flames of hell.

While we have seen that a number of Chekhov's stories of the late 1880's demonstrate the influence and the partial acceptance of some of Tolstoy's ethical views, after 1890 this is no longer true. In a letter to Suvorin, written in March 1894,[13] Chekhov made explicit his growing rejection of Tolstoyanism:

Since I stopped smoking I no longer have any melancholy and nervous moods. Maybe it is because I no longer smoke that Tolstoy's teachings have ceased to move me. In the depths of my soul I feel hostile to them and that is plainly unjust. In my veins courses peasant blood and one cannot impress me with examples of peasant virtues. From my earliest childhood I have believed in progress, and could not fail to believe in it since the difference between the time when I was whipped and the time when I was no longer whipped was a terrible one. I always loved intelligent people, politeness and wit. But I remained as indifferent to the fact that people picked at their calluses, and that their leggings emitted a stifling odor, as to the fact that ladies walk around in curling papers in the mornings. Yet Tolstoy's philosophy touched me strongly and influenced me for some six to seven years. I was influenced not so much by the basic positions of Tolstoy, with which I was acquainted even earlier, but by the Tolstoyan manner of expressing himself, by his sagacity and probably by some kind of hypnotism. Now something in me protests; prudence and justice tell me that there is more love for humanity in electricity and steam than in chastity and vegetarianism. War is an evil, law courts are an evil; but it does not follow from that that I must walk around in bast shoes and sleep on the stove with the workman and his wife, etc. etc. But the question is not whether I am "for" or "against" Tolstoy, but that somehow or other Tolstoy has become more remote from me, that he is no longer in my soul, that he has left my innermost being saying: "I am leaving thy house empty. . . ."

Although the Tolstoyian outlook grew alien to Chekhov, he never lost his admiration of Tolstoy's artistry. In August 1895, Chekhov visited Tolstoy for the first time in Yasnaya Polyana, the latter's country estate; and it is clear from the letters and diaries of both Tolstoy and Chekhov that they exerted a magnetic influence upon each other, and they visited each other intermittently. Chekhov's own letters express this admiration. "In my entire life," he wrote, "I have never respected a single man so profoundly, I might even say so extremely, as Lev Nikolaevich [Tolstoy]."[14] And in 1900, at the occasion of Tolstoy's illness, Chekhov wrote to the publisher M. O. Menshikov:

I am afraid of Tolstoy's death. If he should die, there would be a huge emptiness in my life. First of all, I have never loved a single man as much as I have loved him. I am not a believer, but of all faiths his is the most attractive and suitable for me. Secondly, as long as Tolstoy exists in the world of literature it is easy and agreeable to be a writer. . . . His activity serves as a justification of those hopes and expectations which mankind has in literature. Thirdly, Tolstoy stands like a rock, and as long as he is alive poor taste in literature, impudent or sentimental banality, and crude and angry egotism will be isolated and hidden in the shade. Only his authority is capable of keeping the so-called literary moods and currents on a relatively high level. Without him [the literary world] would be a shepherdless herd. . . .[15]

Tolstoy's mysticism and rejection of science and medicine were attitudes which never attracted Chekhov even in the

short "Tolstoyan" period. Many of Chekhov's most positive pictures were of scientists. To Chekhov, science was an
indispensable aspect of art, although he took issue, in some
of his later stories, with those who would worship science
uncritically. His early study of medicine undoubtedly affected his own artistic views. His almost anatomical dissec-
tion of humanity, his conciseness and his objective approach
to reality in certain works can be cited as examples. Art
and science were in the last analysis inseparable and hence,
his most sympathetic types were often those who were both
scientists and poets such as Dr. Astrov in *Uncle Vanya.*

Nor could Chekhov ever agree with the older Tolstoy's
puritanical rejection of art as sinful and deceitful. Concerning the publication of Tolstoy's *What Is Art?,* Chekhov
wrote that it:

. . . represents nothing of interest. All this is old hat. To say of
art that it has become enfeebled and has entered a *cul de sac,*
that it is not what it should be, and so on and so forth, is like
saying that the desire to eat and drink has become old fashioned
and that it is no longer what it should be. Of course hunger is
an old phenomenon, and in our desire to eat we have come to a
cul de sac; yet nevertheless to eat is necessary, and we shall continue to eat, no matter what the gentlemen philosophers and
angry old men tell us about it.[16]

It is true that Chekhov partially shared Tolstoy's conception of the moral obligation of the artist, as he wrote to his
friend Maria Kiseleva in 1887:[17] "A writer is a man who is
bound and under moral contract by the realization of his
duty and conscience." Yet he did not accept the view expressed by Tolstoy that the aim of art is "first to depict and
then to brand the evils of life and next to point the way to
the goal." "Literature," Chekhov wrote, "is art only because
it paints life as it is in reality. Its aim is unconditional and
honest truth. To narrow its function to such a specialty as

the uncovering of the kernel [of goodness] is just a
as if you were to force Levitan to draw a tree witho
ing the dirty bark and the yellowed leaves."[18] Yet (
did not entirely reject Tolstoy's stricture that art m
what Tolstoy called a "general guiding idea." In 1888 he
wrote to Suvorin:[19]

While I am sometimes a heretic, I have never advocated the
absolute denial of problems in art. . . . I have always insisted
that it is not the task of the artist to solve narrowly specialized
questions. . . . But that in his [the artist's] sphere these questions
do not exist can be argued only by a person who has never
written anything.

Nevertheless, in the same letter Chekhov makes the point
which distinguishes him from the later Tolstoy. While art
must concern itself with significant problems, he says, it
is not the artist's task to solve them. Chekhov takes examples
from both Tolstoy's own work and Pushkin, when he says:

You confuse two problems: the solution to a problem and
the correct statement of the problem. In *Anna Karenina* and
Onegin not a single problem is solved, but they satisfy you
completely, because the problems posed in them are funda-
mentally correct. It is the duty of the judge to put the question
to the jury correctly and it is for the members of the jury to
make up their minds, each according to his own taste.

Still Chekhov was not quite satisfied with this view, and
four years later he wrote to Suvorin:[20] The author must
not only "depict life as it is" but permeate the depiction of
this life with consciousness and an aim, so that "one feels,
in addition to life as it is, also life as it should be." Chekhov's
works reflect, in varying ways, these two aims—a realistic
depiction of life and also a certain search, however groping, for a meaning to life.

As Chekhov became less influenced by the moralism and
romanticism of Tolstoy in his later years, his stories in the

1890's began to take direct issue with some Tolstoyan themes. Certain protagonists, as Gromov in "Ward No. 6," strongly attack non-violence and other Tolstoyan views. Yet, Chekhov's relationship to Tolstoy was always a complex one, and certain characters, even after 1890 continue to be presented somewhat in the spirit of Tolstoy's views. Chekhov's attitude of admiration for the old master, was tempered by his own artistic and philosophical skepticism which found expression in most of his serious works.

Chapter 5 / The Narcissus Theme
"The Princess" and "The Grasshopper"

The stories "The Princess" *(Knjaginja,* 1889) and "The Grasshopper" *(Poprygunja,* 1892), introduce a new variant of the theme of the two personalities: the social personality and the inner one which is revealed by certain significant details. This variant is the theme of the narcissistic and beguiling woman, who deceives herself as well as others. We can observe, in these works, new techniques for depicting the heroine whose self-image is contrasted to the views of her held by those around her.

These women, whose self-love and hypocrisy can lead only to emptiness, if not to personal destruction, are often metaphorically likened to little birds. In the *Odyssey,* Circe warned Odyseus of the sirens who were half-women, half-birds. While Chekhov's women do not overtly destroy, as did the sirens of the Greek myth, the similarity is suggested. Such use of literary allusions is a frequent device of Chekhov's which often contributes irony by an implied contrast between the meaning of the mythical or literary reference and that of the theme of the story.

"The Princess," begun in November 1888, was not finished until March, 1889. Even then Chekhov asked Suvorin, in whose journal—the *New Times*—it appeared, for an opportunity to work further on it.[1] This story is the first of a series which treat satirically the selfish woman in love with herself. Like "The Steppe," and unlike most of Chekhov's works, this story lacks the "curve" by which the line of the narrative deviates from expected outcome. The princess remains unchanged in the story in spite of a disturbing event in which she is unmasked. Other characters serve to place the princess into perspective. The action is simple: the princess arrives at a monastery, acts and sees herself as a goddess dispensing kindness, is exposed as a hypocrite by a doctor, but leaves the monastery unshaken in her self-admiration.

A picture of a hypocritical and sentimental woman is achieved by skillful manipulation of the point of view of the story. While the voice of the narrative is that of the omniscient author, Chekhov develops a more faceted view of the princess by occasionally permitting the reader to see her as others do, and—more frequently—by allowing us to see her through her own eyes. We have, therefore, five different views of the heroine: the author's objective picture, her own, the monks', and finally that of an old women, and that of an accusing doctor. The shallowness of the princess prior to the exposé by the doctor is made evident by a number of metonymic details, each one slightly suggestive and combining with the others to give a general impression.

The story opens without an exposition, as the carriage carrying the princess approaches the monastery gates, a scene viewed through the eyes of the monks. In the first view of the princess she is dismounting from her carriage. This scene is presented from the perspective of the monks and partly, as well, from that of the princess herself.

> . . . She lifted up her dark veil and went unhurriedly (*ne speša*) to receive the blessing of the monks. Then she nodded graciously (*laskovo kivnula*) to the lay brothers. . . .

The phrases "dark veil," "receive . . . blessing," "without hurrying," and "nodded graciously" reflect the princess' romantic picture of herself. Expressions such as "a friendly, meek smile" suggest her hypocrisy and superficiality. Her first remarks follow:

> "Well, have you missed your princess . . . I haven't visited you for a whole month. But here I have come; behold your princess. But where is your Father Superior? My God, I am burning with impatience! A wonderful, wonderful old man! You must be proud of having such a Father Superior!"

The phrase "your princess," a key expression, as well as "I haven't visited you for a whole month," suggests the princess' conceit. Her affected speech is filled with clichés as "I am burning with impatience." Later she notes that the monastery is "far from the giddy world." She remarks to the accusing doctor that "much water has flowed under the bridge [since last we met]," and her expressions of sympathy to him concerning the death of his wife are banal. She speaks in a condescending and mildly gentle manner to those beneath her station, but she may shift to a rapid succession of almost hysterical exclamations if her composure is unsettled. Thus, the gentle tone of her remarks to the monks suddenly shifts to one of uncontrolled excitement when she faces the Father Superior.

> . . . When the Father Superior entered, the princess uttered a shriek of delight . . . and went to receive his blessing.
> "No, no! Let me kiss it!" she said, snatching his hand and

greedily kissing it three times. "How happy I am, holy Father, to see you at last!"

The Father Superior's military phrasing of his replies, "Certainly, your excellency, quite so (*tak točno*)" and his use of the particle -*s* which in Russian indicates subservience (*slušaju-s, ponimaju-s*), indicates their unequal social relationship.

The brief exchange with the Father Superior is followed by a short passage of authorial comment, informing us that the princess loves the monastery and visits it regularly. Then, almost imperceptively, there occurs a shift of perspective to that of the princess.

... The timid novices, the quiet, the low ceilings, the smell of cypress, the simple food, the cheap curtains in the windows—all this moved her, softened her and disposed her to contemplation and to good thoughts. It was sufficient for her to be in these rooms for just half an hour to make her think of herself as timid and modest, and to make her imagine that she also smelled of cypress wood. ... And the princess began to imagine that, although she was only twenty-nine, she was very much like the old archimandrite, and that, like him, she was born not for riches, not for earthly grandeur and love, but for a quiet life, far away from the world, a life of twilight just as these rooms. ...

Now the princess' enraptured picture of herself becomes that of a little bird and a ray of light and sunshine, which lighten the life of the recluse monks, even as "an angel sent from up high":

... It happens that a ray of light shines suddenly into the dark cell of the anchorite absorbed in prayer, or that a bird alights on the window and sings its song; the stern anchorite will smile in spite of himself, and from his breast, from under the heavy weight of his grief over man's sins, like from under a stone, a quiet sinless joy will suddenly flow forth like a stream of water. It seemed to the princess that she brought from the outside world just such comfort as the ray of light or the little bird. Her friendly, gay smile, her timid look, her voice, her jests, in fact her total appearance, her small, graceful figure dressed in simple black, must arouse a feeling of joy and tenderness in simple austere people. Everyone looking at her must think: "God has sent us an angel" . . . and feeling that no one could help thinking this, she smiled even more cordially and tried to resemble a bird.

Soon she sees a black cloud which looks like a veil. Earlier a black veil had served as a detail to identify the princess. Later she sees herself as a cloud. But ironically this cloud of her sentimental revery turns out to be a flock of crows whose cawing mocks the princess' bird-like self-image.

The self-image of the princess, which has been constructed by narrative comment, by the monks' remarks, and by such structural devices of comment as the contrasting, yet similar imagery (the rook-singing bird, the cloud—the rook cloud), is now set against two further points of view, one of indifference and one of open hostility.

When the princess sees an old peasant woman, she thinks dramatically how good it would be to stop the old woman and to tell her "something kind, sincere, to help her. . . . But the old woman disappeared around the corner without even once turning around." Then follows a lengthy scene. In words reminiscent of a Greek choral speech, a doctor whose wife has just died, who used to serve on the princess' estate but was dismissed, insults her in an outbreak of fury. He cites instance after instance in which she played a role utterly opposite to that in which her imagination has cast her. The doctor is one of Chekhov's many honest physicians whose righteous indignation is sometimes exaggerated. The doctor in "The Princess" regrets having lost his temper and apologizes sheepishly afterwards. Typically this doctor, as other of Chekhov's doctors, is characterized by his constant reference to his "honest labor." The use of such external devices as this unmasking scene is less frequent in Chekhov's later works. The doctor's exaggerated depiction of the princess' sinfulness deprives the story of some of its subtlety. Olga Ivanovna in "The Grasshopper," a further development of the princess, is less obviously drawn, and there is no comparably dramatic unmasking scene.

The doctor's harsh words are followed by a brief lyrical interlude, a poetic picture of an idyllic evening as the princess, crushed by the doctor's remarks, is left alone momentarily. A subtext again forms an ironic comment on the princess' sentimental view of herself as a bird. In an earlier passage a flock of crows had served this purpose. Now bats appear: ("Along the white monastery wall bats were flitting noiselessly.") Now the flying beasts do not even have a voice with which to sing, or even to caw; they are not birds but rodents.

The story then turns to the princess' thoughts. As a result of the doctor's indignant words, her self-view suffers an apparent transmutation. She sees herself sentimentally as an unjustly injured martyr. She dreams in clichés of bidding farewell to aristocratic title and worldly goods and of withdrawing into a nunnery "without a word of reproach: she will pray for her enemies and only then will she be understood and people will ask her forgiveness; but then it will be too late. . . ." As she reflects, however, she admires herself in the mirror and powders her face and eats with gusto her favorite "monastery food"—marinated fish, mushrooms, and honey cakes—washing them down with Malaga wine. We shall observe that enjoyment of food and gluttony are among Chekhov's frequently used metonymic devices to suggest *pošlost'*.

But this interlude of self-pity caused by the doctor's words, which had briefly disarrayed the princess' composure, is quickly forgotten. She falls asleep luxuriantly immediately after going to bed, and wakes up with the same happy feeling. Only for a moment does she remember that she is "unhappy." Her misgiving rapidly turns into a daydream, and she smiles inwardly and thinks that if only all men knew her soul they would all be at her feet.

The story ends, as it began, with the little bird the heroine thinks she resembles.

Attempting to resemble a little bird, the princess flitted into the carriage and nodded to all sides. She felt gay, clear and warm in spirit, and she felt that her smile was unusually kind and soft. . . . She thought that there was no greater joy than to bring warmth, light and happiness wherever one goes, to forgive insults and to smile pleasantly at one's enemies. Peasants whom she met on the road bowed to her, the carriage made a soft noise, clouds of dust rose from the wheels and were carried by the wind into the golden rye fields, and it seemed to the princess that her body was wafted not on the pillows of the carriage but on clouds, and that she herself resembled a light transparent little cloud. . . . "How happy I am!" she whispered closing her eyes. "How happy I am!"

The theme of the narcissistic woman is further developed in "The Grasshopper," a story which continues the contrast of the idealized and good physician to a shallow and pretentious woman. Olga Ivanovna, who imagines that she has great artistic talent, marries the young scholar and physician, Dr. Dymov, a man quite outside her circle of bohemian acquaintances. After the doctor discovers his wife's liaison with a mediocre painter, he allows himself to become infected by one of his patients in an act of self-sacrifice which causes his death.

The story opens with a wedding scene in which Dymov and his wife are characterized. The reader sees Dymov through the perspective of Olga Ivanovna.

"Look at him: it is true, isn't it, that there is something in him?" She [Olga Ivanovna] said to her friends, nodding towards her husband, as though wishing to explain why she married a simple, very ordinary, in no way distinguished man.

Her husband, Osip Stepanych Dymov, was a physician with the rank of titular councillor. He worked in two hospitals: in one as a supernumerary practitioner, in the other as a pathologist. Daily, from nine o'clock in the morning till noon, he received patients and worked in the wards, and in the afternoon he took a horse tram to the other hospital where he dissected bodies. His private practice was small and earned him some five hundred rubles a year. That was all. What else could be said about him?

The tone of Olga Ivanovna's discourse indicates her conceit. The phrase "that was all . . ." with which the brief description of Dymov ends, is not the author's comment, as it might seem, but an oblique expression of Olga Ivanovna's own attitude. Further commentary is provided by the next passage, concerning Olga's bohemian entourage, which continues to suggest her inner reflections:

. . . But on the other hand, Olga Ivanovna and her friends . . . were not completely ordinary people. Each of them was distinguished by something and each was a little bit well known, each of them already had a name and was considered a celebrity. Or, if he was not yet a celebrity, at least he gave great promise.

In the ensuing passages Olga's vision of a celebrated *bohème* is deflated. There is the opera singer who tells Olga Ivanovna "with a sigh" that she has a great future; and Ryabovski, the painter and future lover of Olga, about whom we learn initially only that he is "handsome" and has sold his latest picture for five hundred rubles; and the cellist "whose instrument wept." This passage not only satirizes Olga Ivanovna's notion of herself and her friends but also prepares the stage for the less subtle ironic reversal at the end of the story. Olga Ivanovna is obsessed with the hunt for great people who are to be her private discoveries. "Not one of her evenings would pass," we are told, "without [her] trembling whenever the doorbell would ring and saying with a triumphant expression on her face: 'That is he.' " The story ends with the deceived husband's death. Only then Olga Ivanovna discovers that unknowingly she had lived with the only able man, the only celebrity, she had ever known.

... Remembering what her father and all his medical colleagues thought of him [Dymov], she understood that they all saw in him a future celebrity.

Certain details serve to characterize the personalities of the main protagonists. Olga Ivanovna's obsession with "effects" is evident in the arty pretensions in the furnishings of her house.

Olga Ivanovna hung the living room with drawings, her own and her friends', framed and unframed; and near the piano and furniture she created a pretty confusion of Chinese parasols, easels, many-colored draperies, daggers, busts and photographs. She bedecked the dining room walls with bright colored illustrations, bast shoes and sickles. In the corner she placed a scythe and a hay rake, and this made a room in the Russian style. To make her bedroom like a cave, she draped the ceiling and the walls with dark cloth, hung a Venetian lantern over the bed, and set a figure with a halberd near the door.

The disarray of Olga Ivanovna's apartment suggests the cluttered activities which fill her superficial life. The Venetian lantern and the bast shoes are just as incongruous as Olga's *bohème* and her husband. The dark cave of her bedroom suggests the essential isolation of Olga Ivanovna.

Olga Ivanovna is also revealed by her clothes, beguiling and yet false, like her illusions and her unsubstantial friends:

... She and her dressmaker resorted to many ingenious tricks, so that she could appear in new-looking dresses and make an impression with her outfits. Frequently old, dyed-over pieces of cloth, worthless patches of tulle, lace, plush, and silk were transformed into something bewitching, not dresses, but dreams.

When she travels with her artist-lover on a Volga steamer, Olga Ivanovna muses as she looks into the water and at the beautiful shore. She thinks of herself as immortal, and in a narcissistic revery "she imagined crowds of people, fireworks, triumphant sounds of music, shouts of rapture. And she herself in a white dress, and flowers strewn about her on all sides."

The clichés and condescending expressions marking Olga Ivanovna's speech also reveal her pretentiousness. She addresses her husband only by his last name, Dymov, thus indicating the chasm and misunderstanding which separates them. In her embarrassment at her husband's lack of veneer, she carefully constructs for herself and her bohemian friends a special image of Dymov. This view, based on certain externals, is expressed in the affected phrases of Olga Ivanovna as she refers to her husband's "honest hands," to his face "powerful as that of a Bengal tiger," and to his bearlike strength.

Echoing her insincere view of Dymov is her trite description of a village telegrapher whose coming wedding she wishes to celebrate as a pastoral amusement. The telegrapher had "in his face something strong, bear-like. . . . One could use him as a model for a picture of a young Varangian." She reflects that she might paint the young man in a romantic pose which recalls an earlier scene when she painted Dymov with a towel around his head "as a Bedouin."

Olga Ivanovna's flighty mind, like that of the princess, is suggested by her frequent employment of hectic, almost hysterical phrases, such as the brief exclamations and commands—"Listen!" "Come closer!" "Look!" Her description of Dymov's courtship and their betrothal is typical.

"No, but listen, you . . . how could this happen so suddenly? Listen, listen! . . . When my poor father became ill, Dymov watched day and night at his bedside. Such self-denial! Listen, Ryabovski. . . . And you, writer, listen, this is very interesting. Come closer. How much self-sacrifice, genuine compassion! I also did not sleep nights and sat by my father's bed, and suddenly! There we were! I had captivated the brave swain! My Dymov was up to his ears in love. . . . Well, after my father's death, he sometimes visited me, we met in the streets. And suddenly, one beautiful evening—bang! He proposed!

A phrase strikingly conveying Olga Ivanovna's conceit is her remark concerning Dymov's lack of anger over her unfaithfulness: "this man tortures me with his magnanimity," a comment which so pleases her that she repeats it to all those who know of her affair with Ryabovski.

When her husband is dying her first reaction is fear of infection. But soon she regrets selfishly that she has not noticed that:

. . . he had been, indeed, an exceptional man, a rare man, and —compared with all her acquaintances—a great man. . . . The walls, the ceilings, the lamp, and the carpet winked derisively at her, as though they wanted to say, "You have let it slip by you, slip by."

Only then does she rush into her dying husband's room. But her belated regret communicates nothing to Dymov, who is as isolated from her as he dies as he had been in life; his "half-open eyes were fixed not on Olga Ivanovna, but on his cover." The character of Dr. Dymov is depicted with sympathy, and with some idealization. The defenselessness of Dymov in the face of his wife's abuses is almost saintly and in Dymov's goodness and humble self-sacrifice there is even the suggestion of an intellectualized Tolstoyan figure. He is usually silent and does not participate in his wife's bohemian parties. Instead he puts himself in charge of the refreshments, and at every party he flings open the doors of the dining room and "with his good-natured, meek smile he would say, rubbing his hands: 'Gentlemen, come to supper!'" The good-natured smile remains the leitmotif of Dymov, who is thus pictured as remote from his wife's milieu, within which he is ineffectual.

Ryabovski, Olga's artist-lover, is also characterized by mannerisms of speech which indicate his banality. While Olga speaks in excited staccato phrases, Ryabovski's speech sounds languid and is filled with pretentious-sounding observations. On their Volga trip, he tells Olga, as they view the water at night from the boat, that:

... the black shadows on the water are not shadows but merely a dream; that this magic water, with its fantastic reflections, this endless sky, these melancholy, pensive shores which express the vanity of our lives and the existence of something more elevated, eternal, blessed, all call on us to forget ourselves, to die, to become a memory. The past is trivial, and uninteresting, the future insignificant; but this magic, never to be repeated night, will soon end, will disappear in eternity. Why, then, live?

Ryabovski's lack of vitality is also conveyed by an expression which becomes his leitmotif, "I am tired," which he usually utters with closed eyes. His penchant for affected punning and playing with words also suggests the insecure *poseur* e.g., the recurrent "not badsome" (*nedurstvenno*) and the senseless rhyming, *"Nature morte, kurort, sort, čort, port"* (*nature morte,* spa, brand, devil, port).

The princess as well as Olga Ivanovna, are the progenitors of later narcissistic types: Layevski's mistress in "The Duel" (1891), the heroine of "Ariadne" (1895), the would-be musician "Kitten," who temporarily bewitches the hero of "Ionych" (1898). There are as well the many heroes in the mature plays, such as Ranevskaya in *The Cherry Orchard,* and Professor Serebryakov in *Uncle Vanya,* who are similar to these early characters.

Chapter 6 / Early Social Stories

In 1890, after Chekhov's visit to the Russian penal colony on the island of Sakhalin, he became increasingly concerned with a search for a more clearly defined world view and for an answer to the question of the moral responsibility of the writer. He also began to think more seriously of social problems, and his writings voiced a degree of social criticism previously unknown in his work. His observation of the sharp cleavages in Russian society brought about his final disenchantment with the Tolstoyan idealization of peasant life which had briefly attracted him. The only stories of 1890, "The Thieves" (*Vory*) and "Gusev," both completed after the return from his voyage to Sakhalin in 1890, as well as "Peasant Wives" (*Baby*, 1891), "The Wife" (*Žena*, 1892), and "In Exile" (*V ssylke,* 1892), all reveal this strengthened interest in social problems.

"The Thieves" tells the story of a group of horse thieves who are observed by a medical assistant marooned in their hide-out by a snowstorm; finally, after being robbed by them, the medical assistant becomes a thief himself. Suvorin, for whose journal, *New Times,* the story was written, criticized "The Thieves" for its failure to clarify sufficiently the distinction between good and evil. Chekhov's reply is another manifestation of his attitude of objectivity.[1]

You criticize me for objectivity, calling it indifference to good and evil, and absence of ideals and ideas and so on. You wish that I, in depicting horse thieves, should say: the theft of horses is an evil. But this has been known for a long time even without me. Let the jurors judge about this, but my task is to show only what they are like. I write: You are dealing with horse thieves, so you should know that they are not beggars but well fed people, that they are people of conviction and that horse thievery is not only thievery, but a passion. Certainly it would be nice to combine art with preaching, but for myself personally this is extremely difficult and almost impossible because of problems of technique. In order to show horse thieves in seven hundred lines, I always have to speak and think in their tone and feel in their spirit, otherwise—if I add subjectivity—my images will become diluted and the tale will not be as compact as a short tale must be. When I write, I put all my faith in the reader, presuming that the subjective elements which are lacking in my tale will be supplied by him.

Chekhov's depiction in "The Thieves" of the relationship between the medical assistant and the pretty and sensuous girl, who assists in the theft of his horse, comes as close as Chekhov ever does to a Zolaesque naturalistic treatment of sex. The elements of satire and irony, usual in Chekhov's works, are lacking, however, in the treatment of the thieves who are even romanticized in their portrayal as rebels.

Another work, this time of peasant women, which does not lack satire and irony, is "Peasant Wives," published in Suvorin's *New Times* in June of 1891. With his habitual facetiousness Chekhov wrote Suvorin about "Peasant Wives":[2]

I have been torn away from my work on Sakhalin not by the muse of revenge and sadness and not by a thirst for sweet sounds but by my desire to turn a quick penny, for I am literally without a penny. . . . It is dull to write about peasant life.

In July of the same year Tolstoy's friend and collaborator, I. I. Gorbunov-Posadov, requested Chekhov's permission to reprint "Peasant Wives" in the Tolstoyan publication, *The Intermediary* (*Posrednik*). He told Chekhov that he found the story a strong attack on "the type of the Russian Tartuffe, the immoral hypocrite."[3] The story is indeed a study of hypocrisy, as was "The Princess," but it is a more serious treatment. Its chief character, the cruel and cold Matvey Savvich with his pharisaic cant, seems more reminiscent of Judushka Golovlev from Saltykov-Shchedrin's *The Golovlev Family,* than he is of Tartuffe. A peasant milieu is the setting for this study of the hypocrisy of a trader, one of whose victims is a Russian peasant woman. A sub-theme is the subservient position of women in peasant society. "Peasant Wives" is in many respects a thematic prototype for many of Chekhov's later stories which depict the cruel treatment of women among the peasants and the lower middle classes, such as "The Peasants" (*Mužiki,* 1897) and "In the Ravine" (*Vovrage,* 1900).

The explication of the theme by shifting points of view from which the main character is seen, which we have noted in "The Princess" and "The Grasshopper," is also important in "Peasant Wives." Like these stories "Peasant Wives" is a story of one character—Matvey. Other protagonists serve primarily to delineate Matvey more fully.

We first see Matvey Savvich from the authorial view as he enters the courtyard, prays, and sits down to eat. The point of view then shifts to the innkeeper, Dyudya, who acts as a commenting chorus. Matvey's "sedate" and deliberate way of eating suggests to the innkeeper a "businesslike man, serious and aware of his own value." We are reminded of the protagonists of earlier works, and notably of Kuzmichov of "The Steppe" who is characterized by "businesslike dryness."

A third view is Matvey's own, revealed when Matvey boastingly tells the innkeeper and his family the story of his seduction of Masha whose soldier husband was away on army duty. With hypocritical propriety Matvey rejects his mistress after her husband's return. But Masha refuses her husband whom she married without love. When her husband dies of arsenic poisoning, Masha is tried and Matvey condemns her in her trial. Nevertheless he visits her with gifts of food and is indignant when she rejects him. He visited her, he says, out of humaneness. When Masha dies, Matvey Savvich takes her son into his house to save his own soul, he explains. But he treats the son badly, and the adoption becomes thus only another insincere act.

The position of the innkeeper, Dyudya, is of special interest. His brief statements, acting as a commenting chorus, punctuate Matvey's story. "Ah the evil one," he says about Masha, and "a dog's death to a dog" is his remark about her death.

Matvey is also characterized by speech traits. He is initially described ironically by the narrator as "eloquent" (*krasnorečivyj*), a reference to the baroque embroidery of his expressions. Clichés, unnecessary sayings, Old Church Slavic expressions, half-understood Westernisms, and stilted metaphors pervade his speech. When referring to the death of his mistress' mother-in-law, he says that she "had taken herself into upper Jerusalem where there are neither illness nor sighs." But the ecclesiastic language switches abruptly to folk sayings and colloquialisms as he says: "They lived for half a year. Then misfortune came, you must take it.

. . . God's will, you can't do anything about. Sure thing."
When recalling his attraction to Masha, he returns to his
hyperbolic style: "the unclean one, the enemy of mankind,
confused me," and "my brains spun in my head from
imaginings."

The character of Matvey Savvich is further elucidated
by the outlook of Masha, indicated through Matvey's words,
as he describes Masha's love and then hate of him. There is
also the little boy's impression and, finally, that of the
womenfolk in the inn. The women sympathize with Masha
and one of them, Varvara, is fired to heated protest by the
story about Masha.

Again, the simple plot structure of "Peasant Wives" reminds us of "The Princess": the central protagonist arrives
in a carriage, reveals himself by his action and speech, is
seen through varying points of view, and leaves again—unchanged—as he had come. As in "The Princess," a significant gesture introduces and concludes the story on a note of
irony. The princess enters "like a bird" and leaves "like a
bird" and "like a cloud." The initial appearance of Matvey
Savvich is marked as he crosses himself properly; it ends as
Matvey leaves with the same gesture the next morning, but
only after we have heard his cruel tale, which unmasks him.

In 1891, Chekhov took an active part in famine relief,
an experience which provided inspiration for the story "The
Wife" (*Žena*, 1892). This work depicts the indifference of
Russian landowners to the lot of the peasants. The ineffectiveness of aristocratic philanthropy is satirized and
contrasted to the realities of peasant life which is natural-
istically shown in tones which are to characterize some of
Chekhov's later peasant stories:

. . . They live, three or four families in one hut, so the population of each hut is never less than fifteen people of both sexes,
not counting the small children and of course there is nothing
to eat, there is hunger and a general epidemic of typhoid and

typhus; literally everyone is ill. The medical assistant says, "you enter the hut and what do you see? All are sick, all delirious, someone laughs, someone crawls to the wall; the huts stink, there is nobody to give them water or to carry the water from the well, and for food they have only frozen potatoes."

In contrast to this picture there is the ironic characterization of the aristocratic narrator, Assorin, who sends gendarmes after the hungry peasants because they have stolen some of his grain while at the same time he is preparing to give a sizable sum to famine relief. The thought of the famine only annoys him, for it threatens to disturb his life work, a study of the history of Russian railways. Assorin's tearful and hysterical wife is also ridiculed. She organizes famine relief not out of sympathy with the peasants, but in order to spite her husband and to assure herself social recognition. The third aristocrat, Bragin, a flabby old man who boasts of his erstwhile radicalism, is a picture of degeneration and demoralization. His self-effacing remarks, his asthma, his constant alternation between giggling and tearfulness, and his oft-repeated jokes and clichés all contribute to the view of a landowner not unlike so many of Gogol's, but also cursed with an inability to act. And satire is strong, if not subtle, in the description of the gluttonous meal served by Bragin to guests who stuff themselves with many courses while they piously discuss the famine.

A didactic quality detracts from the depiction of the simple country doctor, Sobol, who expresses his ideas of philanthropy:

"As long as our relations to the people are characterized by ordinary philanthropy, as in children's homes or in institutions for war veterans, so long will we only dodge issues, prevaricate, and deceive ourselves and nothing more. Our relations must be business-like, they must be based on accounting, on knowledge and on justice. My Vaska has been a workman on my estate all his life; he had a bad harvest, he is ill and hungry. If now I give him fifteen kopeks a day, I do this because I would like him to be able to return to his previous position of a worker, that is, I preserve primarily my own interests, but at the same time for some reason or other I call these fifteen kopeks a help, assistance, and a good deed. Now let us say the following. By the most modest accounting, figuring on a sum of seven kopeks per person and on five souls per family, in order to feed one thousand families, we would need three hundred fifty rubles a day. This figure determines our business obligations to one thousand families. However, we give not three hundred fifty a day, but only ten and we say that this is assistance, help, and thanks to this assistance your wife and all of us are extremely wonderful people, and long live humanitarianism! That's the way it is my dear! Oh, if only we would talk less about humanitarianism, and would count and judge a little more and carry on according to our conscience in our relationship to our obligations! How many of those humane, sentimental people are there among us, who sincerely run from house to house with collection sheets but fail to pay their tailors and cooks? There is no logic in our life. No, that's all, no logic!"

We must admit to a groping quality in this story, a heavy didacticism as well as a too-obvious character delineation. While the Chekhovian method and technique can be recognized in the disclosure of the hypocrisy of the aristocracy through the means of shifting points of view, speech traits, and distinctive features, we feel that the contrasting pictures of the peasants and aristocrats are oversimplified.

Another work, also concerned with broad social problems, but more subtly drawn, is "In Exile" (*V ssylke*, 1892), which was inspired by Chekhov's observations in Sakhalin of the notorious Russian penal colonies. Here Chekhov describes the suffering of Siberian exiles to whom human dignity is denied. Two exiles of different social background are the protagonists: a young, sick Tatar who yearns for his warm land and his wife, and an old aristocrat, deserted by his wife, who desperately searches for a doctor to cure his hope-

lessly ill daughter. The nobleman's fate composes a critique
of Tolstoy's idealization of simple labor. The aristocratic
exile comes to Siberia with the intention of tilling the soil
and of living "by his labors, by the sweat of his brow"; but
his hopefully repeated phrase, "Yes, even in Siberia one can
live," rings as an ironic commentary to his life of servitude.
The sadly false optimism of the aristocrat is, however, only
a weak echo of the oft-repeated phrases of Semen Tolkovy,
another exile, "May God give everyone such a life," and
"You will get used to it." Semen's acceptance of the evil of
the Siberian life has deprived him of all humanity. He becomes so hardened that he laughs at other people's suffering and shrugs off their sobs with his phrase: "You will get
used to it."

Chekhov must have seen many such brutalized men on
Sakhalin. The reality of the acceptance of suffering, romantically treated by Tolstoy, is implied in a description by Chekhov, which is not unlike those in the first Soviet novel
about Siberian labor camps, Solzhenitsyn's *One Day in the
Life of Ivan Denisovich.*

They all lay down. The door was thrust open by the wind
and snow blew into the little hut. Nobody wanted to get up and
close the door: they were cold and lazy.
"But I feel well!" said Semen falling asleep. "May God give
everyone such a life."
... From outside one could hear noises, similar to the howling
of dogs.
"What is that? Who is that?"
"That is the Tatar who is crying." ...
"He will get used to it!" said Semen and immediately fell
asleep.
Soon they were all asleep. But the door remained open.

Chapter 7 / The Searching Stories I
A Dreary Story, Gusev, The Duel, Ward No. 6

Simultaneous with Chekhov's growing concern about social problems is his search for a definition of his own world view, a quest which is clearly expressed in a series of stories, written between 1889 and 1893, which are concerned more directly than any other of Chekhov's works with specific philosophical questions.

These stories, united by a common theme, the search for a guiding idea, include: "A Dreary Story" (*Skučnaja istorija*, 1889), "The Duel" (*Duèl'*, 1891), "Gusev" (1891), "Ward No. 6" (*Palata No. 6*, 1892), and "The Black Monk" (*Černyj monax*, written in 1893, published in 1894). After "The Black Monk," which terminates the cycle of searching stories, Chekhov no longer shows so intense and restless a concern with intellectual and philosophical questions. In his later works we find that philosophical questions are no longer so directly posed, but are rather suggested as a result of the dramatic and inner action of the work.

One of the most important themes in the philosophical stories is that of man's dedication to intellectualism and science. It has become almost a truism in the critical literature about Chekhov to consider him as dedicated to the scientific view. His clinical probing of characters, his lack of moralizing, and his objective approach to his heroes frequently bring Chekhov close to the methods of the French naturalists, whom he greatly admired, although their influence must not be overstated.[1] Chekhov was intimately acquainted with Zola's *Le Roman expérimental,* as well as with Claude Bernard's *Introduction à la médicine générale* (1865), which so strongly influenced Zola's literary theories.[2]

The many positive depictions of important scientists, and especially physicians, are familiar to all readers of Chekhov. It is frequently the scientist who represents the humane view in the conflict Chekhov depicts between creativity and *pošlost'.* Nevertheless, it would be incorrect to consider the scientist in Chekhov's works as unqualifiedly identified with the ideal. While Chekhov was clearly very much influenced by the spirit of empiricism and scientific optimism of the *fin de siècle,* there is little doubt that he viewed with skepticism a scientistic attitude, not uncommon in his days and very much a part of our own age, which sought, he believed, to place science above man. The emerging conflict between the new science and traditional humanistic values is reflected in the philosophical stories.

In "A Dreary Story" an excessive dedication to science by a very capable scientist is one of the underlying causes for isolation and unhappiness. In "Gusev," the concept of the superiority of intellectualism is satirically presented. In "The Duel," the belief in the superiority of an intellectual and scientific *Übermensch* is voiced by a cold Nietzschean scientist. In "Ward No. 6," the idea of the superiority of the intellectual serves to justify submission to evil. Finally, in "The Black Monk," this theme is most highly developed in the phantom monk's intoxicating vision of the intellectual *Übermensch* who is made all-powerful by the strength of his scientific mind.

The first of the philosophical stories, "A Dreary Story," is the most significant work of the 1880's. Its melancholy tone and intellectual probing reflect the intellectual and emotional crisis through which Chekhov passed at that time.

Chekhov felt that "A Dreary Story" was an entirely new kind of work and referred to it as containing "totally new motifs."[3] He complained, while working on it, of the difficulties it presented and spoke of his constant reworking of the story. Clearly the demands placed upon Chekhov by this ambitious work, one of the most interesting and complex, caused him to question the successful fulfillment of his aims.[4] When it was completed, he wrote that he was dissatisfied with its serious and heavy tone; he feared that the long ideological and philosophical considerations of the old professor harmed the story,[5] and that he had failed in his attempt to reconstruct the feelings of an old man.[6] Yet the work was very well received by those whose opinions Chekhov valued. Tolstoy is reported to have been enthusiastic about "The Dreary Story,"[7] while Pleshcheev praised it as Chekhov's most profound and powerful work.[8]

"A Dreary Story" portrays the tragedy of a noted professor of medicine, who, when he is old and incurably ill, realizes that his life has not been the glorious one he and his admirers had thought it to be; but that, for reasons which he attempts to define to himself, it has been a total failure. The professor feels himself ever more isolated from those around him, from his colleagues, his students, and also his family. Even his ward, Katya, with whom he had a special intimacy, turns away from him in despair when he cannot heed her cry for help.

There are few works of Chekhov's which have been the object of as much discussion as "A Dreary Story." Particularly debated is the question of the cause of the professor's isolation and unhappiness. Chekhov himself wrote of "A Dreary Story" that it contained not "two but fifteen moods,"[9] and there are indeed several reasons for the professor's psychological decline.

The most common interpretation of the work upholds the view that the professor's isolation is caused by his lack of a "general idea," of a "world view," which has prevented his own full participation in life. He is a scientist who, as he himself admits, has always carefully avoided concern with politics. The professor says of himself:

With such a lack [of a unifying idea] it was sufficient to have a serious ailment, a fear of death, or to be affected by circumstances and people, to have all that I formerly considered my world view, which had composed the happiness and meaning of my life, turned upside down and disappear. It is therefore not surprising at all that the last months of my life have been beclouded by thoughts and feelings worthy of a slave and a barbarian, that I am now so indifferent, that I do not even notice the dawn. When man lacks something which is higher and stronger than external influences, then he has only to have a bad cold in order to lose his equanimity and to make him see in every bird an owl and to hear in every noise a dog's barking.

We meet the professor in a moment of crisis, when he sees his life critically for the first time, a view which is expressed in a disdainful attitude toward himself. He is a famous scientist who has so many decorations that the students call him "iconostasis"; he speaks of himself as a professor of world renown, who is "as partial to work and enduring as a camel" and who is a "good and honest fellow." He also pictures himself unflatteringly as a bald-headed man with false teeth and an incurable *tic douloureux,* with a "neck which, like the neck of one of Turgenev's heroines, looks like the handle of a base fiddle, with a hollow chest and narrow back and a dry sing-song voice." He now constantly feels irritated and complains about others. Yet, we learn that earlier when he had observed such an attitude in Katya, he felt that this was a certain sign of personal decline. His growing crisis is also expressed in a more critical attitude toward social problems, and in his belated realization of the ills of his country which comes to him in bitterness as he sits in a hotel room in Kharkov.

As he becomes increasingly dissatisfied, his own impotence makes his position even more helpless, if not grotesque. Hence he fails the only person he loves, Katya, and his isolation is complete. Unlike the professor's unimaginative assistant, who sees only his own small world and is spared painful doubts, the professor is tortured by his inability to form a new and more positive philosophy. Clearly the absence of a "general idea" is an outward expression of the professor's psychological decline and his growing resentfulness. But one cannot agree with critics who advance this as the only cause for the professor's unhappiness. Some Soviet critics find that the absence of political and social awareness[10] causes the professor's decline, while in the opinion of the Russian symbolist writer, critic, and philosopher, D. S. Merezhkovski,[11] it is the professor's scientific positivism, his lack of spiritual values, which destroy him. That the professor shares other values than pragmatic scientific ones is overlooked in this latter view.

The professor does not lack an aesthetic sense; he enjoys lecturing artistically and in beautiful style; when he stands on the lecture platform, he thinks of himself as a conductor who must carry the students away by his eloquence. He is interested in literature and in the theater.

Overlooked by these critics is the fact that the professor's unhappiness emanates not only from his despair in his search for a philosophical direction, but also from the inward isolation brought to him by fame, and by his increasing inability to participate in the superficialities of the life

around him. Every figure in "The Dreary Story" is characterized by banality, emptiness, bitterness, or cynicism. Even
the professor's beloved Katya becomes, after all, a superficial cynic who holds in contempt the one activity which
has meaning for the professor, the teaching of his science.

The professor is estranged from his wife, who has forced
him to live in a way commensurate with his high rank. She
has made it impossible to have the former pleasant family
gatherings around the table. She has deprived her husband
of the ordinary Russian fare he enjoys and has replaced the
Russian maid with a butler. The professor is unable to dis-
cover a satisfying relationship either with his superficial
daughter and her philistine suitor, or with his trivial colleagues, the pedantic assistant and the cynical philologist.
Even his students are mediocre.

Not only is the professor isolated by surroundings which
are repugnant to him, but he also suffers from his own weakness, his inability to understand others. Chekhov remarked
that the professor "is altogether too indifferent to the inner
life of those around him. At a time when people near him
are crying, blundering through life and lying, he pontificates
calmly about the theater and literature."[12]

The internal turmoil and withdrawal of the professor is
augmented as he suffers the premonition of death. He reflects that in a few months someone else will occupy his
lecture platform, possibly even the narrow-minded micro-
scope gazer who is his assistant, and that he will not really be
remembered, or truly mourned, and he is embittered finally
and completely.

The psychological collapse of the once successful and
happy scientist is thus related to many factors. The loneliness of the famous and the despair of the aged—particularly
those who are condemned to the questionings of a searching
mind—the isolation of the individual whose sensitivities
cause him to rebel against the *pošlost'* of society, all con-

tribute to the professor's predicament. Perhaps the underlying problem is the professor's over-committedness to the scientism of his age. Although realized at the highest level, this dedication proved in the end to be inadequate. The professor's assistant does not suffer from the limitations of his commitment, for the small soul of the assistant neither can nor needs to question the correctness and fruitfulness of his circumscribed world. The professor vaguely feels the inadequacy of his science; he faintly yearns for beauty and art. But he cannot realize an integrated wholeness of life.

The failure of the old professor to find lasting satisfaction in a life devoted primarily to science is brought into relief by a contrasting theme, the fate of Katya, which serves as a commentary on the problem of the professor. Katya, like the professor, has committed her life to a specific pursuit, art, which ultimately appears as elusive and unsatisfactory. But Katya's failure and resulting cynicism, unlike the professor's, come early in life and at an immature level. Her frustration is caused not by any awareness of the limitations of her goal. Rather her unhappiness and her resulting inability to act are caused by her unhappy realization of her lack of talent. Hence, Katya's dilemma is more pathetic because of the hopelessness of her inner inadequacy. A realization of this flashes in the professor's mind in the last moments of the story, as he reflects:

I look at her and I am ashamed that I am happier than she. Only shortly before my death, in the evening of my life, have I noticed in me the absence of what my philosopher colleagues call a general idea; but the soul of this poor creature will know no shelter all her life, all her life.

The theme of Katya, an ordinary person with pretensions, is a pathetic echo of the tragic, or near-tragic, notes of the theme of the extraordinary scientist. The professor is constantly drawn to Katya. In Katya, the artist, he sees an escape

from the constrictions of his own life, something free, un-
conventional, natural, and beautiful. She represents to him,
however inadequately, the life of emotions and aesthetics
which he himself cannot realize. Katya, on the other hand,
depends in childlike fashion on the professor, the wise scientist who can, though he never does, help her. They each
seek salvation from their own limitations in the tempera-
ment of the other. Yet, the professor cannot guide Katya,
and she cannot provide the warmth and human contact
which the professor wishes.

In "A Dreary Story," as in all of Chekhov's philosophical
stories, the philosophical level is united with the psychological, as Chekhov examines the problem of man's search
for and inability to find life's wholeness, and man's consequent isolation from himself and from society. The themes
and moods of this story are suggested by typical Chekhovian
use of detail and symbolism, as well as by the structure of
the story. The histories of the growing isolation of the professor and of Katya are closely interwoven and joined together in the critical moments of the narrative. The narrative is related by the professor from his own bitter perspective.

Certain descriptive details metonymically portray the professor. Initially there is the dry and detached tone in which
the professor speaks disparagingly of himself. The image of
isolation is then intensified by a series of encounters between
the professor and his surroundings, each showing that communication is no longer possible for him. His wife enters
his bedroom and utters automatic routine phrases which
habit has made meaningless. Her aged face reminds him of
his own age. His relations with his daughter, Liza, are also
based only on outward forms of an erstwhile intimate relationship. He still kisses her fingers as he had done in her
childhood, and he calls them by the names of her favorite

ice creams. But now he feels nothing when he repeats these words, and is "cold as ice cream."

An encounter with a learned colleague is also without content. Then we meet the student who wants to be passed in an examination he failed, and the young doctor who begs for a dissertation subject.

As the story comes to a conclusion, the now very lonely professor suffers an attack of terror at night and thinks he is dying. In the final scene, when the professor is sent to Kharkov in search of his daughter's fiancé he spends another lonely night in a hotel room, tortured by thoughts of his indifference, feelings of futility, and impending death. This solitude is interrupted by Katya who comes to ask him for help because she cannot go on with her present life. He can only answer her weeping entreaties with "I can not tell you anything, Katya," "Let's have lunch," and "Soon I will be dead." Katya leaves him coldly and he thinks as he watches her departure: "Good-bye, my treasure!"

Throughout the story, and particularly in the last two chapters the impending disasters are augured by audial symbols. As the professor thinks he is dying, he hears a bird calling, then a mysterious moaning, then again there is silence which is broken by the noise of the wicket gates which announces Katya's arrival. Later in the Kharkov hotel room, a feeling of futility is indicated by the recurrent striking of the clock in the hotel corridor, which interrupts the professor's depressed thoughts during a sleepless night.

The predominantly melancholy tone of this searching story marks it forever as one of Chekhov's saddest.

"Gusev," which was published in 1890, combines elements of social protest with some of the philosophical themes noted in "A Dreary Story." The setting of the story is a ship's hospital, a squalid and depressing ward. The impression of suffering is sharpened by frequent contrasts with the peace and beauty beyond the portholes of the ward.

The story presents the conversation of two moribund patients, Pavel Ivanych and Gusev, to whom we are briefly introduced after the laconic opening sentence: "It began to get dark, night would be falling soon." Then the simple peasant Gusev speaks naïvely in phrases filled with folk expressions. When the storm blows, he says that it means the winds, which are usually kept chained at the end of the world like dogs, have broken loose. He accepts life and death stoically and uncomplainingly. But Gusev's humble acceptance of death is dramatically emphasized when his body, after being properly buried at sea with priest and prayer, is devoured by a shark. As Gusev's body is pushed overboard, wrapped in canvas, it "looks like a carrot or a radish, wide at the head and narrow at the feet." He who has suffered from the hand of man, without protest, is now devoured by a shark. Criticism of Tolstoyian humility is also implied by the words of Gusev's ward neighbor Pavel Ivanych, a haggard man who must sleep in a sitting position so that he does not choke as he suffers from the last stages of consumption. Pavel Ivanych, a reversal of the Gusev type and one of Chekhov's rebellious intellectuals, opposes in extreme fashion Gusev's humility:

"Yes, I always tell the truth straight out. . . . I am not afraid of anyone or of anything. In this respect there is a tremendous difference between me and you. You are ignorant, blind, forgotten people, you see nothing and what you see you do not understand . . . you are told that the wind is tearing loose from its chain, that you are cattle, barbarians, and you believe even that; they beat you on the neck and you kiss their hand in return. Some beast in a fur coat robs you and then throws you a five ruble note as a tip and you say, "Please master, your hand." You are pariahs, you are pitiful people . . . but I am different. I live consciously, I see everything just as the eagle and the falcon when they fly over the earth, and I understand everything. I am protest incarnate. I see arbitrariness, and I protest; I see a pharisee and a hypocrite—and I protest, I see a triumphant swine—I protest. And I am invincible, no Spanish inquisition can force me to be silent. Yes . . . cut off my tongue —and I shall protest by gestures, wall me up in the basement— and I shall shout so loudly from there that I shall be heard for a whole verst, or I will kill myself by hunger so that their black conscience shall be heavier by one pud, kill me—and I shall appear as a ghost."

In his passionate protest Pavel Ivanych not only rejects the acceptance of evil, but also suggests the deification of science and intellectualism. In "The Black Monk" this theme is brought to the logical extreme in the monk's vision of the extraordinary man who is immortal because of the power of his scientific mind. Pavel Ivanych feels himself to be omnipotent and even immortal ("kill me—and I shall appear as a ghost").

In this scene, as in a scene in "Peasant Wives," we find the device, so important in Chekhov's plays, of the indirect chorus composed of seemingly unconnected statements which comment on the theme of the story.[13] When Pavel Ivanych has completed his peroration, it is noted that Gusev has not listened to him, but looks out of the porthole, where he sees a Chinese bird seller in his boat who lifts up a cage with canaries and calls out, "He sings! He sings!" The ironic identification between "He sings! He sings!" and the brave speech which has just resounded, is clearly evident. The commentary is further strengthened by the implied contrast between Pavel's self-image as a bird of omnipotence ("I see everything, just as the eagle and the falcon when they fly over the earth") and the caged canary bird. The story also provides an ironic commentary to the assertion of the omnipotence of the superior intellectual: Pavel Ivanych dies and is unceremoniously buried at sea. A further theme

is a more general one of the barriers to communication be-
tween individuals. While Pavel Ivanych talks passionately,
Gusev looks out of the porthole; while Gusev suffers, Pavel
Ivanych feels only the need to assert his own thoughts.

The story ends with the death of both protagonists. The
evocation of nature in the final lines comments ironically on
the death of Gusev. Nature's brief protest is belied by the
ridiculing shape of the clouds. The ocean soon joins the
universe in celebration of its own beauty, which is indifferent to the fate of man:

... At the same time [while Gusev was being devoured] in that
part of the sky where the sun sets, clouds are massing, one re-
sembling a triumphal arch, another a lion, a third a pair of
scissors. . . . A broad shaft of green light pierces the clouds and
stretches to the very center of the sky; a while later, a violet
beam appears alongside it and then a golden one and a pink
one. . . . The sky turns a tender lilac tint. Looking at this magnificent enchanting sky the ocean frowns at first, but soon it
too takes on tender, joyous, passionate colors for which it is
hard to find a name in the language of man.

"The Duel" (*Duèl'*) is Chekov's longest prose work, ex-
ceeding even "The Steppe," from which it is, however, distinguished by its greater dependence on action and dramatic
collisions. Chekhov expressed concern about the length of
"The Duel" while working on it as he had earlier when
writing "The Steppe."; He wrote Suvorin:[14] "I am afraid
that it will be difficult to read even half of it, not to speak of
reading it through to the end." Chekhov's concern about
the story seems justified in part. He was more at home in the
pithy short story than in the longer form of the novella, and
"The Duel" is at times written with the lack of restraint, so
untypical of Chekhov, which we have noted as well in our
discussion of "The Steppe."

"The Duel," a part of the cycle of Chekhov's philosophical stories, continues the theme of an overcommitment to science in the portrayal of the character of the young natural scientist von Koren, who is contrasted to the uncommitted, drifting intellectual Laevski. The latter type becomes an important figure in Chekhov's later stories and plays. The intellectual incapable of action is well-known in Russian literature of the nineteenth century as the "superfluous man": a sensitive individual, alienated from, and bored by, society and incapable of decisive action.

The story concerns the philosophical and personal conflict between von Koren and Laevski. Laevski and his mistress have come to the little town on the Black Sea in which the story is set, in the hopes of a Tolstoyan regeneration through a life of tilling the soil. These plans are never realized, however, and both Laevski and his mistress lead a life of aimless inactivity and moral vacuity. Instead of "tilling the soil by the sweat of [his] brow," as he had imagined he would, he remains a minor official of the Ministry of Finance who does not work. He has even ceased to love his mistress, Nadezhda Fedorovna. Recurrent details serve to diminish Laevski's self-view as a romantic personality, a new Hamlet, a new version of Lermontov's Pechorin, Turgenev's Bazarov, and Byron's Cain. He is a nervous intellectual who bites his fingernails and walks with dragging slippers, showing his darned socks; he is sentimental and speaks in clichés. His mistress has now come to represent for him all the senselessness of his existence. Throughout the story he speaks of escaping, recalling nostalgically the life he once rejected in tones which anticipate the futile call "to Moscow, to Moscow" of the three sisters *Three Sisters*. In his dreams of freedom he imagines that:

. . . he would board a steamer, eat lunch, play, drink cold beer, talk with the ladies on deck, and then in Sevastopol he would get on a train and go. Greetings to you, Freedom! The stations flash by one after the other, the air becomes colder and harsher.

Here are the birch trees and pine trees, here is Kursk, Moscow.
. . . In the station restaurant they have mutton with *kasha,*
sturgeon, beer; in one word this is not Asia but Russia, the true
Russia. The passengers in the train speak about trade, new
singers, and about Franco-Russian friendship; everywhere one
feels alive, cultured, intelligent and a bold life. . . . Faster,
faster! Here finally is the Nevski Prospekt, the Bolshaya Mor-
skaya Street, and here is Kovenski Square where he used to live
as a student, here is the dear gray sky, the freezing drizzle and
wet cab-drivers. . . .

In opposition to Laevski, von Koren is depicted as a puritanical fanatic who believes that Darwin's theory of the survival of the fittest justifies the destruction, in the name of
humanity, of those who are harmful to society. He considers
Laevski such a person, injurious to mankind because of his
inactivity and his sexual immorality. Von Koren's cold and
arrogant worship of the abstract value of science, which
denies the individual, is expressed in a statement by Laevski:

. . . When ordinary mortals work for the common good, they
keep their fellow man in mind: me, you, in one word, Man.
For von Koren, however, people are but little dogs, insignificant beings, too small to constitute the aim of his life. He works
. . . not in the name of the love of fellow man, but in the name
of such abstractions as mankind, future generations, an ideal
race of men. He pleads for the improvement of the human race
and in this relationship he considers us nothing but slaves,
cannon fodder, howling animals; some he would destroy, or
send to forced labor, others he would force into discipline; he
would force them, like Arakcheev, to rise and go to sleep to
the sound of drums. . . .

Von Koren is caricatured by a number of details. In his
first appearance we note his vanity. The young scientist
stands before a mirror where he:

. . . viewed his swarthy face . . . his shirt of dull cotton with
large flowers which looked like an oriental rug. . . . This view

of himself gave him almost greater pleasure than the sight of the photos or of an expensively appointed pistol. He was very satisfied with his face, his neatly trimmed little beard, and his broad shoulders, which served as clear evidence of his good health and strong build. He was satisfied also with his foppish clothes, from his necktie, which matched the color of his shirt, to his yellow shoes.

Von Koren speaks of his desire to destroy Laevski and his opportunity comes when Laevski challenges him to a duel following a violent argument. The duel itself is presented as a parody of all literary duels: no one knows the rules and the seconds try to remember the procedure by recalling famous duel scenes in literature. Yet, the absurd duel is the climax of the story and its turning point. Its results are ineffective and it leads to a general, and quite artificial, reconciliation between Laevski and von Koren and between Laevski and his mistress. Now Laevski can work, and von Koren is chastened. The story ends on a note of qualified hope.

The second conflict of the story, that between Laevski and his mistress, Nadezhda Fedorovna, is presented with gentle satire. While bathing in the tepid sea with his friend, Dr. Samoylenko, and standing in water up to his shoulders, Laevski discusses his moral obligations to his mistress, whom he no longer loves. The conversation ends as a big wave sweeps the friends ashore.

Laevski is beset by guilt because of his desire to flee from his mistress. He fears that such a move might kill her. But, unbeknown to him, Nadezhda Fedorovna harbors the same desires, tempered by the same sense of guilt. Like Laevski's conflict with the scientist, his relationship to his mistress also rises to a quasi-tragic climax. On the night before the duel, Laevski discovers his mistress in a hotel room with a local police official. But the discovery scene leads not to violence but to their later reconciliation. The depiction of

Laevski's flighty mistress recalls the heroine of "The Princess." We find the recurring metaphor of the bird, so often applied by Chekhov to her type. She goes swimming and,

... having freed herself from her clothes, Nadezhda Fedorovna felt a desire to fly. And it seemed to her that she had only to flap her arms and she would fly up into the air.

When she is tipsy, she is "gay and happy and felt light as a feather." Later during a picnic, "she felt small, simple, light and airy like a butterfly." Like the princess, she is caricatured by a typical sentimental expression: "I feel nostalgic" (*u menja toska*), she says repeatedly, expressing the pseudo-emotion she feels is real. At a party her thoughts accompany a letter-writing game as she imagines her moral regeneration in terms of a theatrical martyrdom:

She will live somewhere in the provinces, work and send Laevski money, embroidered shirts, tobacco "from an unknown person," and only in old age will she return to him should he suddenly fall dangerously ill and be in need of a nurse. When in old age he discovers the reasons why she refused to be his wife and left him, he will appreciate her sacrifice and he will forgive her.

Snatches from notes she receives in the game interrupt her reflections and act as commentary. "I love you, love you, love you!" she reads, just as she imagines her martyrdom for Laevski. At the next moment another note tells her "you have a long nose!" Finally, as she imagines her sentimental parting from Laevski ("she will kiss his hand and swear that she will love him all, all her life ... and ... will always think that somewhere she has a friend . . . who keeps a pure memory of her ..."), a brusque note from the police officer, demanding a tryst and hinting at blackmail if she does not satisfy him, abruptly ends her sentimental reflections.

An important position in the story is occupied by the

deacon whose seemingly unrelated remarks act as a commentary. The ridiculous deacon often bursts into guffaws of laughter at inopportune moments, as the philosophical issues of the story are voiced. When von Koren and Laevski engage in their duel, the deacon, who is secretly watching from the bushes, is reminded of a scientific description the zoologist von Koren had given only the night before of how two moles, meeting each other underground, clear away a space of ground and fight; and the deacon mutters to himself "moles!" observing the senseless battle. It is the outcry, a few moments later, of the deacon which saves Laevski's life and thus also frees von Koren from the moral burden of having killed his adversary.

There is a sharp depiction of the busy-body Marya Konstantinovna, who professes to be horrified by the immoral relationship of Laevski and Nadezhda Fedorovna, but whose fascination with the sinful woman is ill concealed. She is characterized by her bitter-sweet (*mindal'noe*) expression. Frequently and at inopportune moments she remarks: "charming" and "extravagant," the latter in criticism of Nadezhda Fedorovna's life.

The kind, self-sacrificing and sentimental scientist Dr. Samoylenko, is, unlike Von Koren, drawn with some sympathy. Nevertheless, his blustering behavior, his naïveté and sentimentalism, and his insistence on being addressed as "Your Excellency," although he is only of modest rank, all create a comical characterization which diminishes the significance of the fact that he has a guiding idea, that of humaneness and tolerance.

"The Duel" is the only one of the searching stories in which Chekhov has attempted to resolve the philosophical conflicts within the dramatic context of the story; and this attempt, as well as the uncharacteristically wordy conclusion, constitute its weakest parts.

The clinical naturalism of "Ward No. 6" (*Palata No. 6,* 1892) may be seen as a continuation of the mood of "Gusev," in which social injustice and human suffering are realistically portrayed. The discussion in this work of Tolstoyan issues relates it to "The Duel." In the years 1889-1891, as we have noted earlier, Chekhov became more critical of some of Tolstoy's ethical doctrines, which are finally rejected in this work.

"Ward No. 6" continues the search for a general idea, and the study of the consequences of an exaggerated intellectualism. The dominant problem, however, is the Tolstoyan one of nonresistance to evil. The themes are developed through the conflict and contrast of two individuals of differing, although not quite opposite, temperaments and outlooks— Ivan Dmitrich Gromov and Dr. Andrey Efimich Ragin. The contrast of two opposing temperaments is a dramatic device frequently used by Chekhov. The two school fellows in "Fat and Thin" (1883), the romantic huntsman and his prosaic wife in "The Huntsman" (1885), the doctor and his sybaritic neighbor in "Enemies" (1887), Gusev and Pavel Ivanych in "Gusev" (1890), Laevski and von Koren in "The Duel" (1891) are all examples.

"Ward No. 6" opens with a naturalistic depiction of a poor provincial hospital. The hospital yard is overgrown with nettles; the building in which the psychiatric ward is located has a rusty roof with a half-collapsed chimney. Rotted wooden steps lead to its main entrance. The whole compound is surrounded by a fence topped with sharp nails to prevent escapes. Chekhov takes us through the yard, warning us not to burn ourselves on the stinging nettles through which a path must be beaten in order to arrive at the building. When the door is opened, the picture of disorder is repeated as we see in the hall a pile of discarded materials— mattresses, old torn hospital gowns, pants, shorts, old shoes.

"All this mess is swept into a high pile . . . and rots and emits a stifling stench."

Thence we are led to the locked Ward No. 6, where the disturbed patients are kept. Here the description, first presented by the nail-studded fence, is repeated: the windows are barred, the beds are fastened to the floor. Dirt and stench are everywhere. Most of the inmates have lost all human feeling. But are they animals in a zoo, as the description of the ward infers, or are they prisoners? Is not the city jail visible through the barred windows of the hospital ward? The association of the ward with the prison is strengthened by the depiction of the brutal guard of the ward, Nikita, a retired soldier who controls the hapless inmates, using his power unreservedly.

One of the patients in the ward is Ivan Dmitrich Gromov, a social protester, an intelligent and sensitive man who will not acquiesce to the brutality and injustice he sees around himself. Like Dr. Lvov in the play *Ivanov* and von Koren in "The Duel," Gromov is relentless in his criticism. Unlike them, however, he does not pretend to moral superiority. He thinks of himself as an ordinary man, but one who is passionately attached to life and to beauty, one who is repelled by ugliness. He recalls the hero of an earlier story, "A Nervous Breakdown," whose protest against the degradation in the Moscow brothels is interpreted by his acquaintances as a neurotic symptom. Gromov's protest is of a more fundamental character and correspondingly he is held to be insane, suffering from a persecution mania. Thus, he is confined to the infamous Ward No. 6. A significant event precipitates Gromov's illness. When walking one morning he sees two convicts conducted in chains by four armed soldiers, an incident which initiates a series of thoughts ending in a nervous collapse. Gromov begins to be troubled by vague feelings of anxiety and guilt. Who can be safe from such a fate these days? "Does not the people's experience for centuries teach us that there is no protection from the army and from jail?" he asks himself. What can protect him from a legal error? Gromov then voices as strong a critique of Russian society and its bureaucratic methods as we shall ever hear from a character of Chekhov's:

"A miscarriage of justice is quite possible under our legal conditions today, and there is nothing queer in it at all. People who have an official, businesslike relationship to the suffering of others, as for instance judges, policemen, physicians, become in time so hardened by habit that, even if they wanted to, they could only act towards their clients in a coldly formal fashion; from this point of view there is no difference between them and the peasant who slaughters sheep and calves in the farmyard without noticing the blood. In the presence of a purely formal, soulless relationship to the individual, there is only one thing needed to deprive an innocent person of all his rights and to condemn him to forced labor: time. Only time, for the carrying out of the various formalities for which the judge is paid his salary, and then—all is finished. . . . How ridiculous it is to look for justice when society looks on violence as a reasonable and expedient necessity. . . ."

While Gromov is shut into Ward No. 6 he continues to long for the life which always escaped him. "I love life, love it passionately. I have a persecution complex, I am tortured by constant tortuous fear, but there are minutes when I am overcome by a thirst for life, and then I am afraid of losing my mind," he tells Dr. Ragin. He bitterly questions Dr. Ragin: "Yes [I am] ill. But do not tens, hundreds of madmen walk around freely, because your ignorance cannot distinguish them from sane people?"

Ironically, Gromov's passionate attachment to life and mankind are in the final analysis attachments to abstractions. In spite of his love for life, Gromov cannot live; and in spite of his love for mankind, he cannot love an individual.

In contrast to the sincere though sterile idealism of Gromov is the hypocrisy of Dr. Ragin, who becomes the administrator of the disorderly hospital in which each person works only for himself. Because he is repelled by the conditions he finds, he withdraws as far as possible from his work, fearing the clash which a struggle against the evils of the hospital would arouse. Ragin's cowardly behavior leads him to an isolation even more profound than that of the protesting Gromov. Ragin is incapable of fighting the evil around him because he lacks, like Goncharov's Oblomov, the strength to act or to command. He can only say "please" and "if you would be so kind" and, consequently, none of the brutalized people with whom he has to work listens to him. He is a humble and submissive individual like Gusev, or Tolstoy's submissive peasant Karataev. Ragin accepts evil meekly. Unlike the truly meek Gusev-Karataev type, however, Ragin's humility is only an intellectual rationalization of inactivity. The philosophies of the Roman stoic idealist Marcus Aurelius and—without ever being named—Tolstoy's doctrine of nonresistance to evil provide for Ragin a convenient excuse for his escape.

The initial description of the doctor—a heavy-set man with a rough peasant build—ironically depicts an exterior incongruous to the doctor's inner impotence. Other details suggest Ragin's weakness. He moves stealthily, is always the first to step aside to make way for another; his voice is thin and reedy; he dresses carelessly. The intellectualism of the doctor is also satirized. He loves "deep" books, especially books on philosophy and history. (The only professional literature he reads is the official medical journal which, for some unexplained reason, he always starts from the end.) The description of Ragin as he reads indicates the dilettante.

He does not read as rapidly and passionately as had Gromov. He reads slowly, frequently stops over a passage which seems to him particularly pleasing or incomprehensible. He always has a decanter of vodka next to his book, and a salted pickle or pickled apple always lies before him, directly on the table cloth, without the benefit of a plate. Every half hour, without taking his eyes from the book, he pours himself a glass of vodka and drinks it. Then, without looking, he gropes for the pickle and bites off a little piece.

Ragin's philosophical idealism, little suited to the pickle-eating, peasant-faced doctor, emerges in his conversation with Gromov. Only with Gromov does Ragin escape from his loneliness and enjoy the delights of philosophical speculations. He attempts to justify his behavior to Gromov by preaching the stoic idealism of Marcus Aurelius. We imagine pain, says Ragin, quoting Marcus Aurelius, and if we make an effort, if we do not complain, the pain will disappear. A wise man is distinguished from the herd by the fact that he despises suffering and is thus always satisfied. A man must look only to himself for happiness and, suggesting Tolstoy, Ragin states, no happiness comes to man from without. If you can find inner happiness, he tells Gromov, then it does not matter whether you are physically free or not, and he gives as an example Diogenes who "lived in a barrel, but was happier than all the kings of this earth." But such ideas are pronounced in the hospital ward of sufferers, of which Ragin is not a part and from which he may freely leave, while Gromov will have to remain, a victim of the beatings of the guard, Nikita.

Gromov assails the doctor's appeal for submission. "Your Diogenes was a fool," he says. He rejects Ragin's Tolstoyan concept of man and counters with a call to the overwhelming importance of sensation:

"External, internal. . . . Forgive me, I don't understand all this. I only know that God has created me with warm blood and nerves. . . . And organic tissue, if it is alive, must react to any irritation. And I do react. To pain I react with shouts and tears;

to foulness I react with indignation, to abomination with re-
pulsion. And this is, I think what life is. The lower the organ-
ism, the weaker its reaction to irritation; the higher the organ-
ism, the more receptively and energetically does it react to
reality. . . . The teachings which preach indifference to riches,
to the comforts of life, contempt of suffering and of death are
totally incomprehensible to the vast majority of men, because
this majority has never known riches or comfort. And to have
contempt for suffering would mean for them to have contempt
for life itself. For the very essence of man consists of a feeling
of hunger, cold, sufferings, losses, and a Hamletian fear of
death. This is life. One can feel it as burdensome, one can even
hate it. But one cannot have contempt for it. . . ."

He who does not react to pain by shouting and protesting, no longer lives, Gromov asserts. Christ himself,
Gromov says, "reacted to reality by crying, smiling, by
being sad, angry, and even melancholy. He did not meet
his suffering with a smile on his lips, nor did he face death
with contempt. On the contrary, he prayed in the garden
of Gethsemane that this cup might pass him by." Gromov
concludes by questioning Ragin's right to urge the acceptance of suffering since he has never suffered himself. No,
you have not only not suffered, but you have not even truly
lived, "you know life only in theory." And all your philosophy, he says:

". . . is a philosophy which is most suited to the Russian idler.
You see, for instance, how a peasant beats his wife. Why inter-
fere? Let him beat her, they will both die anyhow sooner or
later; and he who beats, insults not the one whom he beats, but
himself. To be drunk is stupid and indecent. But you die
whether you drink or not. A woman comes and complains of
a toothache. . . . Well, what about it. Pain is only the concept
of pain, and anyhow, you can't live on this earth without illness,
we will all die anyhow, so let the woman go to the devil, don't
let her keep me from thinking and from drinking my vodka.
A young man asks for advice, how is he to live, what is he to

do? Another one might think before answering. But here the
answer is ready right away: try to understand and to reach true
happiness. But what is this fantastic "true happiness?" That
you cannot say, of course. We are kept here behind bars, we
rot and are tortured. But all this is very lovely and very reasonable, because, after all, there is no difference between this ward
and a warm, comfortable study. A comfortable philosophy indeed: you don't have to do anything, your conscience is clear
and you feel yourself most wise. . . . No, sir, that is not a philosophy, those are not ideas, not broad-mindedness, but pure laziness and hocus-pocus. . . ."

In a final ironic twist Ragin also is considered insane by
the same society that had passed judgment on Gromov. The
more closely Ragin becomes associated with Gromov, the
more he is treated by his erstwhile friends and colleagues
as though he himself were ill. Finally, under the stress of
this conflict, Ragin becomes enraged and wildly curses his
colleagues. This is perhaps the first passionate act of his
life, as—in an action which has obvious symbolic overtones
—he chases his colleagues out of his study, hurling a flask of
bromide after them. The strange sound with which the
flask breaks on the stone floor of the hospital corridor, spill-
ing the calming fluid, marks the end of Ragin's passivity.
When Ragin is tricked into Ward No. 6 and the door is
forever barred behind him, Gromov's prediction that Ragin
would shout if he hurt even his little finger comes true,
as Ragin realizes through the shock of his own sufferings
that he cannot search for inner happiness if he feels pain
and hunger, and he is imprisoned. When he is beaten by
his former subaltern Nikita, the pain of the ex-sergeant's
fists no longer seems an "idea," and Ragin awakens from
his intellectual dreams. In the face of death, he protests
and denies all that he had hitherto stood for, including
Tolstoyan submission.

Chapter 8 / The Searching Stories II
"The Black Monk"

In 1894 Chekhov completed "The Black Monk" on which he had worked during the summer of 1893, the fourth, and last, of the series of philosophical stories begun in 1889 with "A Dreary Story." While in Chekhov's later works philosophical questions are no longer posed so directly as they are in the searching stories, we do not find a complete break between these and later works. Philosophical themes after this period are increasingly integrated into the psychological and dramatic action of the story, but the beginning of this trend can be observed within the philosophical stories themselves. Philosophical problems maintain more independence in "A Dreary Story" and in "Gusev," in which there is little action, than in "The Duel" and "Ward No. 6," in which dramatic conflicts are more important. The trend continues in "The Black Monk" in which philosophical questions, while still of greatest importance, are even more dependent on the artistic form and psychological action of the work.

Chekhov's philosophical searching is expressed in greatest complexity in "The Black Monk," about which there exists many varied interpretations.

"The Black Monk" is the story of a mediocre and ineffective scientist, Kovrin, who comes to the estate of his friends, the Pesockis, to rest his wearied nerves, and there begins to see visions of a black monk who tells him that he, Kovrin, is an intellectual superman. The belief in the scientific and intellectual superman is now posed within the context of the hallucinations of an ordinary man who cannot live without his beguiling delusions. The monk talks persuasively of Kovrin's mission to lead mankind to immortality and to eternal truth, but the charm which the monk casts by his eloquence and conviction is broken when he does not answer Kovrin's question concerning the essence of these problems. "If only you knew how agreeable it is to hear you say these things," Kovrin tells the monk. How strange, he tells the phantom, who might be his *alter ego,* that "you repeat what so often comes also to my own mind . . . it is as if you had looked into, and listened to, my innermost thoughts. But let us not talk about me. What do you mean by eternal truth?" Just at this point the monk fails Kovrin and the hallucination disappears.

The monk did not answer. Kovrin looked at him and could not see his face; his features began to cloud over and to disintegrate. Then the monk's head and arms began to disappear and his body merged into the bench and the dusk—and he disappeared entirely.

While the monk cannot satisfy Kovrin's search for final answers, he can seduce him with flattery and thus still his doubts.

"Yes, you are one of those few who are justly called God's chosen. You serve eternal truth. Your thoughts, your intentions, your amazing science and all your life bear a divine heavenly stamp, since they are dedicated to the reasonable and to the beautiful, that means to that which is eternal."

According to one view "The Black Monk" is a continuation of Chekhov's critique of idealism begun in "Ward No. 6."[2] Such an interpretation assumes a critical attitude by Chekhov toward the imaginary life of Kovrin, the chief protagonist of the story. This interpretation represents an oversimplification, although it cannot be denied that the story does concern itself with this philosophical problem.

The story has also been interpreted as expressing Chekhov's familiar conflict of beauty with banality; beauty being equated with honest and productive labor, which is here said to be represented in the gardening establishment of the Pesockis and the Pesockis themselves, in contrast to the emptiness and isolation of Kovrin.[3] Again, this view bears some truth; yet it leaves out more than it explains.

"The Black Monk" is probably the least successfully analyzed of all of Chekhov's stories, too often oversimplified, and indeed neglected. Some critics have attempted to find a single key to the story, or even to find Chekhov's answer to the problems posed in the work. Yet, in "The Black Monk," Chekhov has not attempted to solve any problem. Rather he has followed the formula which he had outlined to Suvorin, to "pose the question correctly, as the judge should," and has left it to the readers, as the jury, "to make up their minds each according to their own taste." It is in this spirit that we must approach "The Black Monk."

The first question concerns the philosophical problems raised in the story. Just as Dostoyevsky's psychological heroes were symbols of philosophical problems, so in "Ward No. 6" and "The Black Monk" the philosophical and psychological levels are fused. It is only by a process of abstraction, more difficult to carry out here than in "A Dreary Story," that the philosophical content can be considered independently.

In Nietzschean fashion, the monk contrasts Kovrin with the "herd" of ordinary people. Kovrin, he says, is all intellect, all nerves. That is why he sees phantoms. But this, he says, is as it should be, for people who are especially gifted, like Kovrin, have no need for *mens sana in corpore sano.* They are disembodied intellectualism and aestheticism, high above ordinary men with their despicable bodily needs. "My friend," the monk tells Kovrin,

. . . only the ordinary people, the herd, are healthy and normal. . . . Heightened mood, ecstasy—those qualities which distinguish prophets, poets, martyrs for an idea from the ordinary people, are alien to the animal side of humanity, that is to physical health. I repeat—if you want to be healthy and normal, go into the herd.

While the monk speaks of the extraordinary man, addressing his remarks to the scientist Kovrin, he includes all gifted men—artists, poets, as well as scientists. Hence, the aesthetic and the scientific themes are brought to a unity which had already been suggested in the sub-theme of Katya in "A Dreary Story," and which is expressed here by the recurrent leitmotif of music, which always precedes the appearance of the hallucination of the monk.

Kovrin believes in his extraordinary character and talent as do Tanya Pesocki and her father, who feel honored by his presence on their country estate. He compares himself with the great men of history and thinks of himself as striving for all-knowledge, like Faust, an identification which provides its own ironic commentary. For, unlike Faust, Kovrin is a mediocre man who only masquerades as an intellectual giant. He repeats that he cannot live without his work, but he is never able to proceed beyond the out-lines of his writings; and we realize that Kovrin is, in his way, as insignificant as the herd which his monk has taught him to despise.

The depiction of Kovrin is contrasted with that of his friends, the family of the horticulturist Pesocki. While there is something ridiculous about the old horticulturist, his useful labor comments on the fruitless intellectual ef-forts of Kovrin. Pesocki, a simple man, is part of the herd, but in limited respects he is also part of the depiction of the extraordinary man. His excited and vituperative polemic articles on horticulture, and his worry that his garden will perish with his death together compose a simple form of horticultural "scientism." Ironically, Pesocki pic-tures himself of greater worth than the peasants, whom he regrets he can no longer flog, and as above his learned horticulturalist colleagues, whom he accuses of lack of practical experience. Pesocki finds in his natural science of horticulture the perfection of his "Garden of Eden," a value higher than humanity—more important, for ex-ample, than the happiness of his daughter, whose marriage he sees only as a means of securing an heir to continue the work of the garden. Do we have, in the old man, an in-verted picture of Kovrin?

While Kovrin's vaunted intellectual prowess leads him to feel superior, it is Pesocki's practical abilities which cause him to value himself above others. Yet, we are re-minded that both men will perish without leaving a trace of their "extraordinary" talents. Kovrin will not give any lectures, and Pesocki's orchard will be ruined.

Tanya is the only character who lacks pretensions to a special role. But she idealizes both Kovrin and her father because she cannot resist the attraction of their less con-ventional outlook, which she herself does not quite under-stand.

In considering the opinions of the monk, it is difficult to
agree with critics like Gushchin[4] who claim that the monk's
views are treated completely negatively in the story. While
the story destroys the main premise of the monk—the belief
in the intellectual superman and the deification of science
—one could not say that all the monk's beliefs are shown
as delusions. When the monk speaks of "the great and
brilliant future" which lies ahead for mankind in the wake
of a humanely conceived science, does he not express the
hope of Chekhov's most positive heroes? While the monk's
intellectual snobbery is shown to be empty, the mission of
a humane and inspired intellectualism, which is beyond
Kovrin's capacities, is a positive part of the monk's vision.
The themes of the inspiration of genius and the illusions
of the mediocre unite the philosophical dimension of the
story with the psychological.

In Chekhov's stories and plays, the conflict of the exceptional person with his Philistine and banal milieu is a recurrent one. The student in "A Nervous Breakdown,"
Pavel Ivanych in "Gusev," Gromov in "Ward No. 6," the
professor in "A Dreary Story," cannot accept the *pošlost'*
which surrounds them, and consequently are destroyed.
In "The Black Monk" this theme is given a new and bitter
twist. Kovrin's wish to recapture his hallucinations is both
pathetic and ironic.

"How lucky were Buddha and Mohammed or Shakespeare
that well-meaning relatives and doctors did not cure them of
their ecstasies and inspiration! . . . If Mohammed had taken
bromides for his nerves, worked only two hours a day and drank
milk, then this amazing man would have left behind just as
little as his dog. Doctors and well-meaning relatives in the
final analysis will succeed in dulling mankind; mediocrity will
be considered as genius and civilization will perish. If you only
knew . . . how grateful I am to you.

The pathos of life without illusions, be they even delusions, leads almost to tragedy. But Chekhov's hero is not a tragic hero; he is only a little man, the victim of a sensitivity which does not allow him to accept his mediocrity. There is a last ironic note when, at death, Kovrin rediscovers his faith in his greatness, as his hallucination of the black monk reappears. Just as Treplev of the *The Sea Gull* thinks of himself as Hamlet and many situations in the play support this identification,[5] there are in "The Black Monk" indications that Kovrin, who is striving for all-knowledge, is being compared to Faust, an analogy which is supported by the obvious resemblance of the black monk to Mephistopheles. One might also suggest a similarity between Tanya, who is ruined by Kovrin's delusion, and Goethe's Margaret. But the analogy is ironic, since Kovrin has none of Faust's greatness and the black monk is incapable of providing fundamental answers and has none of Mephistopheles' impudent strength.

The social import of "The Black Monk" is more immediately obvious than its psychological and philosophical themes, but it is not less significant in the meaning of the story. The picture of the boredom and frustration of country life, which had been expressed in Russian literature since the appearance of Pushkin's *Eugene Onegin,* is a frequent subject of Chekhov's. Kovrin, a version of the "superfluous man" in Russian literature and society, is an aimless rebel without a role in society, as were his "superfluous" predecessors in Russian letters, such as Pushkin's Eugene Onegin, Lermontov's Pechorin, and Turgenev's Rudin.

"The Black Monk" is not only of special interest as a psycho-philosophical and social study, but also as an example of the use of symbolism. In no previous Chekhov work has the symbolic played so basic a role as it does in "The Black Monk," in which the figure of the gently smil-

ing black monk is all that the frustrated Kovrin desires to
be. Similarly, in Dostoyevsky's early story "The Double,"
there is also a phantom which is a projection of the frustrated ego of the hero of the story.

Nature, as in earlier works of Chekhov's, sustains the
mood of the story. When Kovrin sees the monk for the first
time, the setting sun evokes thoughts of a beautiful future.

[Kovrin] walked down the path which ran along the steep
shore by uncovered roots, frightening the snipe and flushing
two ducks. The last rays of the setting sun were reflected on the
gloomy pine trees. . . . Kovrin crossed the stream by the rocks.
Now a wide field lay in front of him, covered with young rye.
Not a human habitation, not a living soul in the distance, and
it seemed as though, were he to continue on the path, it would
take him to the very unknown and mysterious place of the
setting sun, where the evening red was majestically flaming in
the sky.

When Kovrin loses the comfort of the monk, nature becomes threatening.

. . . Gloomy pines with shaggy roots, which only last year had
seen him here so young, happy and bold, now no longer whispered, but stood motionless and silent as if they did not recog-
nize him. . . .
He crossed the river along the rocks. Where last year there
had been rye, now lay rows of reaped oats. The sun had already
set and a broad red glow on the horizon foretold a stormy
tomorrow. It was quiet. Looking in the direction where the
black monk had appeared for the first time last year, Kovrin
stood for some twenty minutes, until the evening glow had disappeared.

Music also indicates indirectly the mood of the characters. A serenade is mentioned repeatedly. Its text, the implications of which are clear for Kovrin's dream, is the
story of a young girl with a disordered imagination, who

hears mysterious sounds. When he first hears it, the song reminds Kovrin of a strange legend of a black monk and hereafter the serenade is heard before every hallucination, and it also precedes the final appearance of the monk, which leads to Kovrin's death.

> Suddenly . . . beneath the balcony a violin began to play and two soft women's voices sang. All this was familiar to him. The song they sang told of a girl, diseased in imagination, who heard by night mysterious sounds in the garden, and found in them a harmony and holiness incomprehensible to us mortals. . . . Kovrin held his breath, his heart contracted from grief, and the magical, sweet joy, which he had long forgotten, trembled in his breast again.

The monk appears, and Kovrin is dying,

> . . . but an inexpressible limitless joy filled his whole being. Beneath the balcony the serenade was being played, and the black monk whispered to him that he was a genius and was dying only because his feeble mortal body had lost its balance and could no longer serve as the covering of genius.

Interesting parallels to the theme of "The Black Monk" can be found in some of the works of Henry James, another writer in whose stories characters search for a meaning in life. In an early story of James, "The Madonna of the Future" (1873), a mediocre artist believes himself to be an especially sensitive and intelligent interpreter of art and philosophy and the creator of a great masterpiece. He dies when he is made aware of his illusions. In "The Beast in the Jungle" (1903), Marcher, a mediocre man who lives in total isolation and fear, is entertained only by his obsession that he is being kept for something strange, momentous, and perhaps terrible. After the death of Mary Bartram, who personifies his vision, he at last realizes that his fate was to have no passion at all; he was to be the man to whom nothing was ever to happen. His hallucination re-

appears of "the beast" as he flings himself on the tomb of
the woman who "watched with him" for the event that
never happened.

Though the intellectualism, heaviness, and extent of exposition which characterizes the style and method of James
is different from that of the poetic talent and terse style of
Chekhov, both writers tried to express, with an economy of
action, and often by shifting views, a complex perspective of
the inner life of the individual.

Chapter 9 / The Bourgeoisie

Chekhov's notebooks and letters of 1890 express his growing concern about social conditions in Russia. In a letter to Suvorin he noted that: "A workman's labor is practically not paid for at all, and that is why I am well off. I am beginning to understand the delights of capitalism.[1] And in his notebook we find the following entry concerning the peasants:

> In the estate there is a bad smell and a bad atmosphere, trees are planted somehow badly; and far away in a corner the watchman's wife is ironing the guests' laundry all day long—and nobody ever sees her; and those gentlemen are permitted to talk, for days on end, about their rights and about human nobility.[2]

The Russian social scene is of dominant importance in nine stories bearing upon the growth of Russian industry, the new bourgeoisie of the worker, and life in the village. In these stories the sources of human frustration are related to the flaws of a social system in which a great majority of Russians lived in deprivation, and which, Chekhov indicated, gave no satisfaction to the ruling group. In these works we find Chekhov's closest approach to Zola's naturalism.

These stories, written between the years 1894 to 1900, clearly form a series, although one might question Edmund Wilson's assumption that they compose an analysis of Russian society, a miniature *Comédie humaine*.[3] Concern with social phenomena, though fundamental to these stories, is still subservient to Chekhov's main theme—human isolation.

Three of the stories are concerned with industrialization and the emergence of a new bourgeoisie. These are: "A Woman's Kingdom" (*Bab'e carstvo*, 1894), "Three Years" (*Tri goda*, 1895), and "A Doctor's Visit" (*Slučaj iz praktiki*, 1898). Those dealing with social order in the Russian village in the late nineteenth century are: "The House with the Mezzanine," also translated as "An Artist's Story" (*Dom s mezoninom*, 1896), "My Life" (*Moja žizn*, 1896), "The Peasants" (*Mužiki*, 1897), "A Journey by Cart," in Constance Garnett's version: "The Schoolmistress" (*Na podvode*, 1897), "The New Villa" (*Novaja dača*, 1899), and "In the Ravine" (*V ovrage*, 1900).

"A Woman's Kingdom," first printed in the journal *Russkaya mysl'*, in January 1894, tells of the frustration of a woman factory owner, Anna Akimovna, who lives in a provincial industrial town. The familiar theme of human isolation is intensified by the social milieu, which contributes to the unhappiness of the heroine.

Anna Akimovna, herself of humble origin, wishes to regain contact with the workers whom she had known in her youth, but she belongs neither to the workers nor to the upper classes. Her situation is suggested by the two floors of the house in which she lives. On the upper floor, called the "clean or noble" half, aristocratic and educated visitors are received. Humbler visitors are admitted to the lower portion of the house, which is filled with ikons, religious pictures, and "the smell of monks." Anna Akimovna is drawn to the lower portion of the house, where workers and servants come to greet her on Christmas day. But her position forces her to go upstairs and preside at a dinner for an aristocratic neighbor and for her parasitical lawyer, a hypocrite and cynic who has long ceased believing in the platitudes which he pronounces in court; he carries two notebooks with him filled with citations from various authors, but never finds the appropriate quotation when he needs it.

The story discusses love that never finds fulfillment. Anna Akimovna dreams in her loneliness of marrying the foreman, Pimenov. But she and Pimenov are separated by the barrier of her position as factory owner. As ironic commentary, Anna's personal maid, the "upstairs" Masha (there is also a "downstairs" Masha) is hopelessly in love with the lackey, Misha, a figure reminiscent of some of Dostoyevsky's servants. All Misha's behavior toward others is dictated by subservient respect for social position. "He respected and venerated the rich and noble, and he despised the poor and those who came to the house as petitioners with all the force of his lackey's soul." Mocking details hint at Misha's isolation; like the schoolteacher Belikov in "The Man in a Shell," Misha wears flannel underwear under his heavily starched shirt and his ears are always stuffed with cotton. While Anna Akimovna dreams of marriage to the simple workman Pimenov, whom she first sees as he returns from the factory in grimy and ragged clothes, Masha loves Misha because he suggests to her the elegance of the upper classes.

Anna Akimovna is advised, both by the pilgrim woman

called "The Buzz" and by the lawyer Lysevich, to take a
lover. But it is not a lover that Anna Akimovna seeks in
her desire to break out of her isolation. Philanthropy also
fails her as a source of satisfaction. When she enters the flat
of the miserable petitioner Chalikov, in order to give him
money, his self-effacing humiliation and undignified clowning only repel her.

Though "A Woman's Kingdom" is not a story about an
industrial milieu, the urban industrial atmosphere and the
misery of the proletariat is felt. Chekhov has remarked
that "A Woman's Kingdom" is "the description of an old
maid."[4] While not an entirely successful story, it has passages of excellent characterization. Some of the secondary
characters are exceedingly well drawn, such as the miserable
petitioner Chalikov and his tubercular wife, the servant
Misha, and the cynical lawyer.

Chekhov was not to return to the problems of the industrial proletariat and the new bourgeoisie until 1898,
when he published "A Doctor's Visit." But in 1895, the
story "Three Years" appeared. This long work is set in an
upper-class merchant milieu, and expresses the atmosphere
of emptiness and cruelty associated with the new merchant
class which had been so forcefully depicted in Ostrovski's
plays. We are often reminded in this story of Ostrovski's
dictatorial patriarchal merchant families, of his family
tyrants (*samodury*), and of his recurrent theme of the impossibility of happiness and love in the merchant milieu.
But whereas Katerina, in Ostrovski's tragedy, *The Storm*
(*Groza*, 1860), is driven to suicide by the cruelty of the
merchant family relations, no such direct action is part of
Chekhov's more oblique depiction of the degeneration of
the Laptev merchant family which takes place while their
business prospers and outward conditions are apparently
positive.

When Chekhov first commented on "Three Years," he compared it to the novel of his contemporary P.B. Boborykin, *The Pass (Pereval,* 1894). He called "Three Years" "an imitation of *The Pass*"[5] and remarked that "Boborykin's laurels do not give me any rest."[6] However Boborykin's social novel depicts the Russian merchant class as a new, fresh current in Russian life while Chekhov drew a far less optimistic picture. Nevertheless, I cannot agree with Gushchin,[7] who sees Chekhov's story as a polemic directed against Boborykin's novel. Nor can it be seen as a work directed primarily against the evils of capitalism, as has frequently been claimed. Nevertheless it is clear that in "Three Years," as in Chekhov's other milieu studies, unhappiness and lack of mutual comprehension are more directly related to specific social problems than in Chekhov's earlier works, although the more general frustrations in the search for beauty and love, are equally important. The life of a merchant, directed as it is only toward material profit, ruins man's capacity for happiness and love. The Laptev enterprise stands, like an ugly monster, in the background of the destruction of three generations of Laptevs. Father Laptev, the patriarch of family and business, turns into a feeble, blind creature; his daughter Nina dies of cancer after an unhappy marriage, leaving her children orphans; his son Fedor loses his mind; and his other son, Aleksey, the chief protagonist, is ruined.

As in "A Woman's Kingdom," it is the social position of the Aleksey Laptev, which prevents his love from coming to fruition. The plot is relatively simple. Aleksey Laptev has refused to join his family's business firm and has lived the life of an intellectual bohemian, indulging in discussions that criticize established values. Like Turgenev's Bazarov, he and his friends had pictured love as simply a biological phenomenon. Nevertheless, Laptev falls in love with Julia, the daughter of a provincial physician, and his intellectualized theories about love no longer interest him. He timidly proposes and is rejected; but the next day Julia changes her mind and accepts him because she is bored with provincial life. She consoles herself with the idea that love is not really necessary for marriage. Laptev cannot understand why Julia has changed her mind and believes that she marries him for his money. He feels useless and unhappy, while she, in turn, is tortured by his love and unhappy because she knows that he suspects her motive.

"Three Years" is not the story of just one unhappy love. There are also the unsatisfactory relationships of Laptev and his former mistress Rassudina, of Rassudina and her new "lover," and of Nina, Laptev's sister, and her husband Panaurov, who maintains two wives with two sets of children and who deserts them both. Nor is there any friendship between the members of the various families: Julia and her father do not understand each other, and one cannot imagine communication among the members of the Laptev clan.

The problem of isolation and its counterpart, the impossibility of love, is emphasized by the line of the story, which executes a peripety at the end of the story. As the story begins, Laptev's love for Julia leads to their unhappy marriage. He begs Julia at least to pretend to love him. But when he kneels to kiss her foot, he imagines on the next morning that Julia tries to step more lightly on the foot he had kissed. Laptev's love gradually diminishes. After three years, he is cold and indifferent to the world. In an ironic reversal, as Laptev becomes disenchanted, his wife has quietly grown to love him.

Further irony in the relationship of the two protagonists is suggested by Julia's parasol, which is present during significant incidents in the interplay between Laptev and Julia. Forgotten by Julia in the beginning of the story, the parasol provides Laptev with an excuse to return to her house. When Laptev discovers the forgotten umbrella—and it is an old one and not especially elegant—he picks it up, kisses it "greedily," opens it and sits down in the chair, under the parasol, "and it seemed to him that everything around him smelled of happiness." In this ridiculous position he writes a bombastic and sentimental letter to a friend about unrequited love. The incongruous picture of Laptev under the parasol is ridiculous. This impression is strengthened in the scene which follows. When Laptev goes to Julia's house to return the shabby parasol, he "very nervously flew on the wings of love," clutched the parasol to his breast, and

. . . said passionately, irrepressibly, giving himself up again to the same sweet rapture which he had experienced yesterday while sitting under the parasol:

"I beg you, let me have it. I shall keep it as a memento of you, and of our acquaintance. It is such a marvelous one!"

When Laptev proposes, he is again "clutching the parasol to his breast." Toward the end of the story, as the relationship of Laptev and Julia is reversed, the parasol makes its appearance again. Laptev tells Julia that he is now convinced happiness does not exist. "Only once in my life," he says, "was I truly happy: that night when I was sitting under your parasol." Julia then confesses her new feeling of fondness for Laptev, and now it is she who holds the old parasol:

Julia looked at the parasol for a while, recognized it, and smiled sadly.

"I remember," she said, "you were holding it in your hands when you declared your love for me," and noticing that he was preparing to leave, she said: "If possible, please come back soon. I am lonesome without you."

And she went into her room and for a long time she looked at the parasol.

Various views concerning love are satirically treated in this story. The "scientific" explanations of love, which Laptev and his bohemian companions had defended in their youth, are burlesqued in the views of the bigamist dandy Panaurov, who patiently explains love as phenomenon of electricity:

... "In the skin of every human being there are microscopically small pieces of metal, containing an electric current. If you meet a person whose current runs parallel to yours, then you have love."

Panaurov deserts two women with whom he seemingly has parallel electric currents. Equally sterile is Julia's Tolstoyan justification of marriage as a necessary institution for the rearing of children.

Details throughout the story comment indirectly on Laptev's futile search for love and happiness. When, in the evening, Laptev sits in the yard of his father's warehouse, thinking of the destruction of his life and the prosaic business of his father, the night is contrasted to his mood. It is a magical night full of fragrance and sounds, and everything is covered by a mysterious air. Behind the fence, Laptev overhears a whispered declaration of love. He feels uneasily that he must escape the world in which he cannot be happy. But he can no more escape than the black dog that must lie in the yard and can not run at will through the fields. And he thinks that "he and the dog are prevented from leaving the yard by the same thing: the habit of servitude and of bondage."

Moscow has come to represent to the protagonists a meaning in their lives. Panaurov, Julia, Laptev, all dream of Moscow as the center of culture where all their ills can be righted. But the Moscow of the merchant class is just as backward, dull, and empty as the deepest provinces. All expectations appear to be falsely based: Laptev's marriage does not bring him happiness; Moscow is not the hoped-for paradise; Laptev's fears that Julia may be antagonized by the Laptevs' Moscow ménage turn out to be false. Laptev had imagined himself quitting the house with his wife if his father insulted Julia with even one gesture. Instead, he sees from her face how much she is enjoying the pomp and circumstance which accompanies her reception into the family.

Secondary figures compose two groups. One group, the respective families of Julia and of Laptev, are characterized by different kinds of degeneracy and futility. The scientist Yartsev, the lawyer Kostya Kochevoy, and the musician Rassudina, intellectual liberals and free thinkers, form a second group. Their positive outlook and active lives are contrasted to the futility of the lives of the others.

Julia's father, an ineffectual provincial doctor who is dissatisfied with life and jealous of his daughter's suitor, speculates in real estate and cannot resist using his medical practice for economic advantage. Clearly he is not one of Chekhov's self-sacrificing physicians. In his selfishness and greed he is as lonely as Laptev's father, whose life also has been dedicated to economic profit and whose final solitude is physical as well, as he becomes blind. The character of Laptev's eldest brother Fedor Fedorovich is not as simply drawn as is that of Laptev. Although he is engaged in his father's business, we do not know if he has rebelled against it. When he becomes insane, we only sense that he, also, has fallen victim to the monstrous firm, and to what Gromov in "Ward No. 6" calls "purely businesslike relations among men." The depiction of a constricted personality which cannot act is indicated by descriptive details: Fedor has red spots on his cheeks, which are otherwise pallid. His speech is filled with colloquial diminutives. He never speaks about Julia other than as "the little sister" (*sestrenočka*). This strikes Aleksey himself, reminding him of Saltykov-Shchedrin's hypocrite Judushka in the novel, *The Golovlev Family*. Fedor is never without his watch, and frequently opens it. When he becomes insane he simply looks at it "with tense affection, as if he wished to observe the movement of the hand." He clings to the watch as his brother had clung to Julia's parasol.

The most important protagonist of the opposing group, Yartsev, a forerunner of Dr. Astrov in *Uncle Vanya*, is a scientist, as well as a sociologist and a historian. He has not withdrawn from life and defends not only science but also beauty. In a discussion about literature, he upholds its aesthetic functions against the proponents of "purpose" literature. He plays the piano and can sing a little. It is he who has advised Aleksey to rebel against the firm. The most radical character in the story is Kostya Kochevoy who calls for open rebellion and supports the views of the nineteenth century critic Chernyshevski and poet Nekrasov concerning the social purpose of art. The third member of the trio of intellectuals is Laptev's former mistress, and later Yartsev's, Rassudina, a feminist and an individualist. Of the three, she is the most convincingly portrayed. Her brusqueness appears to be only a façade. Gently satirical elements appear in the description of her angular movements and her pointed nose. A metonymic motif, her handshake, which is described as "strong and impetuous, as if she were tugging [the other's hand]," defines her. Laptev is attracted to these three, for they represent to him a way of life unfettered by the pressures of the Laptevs' enterprise. "Three Years" does not, however, present simple alternatives in the contrasts between negative and positive characters of the story. While Aleksey idealizes those who are not bound by their social position, these three are also haunted by doubts and loneliness. Rassudina's abruptness hides a lonely spirit, and Yartsev harbors feelings of unfulfillment.

The opening and closing lines of the work set the theme. In the beginning of the story we meet Laptev sitting outside on a balmy summer evening, surreptitiously waiting for Julia, thinking of his love for her. A romantic scene is evoked.

The street was full of gardens, and linden trees were growing near the fences. They cast a wide shadow in the light of the moon. . . . One could hear the whisper of women's voices and subdued laughter, and someone was quietly, oh so quietly, strumming on a balalaika. There was a scent of linden trees and of hay in the air. The whispering of unseen women and the perfume of the air excited Laptev. And suddenly he passionately desired to embrace his companion, to cover her face, her hands, her shoulders with kisses, to weep and to tell her how long he had waited for her. She smelled lightly, almost imperceptively, of incense and this reminded him of the time when he also believed in God and used to go to evening Mass, and when he used to dream so much about pure, poetic love. And it seemed to him now that, because this girl did not love him, the possibility of that happiness about which he had dreamed in those days was forever lost to him.

When the story ends, the totally changed situation is dramatized in the final setting, externally similar to the first. Laptev can no longer respond to the idyllic background and to the beauty of Julia. It is now Laptev's friend who is aroused while Laptev is deprived of his former dreams and love:

Then he sat on the terrace and watched his wife approaching slowly. . . . She was thinking of something, and there was a sad, charming expression on her face and there were tears in her eyes. This was no longer a slender, fragile, pale little girl, but a mature, beautiful, and strong woman. Laptev noted the rapture with which Yartsev looked at her, and he saw how her new, lovely expression was reflected in his face, which was also sad and ecstatic. . . . And at lunch on the terrace, Yartsev smiled with a sort of joyful and timid smile and never ceased glancing at Julia and at her beautiful neck. Laptev could not help observing them, and he thought that he had perhaps another thirteen or thirty years to live. . . . What was in store for him all that time? What awaits us in the future?

He thought: "We shall live and see."

It was three years before Chekhov again depicted the new industrial bourgeoisie. In 1898, "A Doctor's Visit" was published, a story set in the milieu of a provincial factory town, as was "A Woman's Kingdom." In Chekhov's notebooks there are a number of entries which were later used as material for this story.

A factory. 1000 workers. Night. A guard beats a sheet of metal. Much work, much suffering—and all this for the emptiness that governs the factory. A stupid mother, a governess, a daughter . . . The daughter fell ill. A specialist was called from Moscow, but he does not go and sends his assistant instead. The assistant hears the clanging of the nightwatchman and thinks. Lake pile dwellings come to mind. "Is it possible to work all one's life at this factory merely for these nonentities, for those who have eaten their fill, the fat ones, the empty and the stupid ones?"[8]

We meet the chief protagonists of "A Doctor's Visit" as they realize the absurdity of their lives. The illness of Liza Lyalikova, the daughter of the factory owner, is a symptom of her vague anxieties and can not be helped by medical science. She is drawn to Dr. Korolev, who arrives in the factory town at her call, and she tells him:

". . . I am often treated by doctors, . . . I am of course most grateful and I do not deny the value of medical treatment. But what I need is to talk, not to a doctor, but to someone close to me, to a friend who would understand me, convince me that I am right, or that I am wrong."

"I am lonely," she cries out. But the doctor finds nothing to tell her. He knows that he should persuade her to leave the factory. Not knowing how to find the right words, Dr. Korolev limits himself to a vague statement of optimism. Our grandchildren and our great grandchildren will have a happier life, he tells Liza. But he cannot tell her why and how they will better their lives.

The story begins as well as concludes with a carriage ride of the physician. He enters and leaves the factory town, in two brief scenes of lyricism which contrast to the action of the story in the grim factory town. As the story opens, we learn in vague terms the purpose of the doctor's trip—which is to treat an illness as indefinable as the illness of the town itself.

. . . the daughter of a Mrs. Lyalikova, apparently the owner of the factory, was ill. But more could not be understood from the long and awkwardly composed telegram.

Vagueness remains as Korolev arrives at the Lyalikov's house. The mother avoids the doctor because she lacks education and feels herself inferior to him, and the only educated person in the house, the governess, begins to discuss the reasons for the disease, "but did not say who was ill and what it was all about." The story is disclosed through the conversation and the thoughts of the doctor as he arrives, examines the patient, spends a sleepless night, takes a walk and reflects on what he sees, speaks briefly to Liza, and departs.

As the doctor rides to the village to see his sick patient,

He was captivated by the evening, the settlements, the country villas, the birch trees and the calm atmosphere. It seemed as if, on the eve of the holiday, the fields, the forest and even the sun were preparing to take a holiday with the workers and perhaps even to pray.

The charm of the festive Sunday is jarred as the crowds of workmen whom the doctor encounters bow respectfully, not to the doctor but to the fine horses. The harsh atmosphere of the factory town, the sounds and noises which greet the doctor destroy the supposed idyllic scene. The driver yells warnings to people to get out of his way "without reining in the horses," laundry is hanging on the line. ". . . on everything there was a kind of gray coating, like dust. . . ." Even the owner's house is "freshly painted in gray," and the lilac bushes are covered with gray dust. As the doctor walks around the town at night, everything outside is cold, dreary, and depressing, but "far away . . . frogs were croaking and a nightingale was singing."

The description of the house in which Liza spends her days strengthens the picture of the *pošlost'* of industrial society. The pictures which decorate the Lyalikov house are set in expensive and ostentatious golden frames. "Views of the Crimea, a stormy sea with a little boat, a Catholic monk with a little glass, . . . there was not one beautiful and interesting face in the portraits. . . ." Through the perspective of the doctor, we see the factory town with the sharpness of first perception. The pattern of harsh sounds is repeated as we hear the ring of a piece of metal struck by a watchman to indicate the hour. This sound is heard at critical moments in the story. It interrupts Korolev's thoughts as he studies the inartistic family portraits and the sentimental landscapes. He has never heard such a sound and, at first, does not understand what it is. He knows only that it is disagreeable, and he reflects on the intolerability of life in the factory town. The metallic sound is heard again when the doctor sits outside at night and thinks about the factory, which appears to him incomprehensible, like some terrible mistake. He thinks of the unhappiness the factory has caused: the workers toil in unsanitary conditions and are exploited; Mrs. Lyalikov and her daughter are unhappy.

He begins to think of the factory as a devil who has made use of both workers and master and has cheated them both.

In contrast are heard the sounds of nature, of nightingales and frogs, of sleepy roosters, in the quiet of the spring night. The metallic sound is heard again as Liza tells the doctor of her loneliness.

It seems that all this misery helps only one person—Liza's governess.

. . . only Christina Dmitrievna, an elderly, stupid old maid with a *pince-nez*. So the result is that all these five plants work, and cotton of poor quality is sold in the markets of the Orient, solely and only so that Christina Dmitrievna can eat sturgeon and drink Madeira.

Her veneer of culture hides a crude creature who wipes her mouth with her hand and eats greedily. She thinks the workers are well off, she does not understand Liza's suffering, or the unhappiness in the household. She is the only one who has a good appetite.

"Please, doctor, don't stand on ceremony," said Christina Dmitrievna, eating and wiping her mouth with her fist, and it was clear that she lived here to her fullest satisfaction.

The story ends as the doctor leaves the factory town, unable to help Liza. He thinks vaguely of an undefined future when life will be beautiful and happy. In this departing mood even the factory looks gay to him. As he drives once more through the country, he ceases thinking of the factory. There is no solution, and the doctor leaves the problems of the town behind him.

Chapter 10 / "The Peasants"

> Only the well-to-do peasants were afraid
> of death; the richer they were the less they
> believed in God and in the salvation of
> souls, and only through fear of the end
> of the world did they light candles and
> hold services to be on the safe side. The
> peasants who were poorer were not afraid
> of death. The old father and mother were
> told to their faces that they had lived too
> long and that it was time they were dead,
> and they did not mind.
>
> —from "The Peasants"

The publication of two stories, "The House with the Mezzanine" and "My Life" in 1896, may be said to mark the beginning of the group of stories concerned with the Russian peasant. These were followed by "The Peasants," "The Schoolmistress," "The New Villa," and "In the Ravine." Chekhov's interest in the peasant milieu can be traced to his earlier works, from which it is clear that he knew and understood the peasant milieu better than he did the industrial world. The peasant characters in the early works, "The Huntsman," "Agafya," "At the Mill" (*Na mel'nice*, 1886),

"The Steppe," "Gusev," and "Peasant Wives," are excellently drawn.

In the first two stories of the later cycle concerned with the Russian village, "The House with the Mezzanine" and "My Life," Chekhov examines certain intellectual solutions and attitudes: he explores the Populist view that the peasant can be saved by education and sanitation in "The House with the Mezzanine" and the Tolstoyan tenet of "simplification" in "My Life," but neither is shown to be a solution. In the peasant stories which followed, naturalistic pictures of village life appear more important than social issues.

"The House with the Mezzanine" is only indirectly concerned with the peasant question, but its many discussions of solutions to the village problem justify its consideration as part of the peasant cycle. In this story we find the familiar contrast of beauty and sensitivity to a prosaic, utilitarian attitude to life. An artist, who is the narrator, loves a young, romantic girl, Misyus, but Misyus' sister, Lida Volchaninova, a village schoolteacher, causes this love to be frustrated. Misyus and the artist, who see poetry in nature and in life, are contrasted to Lida, the philanthropist and social reformer, who resents the artist because he does not share her faith in sanitation and medical facilities as a solution to the peasant problem. The first pages of the story present a poetic world in which the artist discovers the estate on which Misyus and her sister live.

. . . It was quiet and dark and only high in the treetops was there somewhere a trembling of golden light which overflowed in rainbow colors over the spider nets. There was a strong, almost choking smell of pine needles.

Light, color, and sound contribute to this sensuous description. When the artist walks home, after seeing the two beautiful sisters for the first time, he feels that he has had a dream as magic as the mysterious evening colors.

He returns to the house of the two girls. He learns that Lida travels from estate to estate collecting funds for peasant victims of a fire. She offers medical aid to the peasants, although she knows nothing of medicine. The artist tells Lida that her medical aid to the peasants will not cure the ills of the peasant. What matters, he tells her, is not to save a few lives, but to realize

. . . that all these Annas, Mavras, Pelageyas must bend their backs from dawn to dusk, are ill from overly heavy labor, tremble all their lives for their hungry and sick children, live all their lives in fear of death and illness, are ill all their lives, fade away early . . . and die in filth and foul smells. And their children, as they grow up, live to the same tune. And thus hundreds of years pass by and billions of people live worse than animals. . . . The whole horror of their position is in the fact that they do not have time to think of their soul. . . . Hunger, cold, bestial fear, constant work have, like snowdrifts, closed to them all roads to spiritual activity, to that very characteristic by which man is distinguished from the animal, and which is the only part of man's life which makes this life worth living. . . .

When Lida replies that man's highest duty lies in service to man, the artist remarks that she can no more expect her remedies to cure these ills than she can expect the light from her windows to illuminate the entire garden. What is needed, he says, in a statement which is as inflexible in its way as is Lida's position, are not palliatives, but far-reaching changes in order to liberate the peasant from the eternal struggle for survival and thus enable him to follow the vocation of Man: "the search for truth and for the meaning of life."

When the artist meets Lida, he is aware of her severe expression and that she hardly glances at him. She talks about the victims of the village fire for whom she is collecting money, but she does not look at her interlocutors. Her matter-of-fact outlook and lack of warmth is stressed by variations of details: "seriously, without a smile, she asked . . ."; "she spoke much and loudly, a habit perhaps acquired as a teacher"; "this slim, beautiful extremely severe girl . . . told me dryly"; her face is "businesslike and preoccupied." In ironic contrast is the phrase, constantly repeated by her mother and sister, "she is a remarkable person," a view which is shared by Lida.

In opposition to her is the somewhat sentimentalized picture of Misyus, who looks at the world with a childlike attitude of wonderment and enthusiasm and wishes to share her frequently naïve impressions.

. . . When I [the artist] would arrive, she would put down her book upon seeing me, blushing slightly as she did so. She would look at me animatedly with her big eyes and tell me what had happened; for instance that there had been a soot fire in the servants' quarters, or that one of the workmen had caught a large fish in the pond.

While Lida dislikes the landscapes which the artist-narrator paints and finds them useless, Misyus watches the artist at work with joy. In contrast to her sister, Misyus is united with the artist by her intuitive response to the world of art. But the artist is disturbed by the practical role of science of which Lida is an example, and by the fact that art only amuses people who lack understanding. He attacks the pragmatism of his day.

. . . Science and art, when they are genuine, aspire not to temporal and private goals, but to the eternal and the universal—they search for the truth and the meaning of life, they seek God and the soul. . . . We have many physicians, pharmacists and lawyers; there are many who can read and write. But we have no biologists, no mathematicians, philosophers and poets. All intelligence, all spiritual energy are used for the solution of temporary and passing needs. . . . Scientists, writers and painters work hard. Because of them the comforts of life are on the increase, the needs of the body multiply. But we are still far from truth and man remains the most predatory and slovenly of animals and everything points to the end that the overwhelming majority of mankind has become degenerate and has forever lost all vitality. Under such conditions the life of an artist is senseless, and the more talent he has, the stranger and more incomprehensible will be his role—for it seems that he is working for the entertainment of a rapacious, filthy animal and upholds the existing order. . . .

The poetic world of the artist and of Misyus is destroyed by Lida's world of pragmatism. When her family discovers that Misyus loves the artist, she is sent away. Nature, in a melancholy mood, suggests the denouement which contrasts with the pine-scented atmosphere in which the first meeting of the artist and Misyus took place.

It was a melancholy August night, melancholy because the smell of autumn was already in the air. The moon, covered by a red cloud, was rising and barely illuminated the path and the dark cornfields which lined it on both sides. Stars were falling frequently.

Misyus leaves, never to return. Inspiration deserts the painter. Only occasionally he wonders what has happened to his poetic dreams, and it is on this wistful note that the story ends with the exclamation, "Misyus, where are you?"

The second peasant story, "My Life," concerned with solutions to the social ills of the Russian village, was published in the same year in the *Monthly Literary Supplements* of the journal *Niva*.[1] In 1897, when both stories were included in a separate book, a subtitle to "My Life" was added: "The Story of a Man in the Provinces" (*Rasskaz provinciala*). In "My Life," as in "The House with the Mezzanine," peasants have only a secondary role, as a kind of documentation of the intellectual argument.

In "My Life," many of the protagonists seek to escape the

boredom of society. Some adopt the Tolstoyan life of simplification. The treatment of this theme is satirical as it was in
the earlier story, "The Duel" (1891). The principal protagonist of the story, Misail Poloznev, who is also the narrator, expounds the redemptive power of physical labor. Misail, the son of a leading architect in a provincial town, rejects the town of his youth and refuses to pursue an occupation in that world. "In the entire town I know not a single
honest man," he muses. And he wonders if there is any sense
to the town which "has existed for centuries, but has in all
that time not produced on useful person—not one."[2] His
father, an architect without talent but with a great respect
for social prestige, takes bribes, as do the other officials in
town. Misail leaves his family and job to become a simple
laborer and later attempts to work the land. But physical
work does not bring him salvation or even relief; and prox-
imity to the peasants shows them to be devoid of the romantic attitudes with which they were endowed by the
Populists and by Tolstoy. They are drunken and brutalized
by constant work and the barrier of distrust which exists between them and Misail is insurmountable. When Misail and
his wife Masha, who has married him to escape the boredom
of the town, try to help the peasants by building a school,
the peasants are unco-operative and even steal the materials.

Masha, now disillusioned with simplification, had said
before their marriage;

"One must . . . harvest ones own bread; that is, one must
plow, sow, cut and thresh, or one must do something closely
connected with agriculture, such as pasture cows, dig the earth,
build huts."

But Misail had entertained misgivings which revealed the
bias of his class:

I loved nature tenderly. I loved the fields, the pastures and
kitchen gardens; but the peasant who ploughed the soil and

urged on his miserable nag, who was wet and tattered with his
neck bent forward, was to me the expression of a coarse, savage,
ugly force, and every time I looked at a peasant's uncouth
movements, I began to think involuntarily of the legendary
life of the remote past, before men knew the use of fire.[3]

Unlike the more passive Misail, Masha decides on a new
course of action. We have worked, she tells her husband, but
all our labors have only helped to make *us* better. Like the
artist in "The House with the Mezzanine," but without his
sincerity, she says that their efforts are "but a drop of water
in the ocean." Individual actions are only palliatives, she
tells Misail. And it is art, in its timeless seeking for the
beautiful, to which she turns with as little understanding of
it as she had of the life of simplification.

". . . Here other methods of struggle are needed, strong, bold,
rapid ones! If one really wants to be of use, one must get out
of the narrow circle of ordinary activity and try to act directly
on the masses. What is wanted first is loud and energetic propa-
ganda. Why is it that art, and music for example, is so living, so
popular and in reality so powerful? Because the musician or
the singer affects thousands at once."

It is soon clear, however, that art is precious to Masha primarily as a new diversion to replace her Tolstoyan life
which no longer attracts her.

"Dear, dear art!"—she continued, dreamily glancing up at the
sky.—"Art gives us wings and carries us far far away! Anyone
who is tired of filth, of petty interests, anyone who is revolted,
wounded and indignant, can find peace and satisfaction only
in the beautiful."[4]

Three of the central characters, Masha, Misail, and Dr.
Blagovo, imply satirical commentaries on the romanticiza-
tion of physical labor. Masha states that she is tortured by
her social position, which she considers morally wrong.

"The educated and the rich," she tells Misail, "must work

like everyone." But descriptive details provide irony and suggest that Masha is another of Chekhov's narcissistic women. This potential "simplifier" dazzles everyone with her fine clothes; she is a "big town girl" (*stoličnaja štučka*). Even her most serious pronouncements are tempered by her inability to remain serious for any length of time. Thus, she tells Misail earnestly that there must be social equality. But the bell sounds announcing a caller, and not wanting to be found talking about such things, she switches to light banter:

"Well, God bless all this philosophy. Tell me something funny. Tell me about house painters. What are they like? Are they amusing?"

Her pronouncements suggest that she is attracted to simplification as a novelty and a clever divertisement. "In your simplification," she tells Misail in one of their first conversations, "there is nothing terrible. On the contrary, you are now the most interesting man in our town." She talks of the benefits of the simple life as she drinks champagne at dinner and takes cognac in her coffee. Misail likens her to a beautiful bird, the frequent symbol for Chekhov's narcissistic women, which has escaped from its cage and is lonely and without shelter. Misail remembers such a bird from his childhood—it was, significantly, a parrot. When, after she has left Misail, Masha writes him asking for divorce, she herself applies the metaphor of the bird to herself, telling him that the formal marriage bonds are the only weight remaining on her "wings." She has now gone a full circle—from a life in society, to "simplification," and back to society. She finds a philosophical "justification" for her flighty life in the inscription of Emperor David's ring: "Everything passes."

". . . Everything passes. Even life will pass. This means that nothing is necessary; or that only the realization of freedom is necessary. For if man is free, he needs nothing, nothing, nothing at all."

In a typically Chekhovian construction Masha's pretentions provide an echo to Misail's protest which has more complex causes and is the result of sincere reflecting. We learn that Misail was a failure in school, that he has lost many jobs, and that he still trembles when his father threatens him. These facts are conveyed by the recurrent use of details, external characteristics, typical gestures, sounds or evocations of sounds, and repeated phrases, which are woven into the narrative.

While Misail believes that he leaves his milieu out of intellectual protest, other contributing factors are hinted at. A lack of maturity is suggested in scenes with his father. Since Misail is the narrator, we observe the world through his eyes, and this in turn defines his character for us. Thus we see that his father appears to him as distant and cold. "His face, which was dry and emaciated, with a shade of blue where it was shaven (his face reminded one of an old Catholic organist) . . . expressed meekness and submission." He speaks pompously, and strikes his twenty-five-year-old son on the face. Certain epithets are repeated when the father is discussed. They are: "dry," "emaciated," and "without talent." But the detail which strikes us most, because of its connection with the father and because of the significance attached to it by Misail, is his umbrella. When the father, upon learning that Misail has lost his job, slaps his face, Misail tells us:

In my childhood, when my father beat me, I was expected to stand straight, with my hands held to my trouser seams, and look him straight in the face. And now, when he beat me, I completely lost my composure and, as though I were still a child, I stood up straight and tried to look him straight in the face.

I staggered back into the hall, and there he grabbed his umbrella and struck me several blows on my head and shoulders. At that moment my sister opened the door from the living room in order to find out what the noise was all about. But she immediately turned away with an expression of terror and pity, without uttering a word in my defense.

The father is a tyrant, and the son feels "as though [he] were still a child" and repeats the childish gesture. The daughter also fears the father. Her first reaction is terror, and only her second is a feeling of pity. The image of the umbrella is henceforth often summoned when Misail meets his father who no longer beats his son. But the umbrella is there—to remind us that Misail is like a child and his "simplification" is the expression of an infantile personality. Sometimes the imagery is varied. Misail sleeps in an old shack, in his father's yard, from the walls of which hang a pair of large crutches. When Misail returns to his father's house for a brief encounter with the architect, he looks into the shack. "The crutches on the wall looked at me grimly and their shadows winked." And when, a few minutes later, Misail stands before his father, again almost at attention, the latter reaches to his drawing board and picks up a ruler. In this encounter Misail gives an impassioned speech attacking the *pošlost'* in the town, which echoes the speeches of Gromov in "Ward No. 6." But the father's ruler reminds us of his tyranny and of Misail's weakness and this little gesture destroys the effect of Misail's speech.

Misail's one attempt to return to a pastoral life does not succeed. Consequently, he adopts an occupation which is only a burlesque of the doctrine of "simplification," that of house painting. We see Misail, as he sees himself, in his paint-spattered suit, carrying his paint bucket and brushes, and his own self-description provides ironical comment to his conscious philosophy. In the conclusion of the story Misail, now sterner, perhaps even less happy, but weary and resigned, becomes a painting contractor and with this action finaly submits to the society he has so long rejected. Shop- keepers no longer splash dirty water on Misail when he passes by; he is addressed with the polite pronoun *vy;* the governor, who had once sternly reprimanded him for betray- ing the aristocracy, now no longer remembers the repri- mand. Misail is humbly grateful that his "great troubles and patience have touched peoples' hearts." But "simplifica- tion" has made him no happier.

The lover and seducer of Misail's sister, Dr. Blagovo, pro- vides a second echo to Misail as he hypocritically expresses his feelings for simplification by such gestures as drinking tea out of a saucer in peasant fashion at a picnic. He praises Misail for his noble sacrifice in relinquishing civilization, and at the same time asks him if he would not better serve mankind in a more intellectual capacity. At their first en- counter, just after the doctor has arrived from the city, Mi- sail sees the doctor as they walk into the garden:

. . . The doctor walked ahead and spoke with enthusiasm: "What air! Holy Mother, what air!" In appearance he was still a student . . . he seemed frail and thin (*židkij*), his beard was thin (*židkij*) and so was his voice—a thin tenor.

The trait of weakness and lack of physical vigor, which is already indicated in the use of the diminutive form for the words meaning beard and tenor (*borodka* instead of *boroda,* *tenorok* instead of *tenor),* and in the repeated adjective *židkij* (thin), remains attached to the doctor. When he touches the piano keys, they respond "faintly, in a tremor- ous, hoarse, but melodious chord."

Opposed to the "simplifiers" are the members of society in the town. Again, small details indicate their prosaic emptiness. There is the family of the Azhogins, patrons of the arts, "progressives," "intellectuals," whose three daughters are never referred to by name, but only as the oldest, the middle one, and the youngest.

. . . They were very serious, never smiled and even when they played in musical vaudevilles, they played without the slightest gayness, with a matter-of-fact attitude, as though they were working on a bookkeeping problem.

Mrs. Azhogin is engaged in a quixotic battle against superstition; she always lights three candles and begins all her undertakings on "unlucky" dates. But when she discovers Misail's sister to be pregnant, her tolerance is forgotten and she demands that Misail remove her immediately.

. . . And the three daughters, exactly like her, thin and flat-chested, stood on one side, huddled together in a frightened way. They were alarmed, overwhelmed, as though a convict had just been caught in their house.

Indirect commentary is also achieved by details attending to other characters. Masha's father constantly asserts that he too once worked with his hands, as he appears smelling of good health and expensive cigars, "with red cheeks, a broad chest, and a well-scrubbed look." He is always taking showers, as if he wished to wash off forever the smell of his worker's past, and he calls all those beneath him "Panteley," not bothering to think of their true names. There is the governor who lectures Misail on his betrayal of the nobility. We see little of him, but his superficiality is quickly suggested when he begins speaking "opening his mouth wide and round, like a letter o."

A commenting function attaches to repeated proverbs and expressions, such as Redka's: "Woe, woe unto us sinners," "Everything is possible," and "A plant-louse eats grass, rust eats iron, but lies eat the soul (*tlja est travu, rža-železo, a lža-dušu*). Sound is characteristically employed to create an atmosphere which also acts as a kind of chorus. During

the last night of Masha's presence in the village, Misail realizes that she will leave him.

> ... As if in answer to my thoughts a desperate shout was heard
> outside: He-e-e-lp! it was a thin woman's voice. And, as if
> mocking it in imitation, the wind whistled in the chimney
> with a thin sound.

It is this sound which brings to Masha the realization that
simplification had been a mistake.

> "It is terrible to live in the village," she said, "and what a
> long night, oh dear." "He-e-e-lp" we heard again, a little later.

In the April, 1897 issue, *Russian Thought* published Chekhov's story "The Peasants." A number of pages were prohibited by the censor. However, Chekhov was able to rein-
state these passages in the first edition of "The Peasants" in
book form,[5] since book publication was not subject to the
same stringent censorship laws as was that of periodicals.[6]
  The protagonists of the story are one peasant family, the
Chikildeevs. Each member of the family has his own tragic
fate, caused by the effects of poverty and the resultant degradation, drunkenness, and brutality. Nikolay Chikildeev,
a Moscow waiter, falls ill and decides to return to his native
village. It is through his eyes, as well as through those of his
wife Olga and their daughter Sasha, that we learn of the
debasement of the remainder of the Chikildeev family who
drink and beg—the men beat their wives and children. All
live like animals, crowded in a filthy hut, tortured by lice,
cold, and stench which prevent them from sleeping.
  These peasants, just as those of Zola in *La Bête Humaine*
and in *La Terre,* are deprived of the slightest trace of romantic veneer. Only the sexual violence of Zola's peasants
is lacking. The naturalistic approach is also evident in the
objectivity and lack of sympathy with the characters which
is carried to an extreme unusual for Chekhov.

While the approach in "The Peasants" is naturalistic, the method of portrayal is Chekhov's usual one. The work consists of a series of episodes which are only tenuously connected, but which create a total impression of peasant life. The story begins with a brief recounting of the illness of the waiter Nikolay Chikildeev and his decision to go to his native village. It is dryly written, almost like a medical case study.

Nikolay Chikildeev, a waiter in the Moscow hotel "Slavyanski Bazar," fell ill. His legs became numb and his gait changed, so that on one occasion, as he was going down the hall, he stumbled and fell down with his tray, on which was a serving of ham and peas.

The waiter has illusions about his village, which he expresses in clichés and folk-sayings: "It is better to be ill at home, and life is cheaper there; it is a true saying that at home even the walls help." The first remarks indicate the irony of the story, for idealized dreams are shattered by the reality of peasant life. Nikolay had thought of the village as a warm, friendly place.

. . . In his childhood memories he had pictured his home [the Russian is "native nest"] as bright, cozy, and comfortable. Now, entering the hut, he was positively frightened: it was so dark, crowded and filthy.

Here two clusters of three adjectives are juxtaposed. And the contrast between those which represent the dreamed-of, but nonexistent, ideal, and those which represent the reality, sets the tone for the enire work. The extent to which the hut differs from Nikolay's memories is further indicated by a number of details: there are many flies, the stove leans to one side, the beams are crooked, bottle labels and scraps of newspaper are pasted on the wall "instead of pictures." Immediately following is a naturalistic description of a neglected peasant child impassive in her misery.

. . . None of the adults were at home; they were all in the fields. On the stove sat a tow-headed girl of about eight, she was un-washed and apathetic. She did not even glance at them as they entered. On the floor a white cat was rubbing against the oven-fork.

"Pussy, pussy" Sasha called to her. "Hey, Pussy."

"She can't hear," said the little girl, "She's gone deaf."

"From what?"

"Just so. She was beaten."

Lyrical nature descriptions are the most frequently used device to set off the lack of beauty in the lives of the peasants. When Nikolay, his wife, and daughter enter the village for the first time, they see an idyllic pastoral scene:

. . . Nikolay and Olga watched the setting of the sun, watched the gold and crimson sky reflected in the river, in the windows of the church and in all the air, which was caressing, still and unutterably pure, as it never was in Moscow. And when the sun had set, the herds passed, bleating and lowing. Geese flew from the other side of the river, all sank into silence, the soft light died in the air and the darkness of the evening began rapidly to move in on them.

But the dissonance of the next paragraph quickly comments.

Meanwhile the old people, Nikolay's father and mother, returned. They were gaunt, bent, toothless. . . . and when Nikolay entered the hut and saw the whole family, all those bodies, large and small, which moved around on the stove, in the cradles and in all the corners, and when he saw with what greed the old man and the women ate the black bread soaked in water, then he knew that it had been a mistake to come here, ill and penniless, and with his family, too—a mistake.

The naïve faith in religious rites is ironically described:

. . . The old father and grandmother and Kiryak all stretched out their hands to the icon and cried, with tears, looking at it greedily, "Defender! Mother! Defender!"

All seemed to realize suddenly that between heaven and earth there was not an empty void, that everything had not yet been pre-empted by the rich and powerful, that there still existed a defense from insults, from slavish bondage, from crushing, unbearable poverty, from the terrible vodka.

"Defender! Mother!" sobbed Marya. "Mother!"

The holiday is over and the description ends with a dry statement:

But the service was finished, the icon was taken away, and everything went on as before; and again coarse, drunken voices could be heard from the tavern.

The attitude of the peasants toward death, for which they often wish, expresses their hopelessness. They tell the old that it is time they were dead and they wait openly and eagerly for Nikolay's death.

Each individual is characterized by a metonymic detail. Nikolay's appearance is not described, but we are constantly reminded of his illness by the mention of his numb legs clad in felt boots, which suggest his impending death. We know only that the old father and mother are bent and toothless and that they greedily eat their bread soaked in water. The most brutal member of the family is Kiryak, who beats his wife and "roars like a beast." He is identified by his animal-like shout, "Ma-a-r-ya!" and by the way he loudly drinks his tea and snores. When he enters, everything is quiet and this calm around him makes him appear even more terrible.

. . . Coming up to his wife, he reached out and struck her on the face with his fist. Stunned by the blow, she did not utter a sound; she only sat down, blood flowing from her nose.

No one comes to her defense. "The old woman sat, hunched over and lost in thought; Fekla rocked the cradle." The only one who has any comment is the old man, but his

remarks are directed only at appearances: "What a dis-
grace ... in front of guests, too!"

The most important character in the story is Nikolay's
wife Olga, who meekly accepts her position. While Tolstoy's
submissive peasant, Akim (in *The Power of Darkness*), symbolizes the forces of good and in his acceptance of evil rises
above it. Olga's outlook can only be viewed as futile. She
defends the landowner and finds solace in religion. Several
details reveal her superficiality. The term "deary" (*kasatka*),
with which she addresses everyone, is an affectation incongruous with the harsh environment in which she lives. She
comforts herself with adages, as "with tears you cannot
diminish grief"; "Bear it in patience"; "In the scriptures it
says: 'if anyone smite thee on the right cheek, offer him the
left one also. . . .' " She walks "like a pilgrim, with rapid,
fussy steps." She reads the Bible every day and understands
little, but the strange Old Church Slavic words "such as
'forasmuch' and 'verily' (*ašče, dondeže*) move her to tears"
and she pronounces them "with a softened, compassionate
and radiant face." Tolstoy, as might be expected, did not
like "The Peasants" and considered it to be without aim.
"The tale [The Peasants] is a sin before the people. He
[Chekhov] does not know the people."[7]

The story ends on a melancholy note. Nikolay has died.
His wife and daughter leave the village to return to the city.
At our last glimpse of them they are standing in front of a
prosperous peasant hut, begging for alms.

Chekhov had originally planned that "The Peasants"
would be a larger work. Two further chapters have been
found, in rough draft, among Chekhov's papers, which tell
of Olga, Sasha, Kiryak, and Fekla and their life in the city.
Olga leaves Sasha with her sister, a prostitute. Sasha also becomes a prostitute, and all live as hopeless and forelorn lives
in the Moscow slums as they had in the village.[8]

In sharp contrast to the naturalistic "The Peasants" is Chekhov's last story in the peasant series, "In the Ravine," published in 1900 in the Marxist journal *Life* (*Žizn'*), for which Chekhov had expressly written the story on the urging of Gorky. Chekhov ranked this work as part of the "peasant cycle" and repeatedly called it his last work concerned with this subject.[9]

He wrote to Olga Knipper, who was to be his wife:

... In the February issue of *Life* my story will be printed. It is a very strange one. Many protagonists, also nature. There is a half-moon, a bittern bird which cries from afar: boo-oo!, boo-oo!—like a cow shut in a shed. There is everything.[10]

We may agree with the statement that this story is a strange one for Chekhov, for in this work he has sacrificed realism in the characterization of protagonists who—in the spirit of some of Dostoyevsky's philosophical figures and also of the late Tolstoy's—are symbols of ideas. The creation of a mood of power, cruelty, and strangeness is the most important effect of this story. Its conflict, simplified and exaggerated as compared with other of Chekhov's works, is essentially that of the clash between natural labor and materialistic greed.

"In the Ravine" describes a family of rich peasants, the Tsybukins, who live in a village which has been reached by industrialization. They have abandoned farming and keep a store in which they secretly sell vodka. The picture of merchant greed connects this story to "Three Years," which describes the Laptev merchant family. But the Tsybukins, who have remained peasants, are not only hypocritical and greedy as are the Laptevs, but also very cruel, reminding us of the peasants in Tolstoy's *The Power of Darkness*.

As the story begins we are introduced into the Tsybukin world. The patriarch of the family hates the peasants. He rides through the streets with an expensive horse to show that he is better than the peasants. The oldest son, Anisim, is a secret agent of the police, but as the story progresses, we find that he is also a counterfeiter.

The juxtaposition of two sets of characters—like those of a medieval mystery play—can be seen to represent the conflict of the kingdoms of darkness and of light. The world of darkness is composed of the Tsybukins—the patriarchal father, his wife Barbara, his son Anisim, and Aksinya, the wife of the feeble-minded younger son—and the various factory owners, who, although important, remain in the background.

To the world of light belong the simple people, Lipa and Kostyl (the "Crutch"), who work with their hands and do not live by the labor of others. Lipa, a poor, but beautiful woman, whose mother works as a cleaning woman, is married to Anisim. But she remains in a position of subservience in the Tsybukin family, and we usually see her on her hands and knees, scrubbing the floors. Conflict comes to a tragic climax in the clash between the greedy Aksinya and Lipa. Aksinya, angered because her father-in-law, Tsybukin, has signed over a plot of land with a factory to his grandson, (Lipa's child), murders the infant by scalding him with boiling water.

"In the Ravine" expresses more clearly than other of Chekhov's peasant stories the themes of beauty destroyed by purely "businesslike relations among men." Beauty is seen in this story as useful labor. This concept, which Chekhov treated satirically in the earlier peasant stories when he related it to a hypocritical adoption of simplification, is nevertheless sympathetically entertained by Chekhov in many of his works. Its spokesman in this story is Kostyl, an old mechanic, whose remarks comment on the main action of the story. Kostyl's saying, "he who works and suffers is better," could be an epigraph to many of Chekhov's later works and plays,[11] and this belief is expressed by Dr. Astrov and Vanya in *Uncle Vanya* and by Tuzenbach in *The Three Sisters*.

Aksinya's murder of the infant is an action which signifies the triumph of the world of darkness. Anisim is sent to Siberia for counterfeiting, and the evil Aksinya gains domination over the house from which the old father is gradually ejected as the Tsybukins can not tolerate old age. While Lipa is not victorious, she alone is able to know happiness. When she walks home with the dead infant, the sympathy she receives from peasants on the road is contrasted to the heartlessness which meets her at home. The old peasant who gives her a lift on his cart consoles her—he understands the meaning of suffering. But when she returns to the Tsybukin's house, no one comforts her, and everyone tries to shift the blame for the infant's death onto her shoulders.

"Ekh, Lipa," (says old Tsybukin) "you did not take care of my grandson."

And Barbara tells her,

"He was a pretty child ... oh, dear, oh dear ... You had only the one child, and even then you did not take care of him, stupid."

The callousness of the Tsybukins is illustrated in a brief description of the funeral feast, through which the guests eat greedily following the burial of the baby:

... after the funeral the guests and priests ate a great deal and with such greed as though they had not eaten for a long time. Lipa waited at table, and the priest, pointing with his fork on which lay a salted mushroom, told her:
"Don't mourn for the child. For theirs is the Kingdom of Heaven."

The story ends as old Tsybukin, cast off, meets Lipa, who now works at Aksinya's brick factory. She comes home, singing, walking in front of the other workers. In this final lyrical scene Lipa's moral triumph is shown.

The village was already submerged in dusk and the sun only gleamed on the upper part of the road which ran like a snake up the slope. Old women and children were returning from the woods, carrying baskets of mushrooms. From the station came women and girls; they had been loading freight cars with bricks, and their noses and cheeks were red with brick dust. They were singing. Ahead of them all walked Lipa, singing in a soft voice, her eyes turned upwards to the sky, breaking into trills as though triumphant and happy that the day was ending at last and she could rest. . . .
. . . . the crowd was met by old Tsybukin and there was a sudden silence. . . . Lipa bowed low and said:
   "Good evening, Grigori Petrovich"!
   Her mother also bowed down The old man stopped and looked at them silently, his lips trembling and his eyes filled with tears. From her mother's bundle Lipa took a piece of pie filled with kasha and gave it to him. He took it and began to eat.
   The sun had now set; its glow had died away also on the road above. It became dark and cool. Lipa and Praskovya walked on and continued crossing themselves for a long time.

The personalities of Aksinya and Lipa emerge again through details which occur repeatedly, but in this story their choice is obvious and their meaning is not subtle. Aksinya is beautiful, well built, and can never stand still. She gets up early and can always be seen running around. She always has "a naïve smile on her lips," and there is no detail which shows her cruelty so directly as the smile which appears again after she kills the baby.

. . . Aksinya picked up the pot with boiling water and threw it on Nikifor.
   Then a shriek was heard such as had never been heard before in Ukleevo. It was hard to believe that so little and

weak a creature as Lipa could shriek so. . . . Aksinya walked into the house silently with her usual naive smile.

Elsewhere Aksinya is described with colors and movements which evoke the image of a snake. Her eyes and head are immobile.

. . . and in those eyes which blinked only rarely, in that little head set on a long neck, and in her slenderness, there was something snakelike. Dressed all in green, but for the yellow on her bosom, a smile on her face, she resembled a viper in the young rye, looking out at the passerby, stretching and lifting its head.

The snake metaphor is repeated although Aksinya is also compared to other animals. Her eyes are described as "green like those of a sheep at night"; she is a "beautiful, proud animal."

Her adversary, Lipa, is a simple woman who is identified by two motifs. She has very large masculine hands, which contrast strangely with her childlike, defenseless physique and she is usually singing. She is compared to a lark which belongs in the fields and meadows, but which has been snared into captivity. Lipa, who by marriage has become a part of the Tsybukin family, remains a stranger. This fact is forecast during the wedding of Lipa and Anisim, when a child's voice is heard during the ceremony: "Mummy dear, please take me away from here. . . ."

Sound, as always in Chekhov's works, is an important part of the story. In the first chapter, as Aksinya washes herself, "the samovar . . . hummed, foreboding something evil." Sound as an omen of tragedy is again heard during the wedding feast: ". . . there was some horrible, wild mixture of sounds from which one's head began to spin." Sometimes sound comments like a chorus. When news comes that Anisim has been sent to Siberia, "the cook . . . began to wail as if at a funeral, using the traditional wailing formulae, and, as if in answer, the dogs in the yard began to set up a howl." Sound also furthers the atmosphere and mood created by visual impressions in the scene in which Lipa is walking home from the hospital with her dead infant in her arms:

... The sun lay down to rest, wrapped in golden and red cloth, and the long clouds, red and purple, stretched across the sky, guarding its sleep. Somewhere in the distance a bittern cried, like a cow shut up in a barn, with a melancholy and hollow sound. The cry of that mysterious bird was heard every spring, but no one knew what it was like and where it lived. Up near the hospital, in the bushes by the pond, . . . the nightingales were singing at the top of their voices. A cuckoo was counting someone's years, kept losing count and starting over again. Angrily the frogs were calling to each other in the pond and one could even make out the words: "that's what you are, that's what you are." What noise! It was as though all these creatures were singing on purpose so that no one would sleep on this vernal night, so that all beings, even the angry frogs, would appreciate and enjoy every minute of it; for life is given only once.

A silvery pale half-moon was shining ... and the same cuckoo was calling already with a hoarse voice, with a chuckle, as though teasing her: "Watch out, you'll lose your way!"

The sounds accompanying Lipa suggest loneliness and mystery as she walks with her dead son. Then voices momentarily break the spell as we hear the simple "put the horses in, Vavila." Lipa is comforted, but when the strangers leave and Lipa approaches the town, the sad and senseless animal sounds reappear. In the final passage it is again sound, the singing of Lipa, which expresses the beauty of her world as compared to that of the Tsybukins.

"In the Ravine" concludes Chekhov's peasant cycle. Its moralism and romanticism sets it apart from the objectivity and realism of the other stories of this group, as well as

from Chekhov's works in general. Tolstoy, who had criticized "The Peasants" for its objectivity, was enthusiastic
about "In the Ravine,"[12] a work which has many similarities to his own *The Power of Darkness*.

Chapter 11 / Beauty and Banality

We have grouped certain of Chekhov's writings as philosophical stories, others as milieu stories. The last of Chekhov's intensely philosophical stories, "The Black Monk," was written in 1893 and published in 1894, the year in which the first milieu stories appeared. In the same year there appeared two stories, "Rothschild's Fiddle" (*Skripka Rotšil'da*) and "The Teacher of Literature" (*Učitel' slovesnosti*), which express a recurrent theme—that of beauty in contrast with banality—a theme which becomes increasingly important in Chekhov's later writings.

Thematic classifications of Chekhov's stories are useful in suggesting certain dominant trends in meaning, but such generalizations must not becloud our perception of the many themes which are suggested in any single work of Chekhov's. The main theme which we now discuss demanded the employment of all the devices which Chekhov had gradually developed.

In "Rothschild's Fiddle," a story of premature death, life and death are counterposed in the depiction of the antagonism between "purely businesslike relations among men" and beauty, expressed somewhat obviously by music. The character of Jacob the coffinmaker, who can play the violin beautifully, is the subject of study.

The struggle for a bare living building coffins has caused Jacob to see everything in terms of his business. He accepts orders for children's coffins grudgingly since the profits are small. He grumbles that people die out of town. While his wife is dying, he takes her measure before she can lie down, makes the coffin in the same room and enters it into his profit-and-loss ledger. But when he returns from her funeral, he feels a momentary nostalgia. Like other of Chekhov's heroes, he is brought to a sudden, but momentary, awakening through an external shock. Now he remembers their dead child, of whom his wife had spoken just before her death. When Jacob himself must die, he takes his violin and improvises a melody so beautiful that Rothschild, the Jewish flutist, weeps. And after Jacob's death, every time that Rothschild plays this melody on the violin Jacob had bequeathed him, he and his audience must cry.

The antiphony of the themes of life and beauty and of death and greed is orchestrated by the composition of the story which, like that of "The Steppe," is based on an interplay of a number of motifs and images representing both themes. In the first paragraph, which forms the exposition of the story, the theme of Jacob and his greed is introduced. The neutral tone of this passage is modified, however, by the subtext which indicates the constricted outlook of the coffinmaker:

The little town was small, worse than a village, and inhabited almost only by old people who died so rarely that it was even annoying. In the hospital and the prison few coffins were ordered. In one word, business was miserable.

While the facts concerning the kinds of people who inhabit the town are simply stated, verbal disharmonies in some remarks suggest not a neutral observer, but the complaining coffinmaker. Pleonasms such as *počti odni tol'ko stariki* (lit.: almost solely only old men); the alliterative strengthening of the adjective *dosadno* (annoying) by the semantically superfluous *daže* (even), *umirali tak redko, čto daže dosadno* (lit.: they died so rarely that it was even annoying), all contribute to a shifting of the passage to Jacob's point of view.

There are many motifs which point to narrowness, materialism, and death. Jacob is surrounded by coffins, hates Jews, and especially the musician Rothschild. He is cold to his wife and subservient to the medical assistant when his wife is dying. The detail which metonymically indicates Jacob's crassness is his favorite expression "deficit" (*ubytok*). Jacob's view of life as a race against "deficits" leads him to a final absurdity, for when he is dying he finds death the most rational and economical state.

. . . he thought that death could only be beneficial: one needs no more food and drink nor does one need to pay taxes, nor insult people. And since a man lies in his little grave not one year, but hundreds, thousands of years, one must figure that there is really a tremendous profit.

Jacob concludes with ridiculous consistency: "Life brings man only deficit, but death brings profit."

In contrast to the varied motifs expressing negative themes, are those of life, beauty, and art, expressed most directly by the motif of music. When Jacob lies awake in bed thinking of "deficits," he touches the strings of his fiddle and feels comforted. When his wife is dying, she reminds Jacob of their youth and their child, and the willow tree under which they used to sing.

The two opposing groups of themes have their own complexities and contradictions. The themes of *pošlost'* and materialism may strangely deform even those of beauty and life. Even music may have a bitter and ironic flavor; it is first stated in terms of the material income it brings Jacob. The stifling atmosphere of the little Jewish orchestra is seen through Jacob's view, in a picture which points only to Jacob's hate:

Kogda Bronza sidel v orkestre, to u nego prežde vsego potelo i bagrovelo lico; bylo žarko, paxlo česnokom do duxoty, skripka vzvizgivala, u pravogo uxa xripel kontrabas, u levogo—plakala flejta. . . .

When Bronza sat in the orchestra, his face was sweaty and red. It was hot, there was a choking smell of garlic. The fiddle was screaming, the double base sounded hoarsely at the right ear; at the left ear, the flute was weeping.

Here a variety of synesthetic images conjure a picture of dissonance and ugliness. These are strengthend by alliteration and assonance which achieve a pejorative onomatopoeia. (*Skripka vzvizgivala . . . xripel kontrabas . . . plakala flejta*.) The assonance of high-pitched *i* and the alliterative repetition of the sibilants *s, z* for the violin, the alliteration of the vibrant *r,* the frequency of the explosives *p, k, t, b* for the double bass, and the predominance of the liquid *l* for the flute, seem to create a caricature of sound.

There are other instances in which the motif of music is thus modulated toward the theme of materialism: ironically, Jacob, who hates children, plays at weddings. Ironic also is the final reversal of the story; Jacob's beautiful improvization had moved Jacob and Rothschild to a reconciliation, and in doing so had impelled Jacob to the only selfless action of his life, the bequest of his fiddle to his erstwhile enemy, Rothschild. But, after Jacob's death, when Rothschild plays the tune on Jacob's fiddle, this music is

again stated not only in terms of beauty, but also in those of
profit, for "this new song so pleases everyone in town that
traders and officials never fail to engage Rothschild for their
social gatherings and force him to play it as many as ten
times."

The old willow tree is a positive symbol, which brings
memories of erstwhile happiness to Jacob after his wife's
death, but is tempered by the crows which inhabit it. ("And
here was the old willow tree with the gigantic hollow in it
and with its crows nests.") The fleeting mood signaled by
the willow tree is soon lost as Jacob wonders how much
profit he could have made from the river by fishing, breed-
ing geese, and by transporting himself on it with his fiddle
to play in distant villages. "But he has muffed all these opportunities. Oh, what deficits! What deficits!" The mood
evoked by the willow tree is further counteracted in this
scene by a general disharmony: the sun is too brightly reflected in the river and hurts the eyes; the children shout
Jacob's nickname after him; a fat, red-cheeked lady going
to bathe in the river makes Jacob think of a sea otter. Sound
effects created by harsh onomatopoetic alliterations and as-
sonances—the hissing of sibilants, the explosions of the
k's and *b*'s, and the sharp shrillness of the front vowels—are
opposed to the lyrical image of the willow tree:

. . . Tut *s* pis*k*om no*s*ili*s*' *k*uli*k*i, *k*rja*k*ali u*tk*i. Soln*c*e *s*il'*no*
pri*p*e*k*alo, *i* ot vody šlo ta*k*oe *s*ver*k*an'e, čto *b*ylo *b*ol'no *s*motret'.

. . . There snipes were whittling, ducks quacking. The sun was
baking hard and there was such a reflection from the water that
it was painful to look.

Frequently, however, sound techniques have more complex functions. When the Jewish orchestra plays, sound
images in the passage describing Rothschild contribute
to the atmosphere of Jacob's hate:

... ryžij, toščij žid, s celoju set'ju krasnyx žilok na lice, nosivšij familiju izvestnogo bogača Rotšil'da. ...

... a ruddy, gaunt Jew with a whole network of red veins on his face, who bore the name of the well-known rich man Rothschild. ...

The repetition of the harsh sounds, $c, \check{c}, \check{z}, \check{s}, \check{s}\check{c}$, the frequency of other sibilants and the play on the combinations $\check{z}i, \check{s}\check{c}i, \check{s}i, ic$, reinforce the pejorative expression for Jew ($\check{z}id$) with which Jacob thinks of Rothschild, and thus helps create a picture of Jacob's attitude to his antagonist.

"The Teacher of Literature" suggests a certain parallel to "Rothschild's Fiddle" in the treatment of the theme of the conflict between beauty, which is here represented by the love of the teacher Nikitin for Masha Shelestova, and *pošlost'*, suggested not only by the world of Masha and her family, but also by the conflict within the character of Nikitin himself. As the story progresses, it becomes clear that the chief protagonist, the teacher Nikitin, is infected by the same crudity and lack of ethical standards which seem to him to have destroyed his happiness.

"The Teacher of Literature" is a sequel to "Philistines" (*Obyvateli*), published in November of 1889 in Suvorin's *New Times*. Chekhov, in a letter to his publisher, called the story "a tale from the lives of porpoises."[1] "Philistines" is the story of the love of the young teacher Nikitin for Masha Shelestova, the daughter of one of the members of society in a small provincial town. Nikitin is unable to see the emptiness of the lives of the Shelestovs. The story ends with his declaration of love for Masha. Five years later, the sequel to this story, entitled "The Teacher of Literature," was published in *Russkie Vedomosti*. In it the gradual disillusionment of Nikitin is depicted. In the same year, the two stories were published together in a collection of Chekhov's

short stories[2] under the joint title "A Teacher of Literature." The central theme of the complete story depicts the
contrast between Nikitin's idealized vision of Masha and the
Shelestovs, and the stagnation and pretense of their lives.

Each of the two chapters is constructed of four dramatic
scenes. Each scene is acted in a specific locale, which is
changed like a stage set with the subsequent scene. Motifs
evocative of *pošlost'* and of beauty form a complex interplay,
as the center of emphasis gradually shifts from expressions
of beauty and happiness to expressions of materialistic crassness.

The first chapter opens on an idyllic note, although one
subtly infused with signs of crassness. Nikitin and Masha
participate in a romantic horseback ride, as Nikitin dreams
of his love for an idealized Masha. The sensuous introductory picture of beauty in which impressions of sound, color,
and smell intermingle, is fortified by Chekhov's polyphonic
use of language. The opening paragraph, which describes
the cavalcade, is strengthened by a high concentration of
sound images:

Poslyšalsja stuk lošadinnyx kopyt o brevenčatyj pol; vyveli iz
konjušni snačala voronogo grafa Nulina, potom belogo Veli-
kana, potom sestru ego Majku. Vse èto byli prevosxodnye i
dorogie lošadi.

The thumping of horses' hooves was heard on the wooden
floor; first to be led out of the stable was the black Count Nulin,
then the white Giant, then his sister Mayka. They were all excellent and expensive horses.

We can note the onomatopoetic imitation of the sound
of horses hooves on the stable floor in the predominance of
plosive *p, b, t,* liquid *r* and *l* and back vowels, and also a
verse-like rhythm of the opening phrase: *"poslyšalsja stuk
lošadinnyx kopyt / / o brevenčaty j pol."*

Punning or other verbal affectations are, as we have

noted, frequent satirical devices employed by Chekhov to indicate the dullness of *pošlost'*. In "The Teacher of Literature" the first spoken words are those of Masha's father:

"Nu, Marija Godfrua, idi sadis'. Oplja!"
"Well Maria Godefroy, mount. Hopla!"

The senseless use of the foreign name Godefroy as a nickname, which has been Masha's ever since she had become enamoured of a traveling circus, combined with the "hopla" derived from the language of the circus, sets the tone for the Shelestov family and anticipates the grossness which pervades their household. How closely Masha is associated with this atmosphere, in spite of Nikitin's idealized picture of her, is already hinted at by her repetition of her father's "hopla," as she mounts her horse.

Animal images, which will pervade the story increasingly, already begin to twist the lyrical atmosphere of the opening scene. It is with a view of animals, rather than human protagonists, that the story begins ("the thumping of horses hooves was heard . . ."). Significantly, Masha's first words to Nikitin, and her entire conversation with him in this scene, concern horses, and her horse talk forms a commentary on Nikitin's romantic dreams and the poetic atmosphere.

As the cavalcade continues, a beautiful atmosphere is described:

. . . here the acacia and the lilac no longer smelled, music was no longer heard; instead the smell was of fields; young rye and wheat stood green, marmots were whistling, crows were cawing. Wherever your eye fell there was green.

Only to be tempered by an antistrophe immediately following:

. . . only somewhere there could be seen the blackness of melon fields, and far on the left at the graveyard, one could see the white of apple trees whose blossoms were beginning to wilt.

They passed the slaughterhouse and then the beer brewery . . .

Vernal nature and life are here contraposed to blackness
and death (the graveyard and the apple trees just loosing
their bloom) and then to the slaughterhouse and the
brewery. Death, food, and drink, again indicate metonymically the Shelestovs. At the end of the scene the brewery is
again presented, as part of the background of Nikitin's
ecstatic dream of happiness:

. . . Manyusya also was silent, and he felt the reason for her
silence and for her riding at his side; and he was so happy that
the earth, the sky, the lights of the town, the black silhouette of
the beer brewery—all blended for him into something very
pleasant and comforting. And it seemed to him as though his
Count Nulin were stepping on air and would climb into the
crimson sky.

Nikitin's insensitivity has been subtly suggested. Beauty
and the brewery blend into an agreeable sensation. He does
not sense the conflict, just as he will not sense Masha's
emptiness until it is too late.

The scene shifts to the Shelestov household. In contrast
to the first scene, motifs of *pošlost'* now dominate and are
only occasionally relieved by lyrical motifs. The atmosphere
is indicated by two details with which the scene opens. The
first is of food. "They arrived home. On the table in the
garden the samovar was already boiling. . . ."

There is a second detail in this introductory paragraph.
As Nikitin enters the house he hears, "It's loutishness,
loutishness and nothing else" (*Eto xamstvo! Xamstvo i bol'še
ničego*), uttered by Masha's father. This expression, oft
repeated by the father, comes to denote the Shelestov family
and it often sounds as a chorus to the story. When Masha's
sister, Varvara, argues that Pushkin knew nothing of psy-
chology and someone attempts to support Pushkin by mistakenly citing some lines from Lermontov, the word
"loutishness" is pronounced from the other end of the hall,

expressing the pretension of provincial conversation. It is heard again when Varvara is left by her suitor, Captain Polyanski. Now, however, her father's "That is loutishness!" refers not only to Polyanski's action, but also to the flirtatious game by which Masha had enticed the now disenchanted Nikitin.

Animal motifs are now presented in a more concentrated fashion and the identification of the Shelestovs with the animals is clearly suggested. The Shelestovs live with a menagerie of dogs, cats, and "moaning" pigeons, which take part in the action. There is the dog, so inappropriately called Mushka ("little fly"), who voices his disapproval of Nikitin's courtship of Masha by his frequent growling.

The association of dogs with the family is furthered by Masha's sister, Varvara, a dry, vulgar woman, somewhat reminiscent of Misyus' sister in "The House With the Mezzanine."

. . . If someone joked or punned, you could immediately hear her voice: "That's an old joke!" or "that's trivial!" And if an officer was joking, she would grimace contemptuously and say: "Arrrmy joke!" (*Arrrmejskaja ostrota*)

And this "rrr" . . . sounded so convincing, that Mushka would immediately answer from under the table: "rrr . . . nga-nga-nga . . ."

The association of Varvara with the dog is repeated again in the second part of the narrative.

The scene ends with Nikitin's departure from the Shelestov's house and his as yet naïve reflections on the house and the moaning pigeons.

"What a house!" thought Nikitin crossing the street. "A house where only the Egyptian pigeons moan, and these only because this is their way of showing their pleasure!"

The third scene is set in the quarters which Nikitin shares with his colleague, the geography teacher Ippolit

Ippolitych Ryzhitski, a crusty pedant and a precursor of the teacher Belikov in "The Man in a Shell" (*Čelovek v futljare*). He is characterized again by Chekhov's concentrated use of synecdochic detail: he speaks only in platitudes and "always says what everyone knows already." His disinterested replies to Nikitin's romantic exclamations are deflatingly ironic. Still under the spell of his happiness, Nikitin breaks into the room. He greets Ippolit Ippolitych with "What splendid weather we are having!" And Ippolit replies,

"Yes, the weather is fine. It is May, soon it will be summer. And summer is different from winter. In winter we must heat our stoves, but in summer it is warm without stoves. In summer one opens the windows at night and it is still warm; but in winter we have storm windows, and it is still cold."

Ippolit Ippolitych's apparently vacuous statement is, however, inadvertently meaningful. The summer of happiness of which Nikitin dreams will only be superficially different from winter. In the end nothing will change. In the narrative, Ippolit Ippolitych is a steady point of reference against which Nikitin's gradual disillusionment is contrasted. As the two confront each other, Nikitin, who is in love and happy, feels superior to the passionless geography teacher.

Nikitin dreams of future happiness with Masha. But here again discordant motifs distort the atmosphere. Nikitin dreams that he writes a letter to Masha. But he composes only the salutation—"My dear little rat!" The Russian *"milaja krysa"* is here used as an endearment, but the significance of the animal motif is clear. The scene ends with Nikitin's return to the Shelestov's house, determined to propose.

In the last scene of the first chapter Nikitin proposes, but not according to his romantic plan to approach Masha in the poetic atmosphere of the garden. He had prepared a speech "with a preamble and a conclusion." Instead, he can hardly speak from excitement, and the proposal takes place not in the garden, but in a narrow, dark corridor in the Shelestov house, surrounded by expressions of *pošlost'*: cats sleep on the staircase leading from the hall, a seamstress is heard clattering with a pair of scissors. A brief interlude of lyrical harmony follows when the two lovers run into the garden. But presently they return to the house, that picture of empty provincialism. Old Shelestov reacts to the proposal with his habitual *"xamstvo"* ("loutishness") and with deflating remarks ("What kind of pleasure is it to put on chains when you are still so young!"). Varvara breaks into the conversation between Nikitin and his future father-in-law by announcing the arrival of the veterinarian. Nikitin's romantic hopes are further denigrated by the prosaic caution clichés of Ippolit Ippolitych:

"Marriage is a serious step . . . one must first consider everything, weigh the evidence, you can't do it simply so. Prudence has never hurt, especially when it is a question of marriage, when man leaving his bachelorhood begins a new life."

The first part of the narrative closes with an almost verbatim repetition of the phrases which had introduced the story. Nikitin

. . . dreams of the thumping of horses' hooves on the wooden floor; he dreams that first they led the black Count Nulin out of the stable, then the white Giant, then his sister Mayka. . . .

The second chapter depicts the life of Nikitin and Masha after their marriage, in which Nikitin is rapidly disillusioned and succumbs to the environment of *pošlost'*. Four scenes again chart the successive stages of Nikitin's disintegration.

In the first section there is an entry from Nikitin's diary which affords an insight into his egotism and sentimentality.

("I thought how my life has blossomed, how poetically beautiful it has become!") The marriage ceremony, as described
by Nikitin, is filled with *pošlost'*:

It was very crowded and noisy in the church; and once someone even cried out and the priest who was marrying Manyusya
and me looked over his glasses at the crowd and said severely:
"Don't walk around and make noise, be still and pray! You
ought to fear God."

The view of the wedding introduces the now predomi-
nant prosaic mood which is to replace the atmosphere of
Nikitin's former romantic happiness. A succession of motifs
indicates the falseness of Nikitin's dreams: he writes in his
diary that the dowry consists of "a plain unplastered two-
story house, a wasteland farm filled with chickens and ducks
running wild." After the wedding Nikitin, in a gesture
which is prophetic of his impending deterioration, "spralls
on the couch in his new study." The scene ends with a nature picture which, in its contrast to the earlier nature
scenes, reflects Nikitin's new somber mood: ". . . the trees
rustle, there will be rain; crows are cawing, and my Manya,
who has just fallen asleep, for some reason looks sad."

In the next scene we return to the authorial view. The
deceptiveness of Nikitin's happiness is signaled by a number of motifs. The lunch which Masha sends to Nikitin at
school appears to Ippolit Ippolitych to epitomize the joy
of married life; Masha is now pictured as parsimonious and
efficient. We also note that Nikitin's remarks no longer
seem sincere. "I am unendingly happy with you, my treasure," he tells his wife. But he tells her, in a didactic, egotistic
vein:

". . . I do not regard my happiness as something which has come
to me accidentally, from heaven. This happiness is a completely
natural phenomenon; it is consistent and logically correct. I

believe that man is the creator of his own happiness, and now I am taking what I have myself created. . . ."

An ironic note is struck here. For it becomes clear that Nikitin is not even the "creator" of this semblance of happiness. Rather he has been caught in Masha's well-prepared net. In Nikitin's second diary entry he describes the death and burial of Ippolit Ippolitych, for whom he fears to make a graveside speech because he knows that the school director did not like the geography teacher. This is the first direct indication of Nikitin's failing character.

The subsequent scene is introduced by a somber nature picture:

Zima byla vjalaja, bez morozov, s mokrym snegom; pod Kreščen'e, naprimer, vsju noč veter žalobno vyl po-osennomu, i teklo s kryš. . . .

The winter was a half-hearted one, there were no frosts, the snow was wet; at Epiphany for instance, the wind howled sadly all night like in autumn, water ran down the roofs. . . .

The animals suggest the disharmony.

Only one thing angered and upset him at times and seemingly prevented him from being perfectly happy: this was the cats and dogs which he had received as part of his wife's dowry. The rooms, especially in the morning, always smelled like a menagerie and nothing could destroy the odor.

Nikitin's disillusionment becomes clear in a brief scene which precedes the denouement, as Nikitin sees Masha lying in bed languidly, snugly satisfied, while a white tomcat purrs at her side. The whole picture is underscored again by sound repetition:

Kogda on prišel domoj, Manja byla v posteli. Ona rovno dyšala i ulybalas' i, povidimomu, spala s bol'šim udovol'stviem. Vozle nee ležal belyj kot i murlykal. Poka Nikitin zažigal sveču i

zakurival, Manja prosnulas' i s žadnost'ju vypila stakan vody.
"Marmeladu naelas' " skazala ona i zasmejalas'. . . .

When he came home, Masha was in bed. She breathed evenly
and smiled and apparently slept with great pleasure. Next to
her lay a purring white tomcat. While Nikitin lighted a candle
and began to smoke, Manya awoke and greedily drank a glass
of water.
"I have eaten too much jam," she said and smiled. . . .

The predominance of liquid *l*'s in this passage contribute
to the impression of Masha's languidness. Now animals
have displaced Nikitin even in the marriage bed. In indirect fashion we are led to the finale which the animal association has made us anticipate. Masha angrily tells Nikitin
that Captain Polyanski has abandoned her sister Varvara.
Her irritated rhetoric question, "Why did he come to the
house so often? If one has no serious intentions, that is not
done!" forces Nikitin to realize that he also had been expected to marry Masha when he frequented her house. He
had dreamed of romantic love, and it had seemed to him
accidental that, on the first horseback ride, his and Masha's
horses should ride next to each other; he had imagined that
his horse was flying through the clouds. Suddenly his romance with Masha loses its charm.

Throughout the story, the lives of Polyanski and Varvara
are contrasted to those of Nikitin and Masha. Bitterly
Nikitin begins to think with envy of the captain whom he
had always despised; for the captain had eluded the trap
which has captured him. There is another ironic sense in
which the scene of the early ride of Nikitin and Masha suggests a conclusion which is in the end not fulfilled. Nikitin's
horse is named Count Nulin, a name which has a literary
significance which no Russian could fail to note. Count
Nulin is the hero of a narrative poem by Pushkin ("Count
Nulin," 1825), who attempts, albeit unsuccessfully, to se-

duce the beautiful wife of a country squire. The horse's name also suggests the role of seducer for Nikitin, whereas in reality it is he who is seduced, as he finally realizes.

In the last scene, Nikitin has been defeated by the world of crassness and vacuity. Images of *pošlost'* are now pervasive as the narrative recalls the plain two-story house, the greedy eating of father Shelestov and the final sounding of his *"xamstvo"* (loutishness).

As the story ends it is spring again, as it was when the story began. But now Nikitin has lost all his dreams, rejects Masha's world entirely, and wishes to return to the kind of life he had pursued and which he had so gladly left when he married Masha. The story has completed a full circle and has fulfilled the implied prediction of Ippolit Ippolitych that Nikitin's dreams of the romance of spring were illusions.

In three stories written in 1895, "Anna on the Neck" (*Anna na šee*), "The Wife" (*Supruga*),* and "Ariadne," the theme of the incompatibility of love and *pošlost'* is further explored.

The first outlines of "Anna on the Neck" appeared in Chekhov's notebook:[3]

A poor girl, graduate of a gymnasium, with 5 little brothers, marries an old civil servant, who nags her about every little piece of bread, demands obedience, gratitude (he has lifted her up), makes derogatory remarks about her relatives. "Every person must have his duties." She stands it all, is afraid to contradict him, is afraid to return to her former state of poverty. Invitation to ball by superior. She creates sensation. Important person falls in love with her, she becomes his mistress (she is secure now). When she sees that husband's superiors seek her

---

* There are two stories which are translated as "The Wife," although the Russian titles are different: *Žena* (1892) and *Supruga* (1895). English does not have an equivalent of these two Russian nouns, both meaning "wife."

favor, that her husband needs her, she tells her husband contemptuously: "Go away, fool!"

In October of 1895, the little story of Anna, a girl of 18,
appeared in the journal *Russkie Vedomosti*. The story
largely follows the outline sketched in Chekhov's notebook.
It is based on the familiar themes of ill-matched and loveless
marriages and adultery. We know that Chekhov was well
acquainted with Flaubert's *Madame Bovary* and, of course,
with Tolstoy's *Anna Karenina,* both of which involve these
themes. Later we shall discuss the special significance of
Tolstoy's novel to Chekhov's story. In *Anna Karenina,* as in
Madame Bovary, unequal marriage and adultery bring
tragedy. But "Anna on the Neck" is ironic rather than
tragic, as a superficial version of Tolstoy's Anna wins in the
end by conquering her husband's world.

Anna, the daughter of an impecunious teacher who is
addicted to alcohol, marries a pompous, elderly civil servant, Modest Alekseich, in the hopes of improving the material position of her family. She fears her husband. But at a
charity ball her beauty wins her success, the roles are reversed, and it is her husband who cringes before her. Anna,
knowing that her husband's career now depends on her,
rules him and leads a gay and irresponsible life.

The story is composed of two parts. In the first there are
hints of tragedy for Anna in her loveless marriage, whereas
the second part provides the peripety which brings Anna
triumph; but it is bought at the expense of her humanity.
The title refers to the anecdote of "Anna on the Neck,"
which Modest Alekseich tells Anna on their wedding
day as a moral admonition. When a colleague of Modest
Alekseich's was awarded the decoration of St. Anna, the
official awarder, "His Excellency," had remarked: "You
have now three Annas, one in the button hole and two on
your neck."[4] The second Anna "on the neck" referred here

to the official's wife, also named Anna, "a quarrelsome wife of giddy disposition." This anecdote serves as the theme of the work, around which the two parts of Chekhov's story form variations.

On their wedding day, after Modest Alekseich had related his tale of the Annas on the neck, he had remarked pompously: "I trust that when I receive the Anna of the second class, His Excellency will have no cause to say the same to me." But in the reversal accompanying the conclusion, "His Excellency" repeats the same remark to Modest Alekseich, who smiles subserviently, only grateful for the same joke which had seemed so degrading to him before.

The opening passage of the story suggests the atmosphere of foreboding which accompanies the marriage.

After the wedding not even light refreshments were served; the young couple drank a glass each, changed clothes and went to the station. Instead of a gay wedding ball and dinner, instead of music and dancing, there was only a pilgrimage. . . .

The ever-repeated adjective *molodye* (the young ones) which is used here and throughout the first chapter whenever the newlyweds are mentioned, acquires an ironic ring. For while *molodye* is used here in the sense of "newlyweds," its primary meaning is "the young ones"; and this double meaning is a play on the inequality between Anna and her husband. The first passage prepares for the ironic variation with which the theme will be played in the second part. While the wedding is characterized by the absence of merriment ("Instead of a gay wedding ball and dinner, instead of music and dancing, there was only a pilgrimage."), it is just the merriment missed here which, in the second part, forms the backdrop to Anna's triumph.

Modest Alekseich, who dominates the first chapter, is revealed in comic distortion, reminiscent of Gogol, as a

. . . civil servant of medium height, rather corpulent (*polnyj*), puffy (*puxlyj*), looking very well-fed, with long sideburns and without mustache; his clean-shaven, round, sharply outlined chin resembled a heel (*poxodil na pjatku*). The most characteristic feature of his face was the absence of a mustache, the freshly shaven bare place which gradually passed over into fat cheeks, trembling like jelly (*žirnye drožaščie, kak žele ščeki*).

The fat cheeks suggest the motif of gluttony, a recurrent token of *pošlost'* in Chekhov's work. The gluttony is often strengthened by the repeated use of the adjective plump (*puxlyj*). This is underlined by the repetition of labial consonants which suggest lip smacking,

She also smiled, frightened by the thought that this man might at any moment kiss her with his full moist lips. (po*l*nymi v*l*aznymi gu*b*ami) (p-l,v-l,b)

And a few lines further:

The smooth movements of his plump body frightened her. (*Mjagkie dviženija ego* pu*x*logo tela pu*g*ali ee) (pu-, pu-)

Finally, the motif of gluttony is presented directly:

At dinner time Modest Alekseich ate very much and talked about politics, appointments, transfers and rewards; he would say that one ought to work, that family life is not a pleasure but a duty, that the kopek protected the ruble and that religion and morality were the most important things in life for him. And holding his knife like a sword in his fist, he would say: "Every man must have his duties!"

The pious-sounding clichés in this passage are characteristic of Modest Alekseich. He speaks in an exaggerated civil-service jargon, overusing the participial forms usually eschewed in spoken Russian. Excessively long phrases, stilted double negatives, such as *ne mogu ne napommit'* (lit. I can not not remind you), and bureaucratic formulas as "in proportion to" (*po mere togo*), "in view of the afore-said" (*vvidu tol'ko čto skazannogo*) fill his remarks.

As the newlyweds are seated in the railway compartment, the contrast between Modest and Anna is further under-lined by alliterative imagery. The most significant phrase is a bifurcated one, which depicts both partners as isolated.

With the clumsiness of a man of good reputation who is unaccustomed to dealing with women, Modest Alekseich touched her waist and lightly patted her shoulder; but she thought about money, about her mother, about death.

The break between the two parts of the sentence occurs just before the word "but." In Russian, alliteration of key words before and after the break serves to emphasize the contrasting moods more clearly than the translation can render it:

Modest Alekseič . . . *p*oxlopyval *po p*leču; / / a ona *d*umala o *d*en'gax . . .

Modest Alekseich . . . patted her shoulder; / / but she thought about money . . .

Not all the atmosphere of the first chapter, however, sug-gests impending tragedy. A fleeting glimpse of another Anna, who later will triumph over Modest Alekseich, briefly appears as the train carrying the couple to the mon-astery halts at a railway station. Here Anna, distracted by the music and the elegant crowds of vacationers, momen-tarily loses her fears. She flirts and strikes affected poses. This glimpse not only anticipates the later ballroom scene, but also provides insight into the personality of Anna, which is not that of the traditional tragic heroine who is victimized by a loveless marriage.

During their early married life, Modest assumes a posi-tion of threatening proportions. Anna realizes that her sac-rifice has been in vain, since it has not brought her the means to provide for her father and brothers. The first chapter ends on a note which seems to indicate the completeness of Modest's domination of Anna:

> But he did not give her money. Instead he gave Anna rings, bracelets and pins, saying that it would be good to hold these things for a rainy day. And he often unlocked her bureaus and inspected them to see if everything was still there.

In the second chapter there is the reversal of the story. The climactic scene is set at the charity ball. The connection of the earlier railroad scene and the scene in the ballroom lies not only in the fulfillment of Anna's triumph, but also in the participating personages, many of whom have been first noted at the railway stop. After the ball, Anna looks at her husband and says, "Get out, you idiot!" Her husband accepts the new tone of his wife, because he notes that "His Excellency" has taken a liking to her. The husband is painted with a few satiric strokes.

> . . . He stood before her now with that ingratiating, sugary, cringingly respectful expression that she was accustomed to see on his face only in the presence of the illustrious and the powerful.

Comic distortion of the characters in this story recalls the earlier anecdotal works of Antosha Chekhonte. Caricature has already been noted in the sketching of Modest Alekseich. Secondary characters are similarly distorted. Anna's alcoholic father alternates between sentimental effusions and brusque talk. Anna's future lover, the merchant Artynov, looks unlike a romantic lover (his eyes bulge and he suffers from asthma). "His Excellency," who awards the decoration, "smiled saccharinely and chewed his lips" on seeing a beautiful woman. His wife is also described in caricature: by her nasal, singsong speech and her disproportionately large lower face, which looked as "though she held a big stone in her mouth."

The role of the *Anna Karenina* theme in "Anna on the Neck" is a notable example of Chekhov's particular use of literary allusions. The use of literary and mythological echoes in Chekhov's works has been briefly suggested in our earlier discussions. They often contribute many-leveled meanings, irony and satire, as well as pathos and emotional depth. Their use may be direct and obvious as in the cases when heroes clearly reflect mythological archetypes. Thus the myth of Narcissus is echoed by protagonists in Chekhov's "The Princess," "The Duel," "The Grasshopper," and in the play, *The Seagull.*

Frequently, however, Chekhov's use of literary and mythological archetypal patterns is more complex. They may be alluded to only indirectly, and frequently they may be inverted. Implied archetypal parallels may encourage certain expectations which are then not fulfilled in the development of the story. The tensions thereby engendered serve to contribute to a tone of irony and to the "curve" of Chekhov's stories. The Chekhovian hero who echoes an archetypal hero is frequently only a weakened version, a pathetic echo, a satire, or parody of his prototype.

Among the archetypal patterns employed by Chekhov which are of literary, rather than mythological, origin, those drawn from *Hamlet, Faust,* and *Anna Karenina* are of particular importance. Chekhov's use of motifs from *Hamlet* is notable in his play *The Seagull,* where Treplev is identified with Hamlet, his mother, Arkadina, with Gertrude, and Nina with Ophelia.[5] The casting of Chekhov's characters into situations similar to those of Shakespeare's prototypes acts as an ironic commentary in which the relationship of *The Seagull* to Shakespeare's tragedy is an inverted one. Treplev, who thinks of himself as Hamlet, is revealed to be only a pseudo-Hamlet who fails as an artist because of his own mediocrity and not because of a tragic flaw.

Perhaps the most frequently employed literary archetype in Chekhov's works is that of Tolstoy's *Anna Karenina*, examples of which can be noted in at least five stories: "The Duel" (1891), "Anna on the Neck," "About Love" (*O ljubvi*, 1898), "The Lady with the Pet Dog" (*Dama s sobačkoj*, 1899), and "The Betrothed" (*Nevesta*, 1903). Echoes from *Anna Karenina* are perhaps nowhere clearer than in "Anna on the Neck" and "The Lady with the Pet Dog," both stories of adultery in which the adulteress bears the name of Tolstoy's tragic heroine, Anna. In both stories the line of the work initially parallels that of Tolstoy's novel, only to deviate from the prototype. The moral censure in the epigraph to *Anna Karenina* ("Vengeance is mine and I shall repay.") is replaced by Chekhov with satire in "Anna on the Neck" and pathos in "The Lady with the Pet Dog."

In "Anna on the Neck," the parallels to characters and situations in Tolstoy's novel are too numerous and striking to be denied. Anna, like Tolstoy's heroine, is married to a pompous bureaucrat and commits adultery. Her husband, Modest Alekseich, is a lowered version of Tolstoy's Karenin. The name and patronymic of Anna Karenina's husband is Aleksey Aleksandrovich, and that of the husband of Chekhov's Anna is Modest Alekseich (*i.e.* the son of Aleksey), which seems to imply even a genetic relationship. Modest Alekseich shares, however, only in Karenin's negative qualities and not in his limited nobility. Both men are what Modest Alekseich calls "men of rules" and careerists who place their official lives above private concerns. Like Karenin, who disapproves of the love affair of Anna's brother, Stiva, Modest mercilessly criticizes Anna's father for his drunkenness. Also, like Karenin, Modest speaks in stilted platitudes. We can also note the similarities between Tolstoy's Vronsky and Chekhov's Artynov, the lovers of the respective Annas. In *Anna Karenina* the fateful liaison is preceded by a meeting between Anna and Vronsky at the Moscow railway station and later by an encounter at a society gathering. In Chekhov's story, Anna also meets her future lover at a railway station and their relationship is later sealed at a society ball. But the unattractive Artynov with his protruding eyes and asthma, is a caricature of Vronsky, and the relationship between Anna and Artynov is only a superficial reflection of the passions of Anna and Vronsky.

As Chekhov's Anna reflects on her marriage, she thinks that her husband and people who are like him threaten her, "as a terrible power moving on her as a cloud, or as a locomotive ready to crush her." Tolstoy's Anna was crushed by a train in the suicide caused by the suffering engendered by her adultery, but Chekhov's Anna does not suffer. The foreboding of Chekhov's Anna about the locomotive does not materialize. Instead, in the final scene, she is shown gaily riding about town with her lover. Thus, the parallels of theme and plot to Tolstoy's novel, which lead to unfulfilled expectations of tragedy, make the reversal of Chekhov's story more pointed.

"The Wife" (*Supruga*), about which Tolstoy is reported to have been enthusiastic,[6] is a subtly drawn sketch of a fickle woman, Olga Dmitrievna, who deceives her physician husband, and who begins herself to believe in the role she is playing. Chekhov had already depicted this type in "The Princess" and in "The Grasshopper." Like Anna of "Anna on the Neck," Olga Dmitrievna is an inverted Anna Karenina, to whom she is contrasted. In the oft used Chekhovian metaphor, Olga Dmitrievna is seen by her husband as a bird which has accidentally flown into his home and is beating its wings against the wall and the windows. She is unwilling to accept her husband's offer of divorce, because she cannot do without the prestige which marriage to the doctor gives her, and thus she prefers to torture her husband with her faithlessness.

"Ariadne," which represents a more complicated development of the theme of "The Wife," is also concerned with the effect of hypocrisy on love. The heroine of the story, as Olga Dmitrievna in "The Wife" and Olga Ivanovna in "The Grasshopper," is obsessed by the desire to conquer, to please, and to be loved. In an apparent wish to escape her own coldness, she wants to be taken by storm. The story opens on a steamship as the chief protagonist, Shamokhin, one of Chekhov's disillusioned intellectuals, tells the story of his enchantment and disenchantment with the beautiful Ariadne, who was his mistress.

Throughout the story a secondary theme, that of sexual abstinence, appears to comment on the views of Tolstoy. Shamokhin believes man should overcome his sexual impulses, and he speaks for a platonic attitude to love. But this view is mocked by the story since Shamokhin seeks a "platonic" love not from a simple, pure woman but from the sensuous and flirtatious Ariadne. This naïve man is shocked when he discovers that Ariadne is the mistress of the man with whom she has traveled to Italy. But when she calls him to her, he answers, adopting the role of her protector, which soon yields to that of her lover. For several weeks he succumbs to the sensual pleasures of their relationship. Irony again accompanies the conclusion as Shamokhin, who saw marriage as the only moral solution for his and Ariadne's relationship and who dreamed of such a marriage, finds that when it is within his reach his romantic illusions are destroyed. It is too late and he is tired of Ariadne. His last words express his hope of escape as he hears that Ariadne might enter into a rich *mariage de convenance* with another man.

The story is related by means of a double narration. The external narrator recounts the tale which Shamokhin has told about himself. The point of view of the story shifts several times from that of Shamokhin to that of the external narrator, a device, we have noted earlier, which contributes greater depth. Still another dimension is provided by a flashback. We are introduced to Shamokhin, the internal narrator, at the time of the denouement of the story which he is about to narrate. He is now disillusioned with Ariadne, whom he had once desired. Furthermore, before Shamokhin begins his tale, we gain a glimpse into the future as we see Ariadne, not as she first appears to Shamokhin, but through the eyes of the external narrator, as she quarrels with the custom official. The impression of her pettiness remains with us as Shamokhin offers his idealized vision of Ariadne.

When the story ends, again on the boat, we have passed with Shamokhin through love and disenchantment. We again see Ariadne through the eyes of the external narrator, and her total stance emerges in two details. She thanks the narrator for the pleasure his books have given her. But she has never read anything he has written. She thinks of herself as a bird, like so many of Chekhov's hypocritical heroines. She says, "with the expression of a naughty fretful child: 'Jean, your little bird has been seasick.'" At the beginning of the story the bird metaphor gave us a different picture, as Shamokhin tells the narrator: "When she talked to me of love, it seemed to me that I heard the singing of a bird of metal."

Another example of Chekhov's use of archetypes is the evocation in this story of the Greek myth of Ariadne which contributes hidden levels of meaning. The Greek Ariadne fell in love with the mighty Theseus, the slayer of the minotaur, and after Theseus deserted her on Naxos, she became the wife of Dionysos, the god of fertility and wine. The parallels and contrasts with the two Ariadnes, between Theseus and Lubkov and between Dionysos and Shamokhin are easily established. Chekhov's Ariadne is obsessed with the desire to conquer. She becomes the mistress of Lubkov and, after being deserted by him, finds another lover, Shamokhin. This scheming, egotistical Ariadne is an inversion of the Greek Ariadne, the personification of spring, and her lovers are also antithetical to their Greek prototypes. Lubkov, who deserts Ariadne just as the mighty Theseus had deserted his Ariadne, is only a petty bureaucrat who wears a pince-nez. He suffers from a speech defect and always pokes self-effacing fun at himself. Moreover, the puritanical Shamokhin, who even hates to see pregnant women is, indeed, a poor echo of Dionysos, the god of fertility and wine.

Ariadne's superficiality and egotism are disclosed by the falsely elevated style in which she speaks. After she has eloped with Lubkov, she signs her letters to the jilted Shamokhin "your forsaken Ariadne" and "your forgotten Ariadne"; she speaks with affected Gallicisms, calls Shamokhin "Jean" and tells him that in Abazzia, which Shamokhin had described as a godforsaken spot, one had to be *komil'fo (comme il faut)*.

It is Shamokhin, the primary narrator, who is depicted most clearly by his speech mannerisms as he relates the story of his early love for the crass Ariadne, while looking back with dispassion on the past. The Russian critic A. Derman[7] has noted the use of affectedly stilted language which is sometimes punctured by a sudden lowering of style which is cited by Derman as an illustration of Chekhov's method of deflation of the prose of his predecessors, notably of Turgenev's. While this parodic device may be viewed as a way of combatting earlier styles, the importance of this technique in character delineation is equally significant. An elevated style broken by lowerings may characterize the speaker as pompous (Ionych for instance). In the example of Shamokhin, an elaborately elevated style interrupted by lowered remarks seems to be consciously employed by the speaker to mock himself as well as to suggest his remoteness from the events which once stirred his passion. When he talks of his affair with Ariadne, Shamokhin begins in a romantically elevated style:

... For a month at least I was like a madman, conscious of nothing but rapture. To hold in one's arms a young and beautiful body, to take delight in it, to feel her warmth every time one awakened and to remember that she was there, my Ariadne!—Oh, it is not easy to get used to that!

At this point of high rhetoric, there is a sudden lowering of language:

... And yet, I did get used to it.

But the switch to matter-of-fact language which betrays the condescension and contempt which Shamokhin now feels for his erstwhile passion, is even more pithy in the original Russian: *O, k ètomu ne legko privyknut'! No ja vse-taki privyk.* More commonly it is not contrasts but simply the elevated style which indicates Shamokhin's self-mockery. When he recalls the proclivity of the Russian intellectual for lengthy discussions of serious questions, he uses the archaic *izrekaem* instead of the common Russian *govorim* (we say). The dry comment suggesting derision, "A new person appeared on our horizon," indicates Ariadne's entrance into his life. He also employs Gallicisms (*tretiruetsja*—is being treated); he spikes his speech with fillers as "you can imagine" (*možete sebe predstavit'*), "I must tell you" (*dolžen ja vam skazat'*), "I must call to your attention" (*nado vam zametit'*), "[I am] Ivan Ilich Shamokhin, a Moscow landowner, in a manner of speaking" (*nekotorym obrazom*).

The personality of Ariadne herself is often lowered by Chekhov's frequent signal for *pošlost'*: a preoccupation with food. Gluttony is associated with Ariadne, her brother, and her lover Lubkov: "[Ariadne] with a serious, inspired face

would make out an order list of oysters, champagne, choco-
lates. . . ."

The breath of Ariadne's brother, an occultist, smells of
boiled beef. The greatest concentration of food motifs occurs when Ariadne, Lubkov, and Shamokhin travel in Italy:

> We ate terribly much. In the morning we were served *café
> complet*. At one o'clock lunch: meat, fish, some omelette, cheese,
> fruit and wine. At six o'clock dinner consisting of eight courses
> with long intervals during which we drank beer and wine.
> At nine o'clock tea. Before midnight, Ariadne would announce
> that she wanted to eat and ordered ham and scrambled eggs.
> For company we ate with her. And in between meals we would
> run from one museum and exhibition to another, always worry-
> ing lest we should be late for dinner or lunch. . . . Like sated
> boa constrictors we noted only the most brilliant objects. . . .
> The same in Rome. . . . After a heavy lunch we went to in-
> spect St. Peter's and because of our full stomachs and perhaps
> because of the bad weather, it made no impression on us.

When Shamokhin enters Ariadne's bedroom after he
has discovered that she is living with Lubkov, he notes that
"on her table were tea dishes, a half-eaten roll, egg shells . . ."
And when he finally becomes her lover, Shamokhin describes her:

> . . . She slept every day till two or three; she had breakfast and
> lunch in bed. For supper she consumed soup, lobster, fish, meat,
> asparagus, game; and when she had gone to bed, I would bring
> her up something, for instance roast beef, and she would eat
> it with a sad worried expression; and when she woke up at
> night, she would eat apples and oranges.

The story terminates, without resolution. The external
narrator meets Shamokhin, who tells him he hopes Ariadne
will marry an old prince so that he can regain his freedom
and leave. But the narrator's last remark is: "What happened to Shamokhin's affair, I do not know."

Chapter 12 / Life in a Shell
The Little Trilogy, "Ionych"

> ... but how many of such people in shells
> still remain . . . how many of them are
> still to come . . . ?
>
> —from "The Man in a Shell"

> Man needs not six feet of soil, not a farm,
> but the whole earth, all of nature, where
> unhindered he can display all his capa-
> bilities and the properties of his free spirit.
>
> —from "Gooseberries"

In 1898, the journal *Russian Thought* published three
stories by Chekhov which, because of their close thematic
and structural relationship, we consider to compose a trilogy. "The Man in a Shell" (*Čelovek v futljare*), "Gooseberries" (*Kryžovnik*), and "About Love" (*O ljubvi*), were
first conceived as the opening group of a series of stories
which were to compose a longer prose form. Such plans are
mentioned by Chekhov in a letter to A. F. Marx, the publisher of his *Collected Works,* in which he protested publica-

tion of the three stories in book form before the series was completed.[1] But Chekhov was never to add to this group of stories, although later works show some thematic links to this cycle.

These three exemplary tales, each illustrative of a special kind of constricted life, are united by the persons of their narrators who relate the tales to each other as was traditional in the genre of frame stories (*Rahmenerzählung*). The protagonists suffer from the insularity of their lives—from isolation and an inability to feel alive. The theme of dedication to too narrow a segment of life, which has been observed as one of the unifying themes of the "searching stories," appears now to be only one aspect of the more general problem of man's pervading limitation of spirit. The phrase from "Gooseberries," a reference to Tolstoy's story, "How Much Land Does Man Need?," quoted as an epigraph to this chapter, states a theme of the trilogy. "Man needs not six feet of soil, . . . but all of nature, where unhindered he can display all his capabilities . . . of his free spirit." The chief protagonists of the stories are constrained by a shell, a mental "six feet of soil," which prevents each from living a full and satisfactory life.

The theme of the trilogy is presented in the introduction. Two huntsmen, the schoolteacher Burkin and the veterinary surgeon Ivan Ivanych Chimsha-Gimalayski, who are the narrators of the first two stories, are resting in a barn after a day of hunting. Their conversation leads to Mavra, the wife of the village elder in whose barn they are resting, who has never been beyond her native village. Burkin remarks that this is not surprising as there are many such unsociable people "who try to withdraw into a shell like a hermit crab," a thought which leads him to tell a story of his colleague, the gymnasium teacher Belikov, which is related in "The Man in a Shell." This story, intended as an *exemplum* by its narrator, extends the theme of "life in a shell" from the incident of Mavra to a story of symbolic proportions in which a man so fears life beyond its outward forms that he seeks various kinds of physical escape. In "Gooseberries," a different type of narrowness is exemplified in the morbid yearning of the hero for his own little plot of land which must have on it a gooseberry bush. We see his complacent pleasure when he has obtained this goal, but its achievement makes the hero even smaller and more selfish. In "About Love," a deadening conventionalism and an emotional paralysis prevent realization of an incipient love affair.

The character of each narrator emerges through his own story and through the mood it expresses. Burkin, the narrator of "The Man in a Shell," expresses only pessimism. Ivan Ivanych, who tells "Gooseberries," is moved by it to protest and to a vague search for a better life. Finally, Alekhin, who tells his own mournful tale of a *vie manquée*, of love passed by, realizes that it was his own failings which prevented him from living a full life.

"The Man in a Shell" is the story of Belikov, the teacher of Greek, an academic Sergeant Prishibeev (Ch. 1), who tyrannizes the entire town in his self-appointed role as guardian of the "proper" forms of life. When Belikov becomes engaged to a pretty and vivacious young girl, Varenka, the results are disastrous for him. His outlook clashes with that of the lively and fun-loving Varenka, who shocks him by riding a bicycle. After a violent argument, Varenka's brother throws Belikov down the stairs. This fall signifies the shattering of Belikov's fragile self. He locks himself in his room and dies.

Belikov is separated from life, except from its external forms, by his insulating shell. When he visits his colleagues, in order to maintain "good relations," he sits silently for an hour and then leaves, a painful duty religiously performed. Any infringement of "the rules, any deviation from them,

plunged him into gloom." Thus he watches over the behavior of colleagues and pupils alike.

. . . Only government regulations and newspaper notices in
which something was prohibited were clear to him. If some
ruling forbade that pupils be outside after nine o'clock at night,
or if some article prohibited carnal love, then this was clear
and definite to him: it was forbidden and that was that! But in
any permission or authorization there remained for him always
an element of doubt, something not fully expressed, something hazy. When a dramatic circle was permitted in town, or a
reading room, or tea-house, he would shake his head and say
quietly:
    "That is of course all very well, to be sure, all this is very
good, but I hope there won't be some consequence."
    . . . If one of his colleagues was late for Mass, if there were
rumors of some prank played by the students, if a female teacher
was seen late at night in the company of an officer, he would
be very disturbed and repeat that he hoped there wouldn't be
some consequence.

    In considering love, Belikov repeats clichés, such as "mar-
riage is a serious step; one must first weigh the impending
duties and responsibilities," and "I hope there won't be
some consequence." Belikov's compulsive attachment to
norms of behavior destroys his timid marriage plans. When
he sees Varenka riding a bicycle his moral indignation leads
to the climactic clash with her brother, who throws him
down the stairs, bringing Belikov's decline and death. Belikov's first action on reaching the bottom of the stairwell is
to feel whether his dark glasses are intact. The worst has
now happened, as Belikov becomes ridiculous. Varenka's
ringing laughter, as she comes upon him tousled after his
fall, "put an end to everything: to the unexpected marriage and to Belikov's earthly existence." He withdraws to
his bed behind the curtains, covered by a heavy quilt,
hiding himself as he dies. In the denouement, as Belikov

lies in his coffin shielded forever from the perils of contact with life,

. . . his expression was meek, pleasant, even gay, as though he were glad at last to have been placed in a shell which he would never leave again. Yes, he had achieved his ideal.

Like Jacob in "Rothschild's Fiddle," Belikov is so estranged from life that he can find happiness only in death.

The Belikov theme is expressed in an entry in Chekhov's notebook: "He who is estranged from life, who is not able to live it, has nothing left except to become a bureaucrat." This picture of isolation is expressed by the trivialities behind which Belikov hides his soul. He is never without dark glasses, galoshes, and a quilted coat, no matter what the weather; his face is always hidden by a high collar and his ears are stopped up by cotton; at home he is always wrapped in a dressing gown and covered by a nightcap; the curtains and shutters of his rooms are kept closed, his door and windows securely bolted. Belikov will not ride in an open carriage; his umbrella, his penknife, and his watch are protected with cloth covers. He prefers to think of the past and not of the present:

. . . Actuality irritated and frightened him, kept him in constant anxiety; and perhaps to justify his timidity, his aversion for reality, he would always praise the past and things which never had existed. And the ancient languages he taught were actually for him the same galoshes and umbrella behind which he sought protection from the realities of life.

When praising Greek for its sonority he would, "as if to prove his statement, screw up his eyes, lift up a finger and pronounce: 'anthropos,'" "man," about whom Belikov knew nothing.

This story, as well as "Sergeant Prishibeev" and "Ward No. 6," might well be read as an allegory of the reactionary

regime, and the oppressive character of the Russian bureaucrat. As Burkin, the narrator, says, "Under the influence of
people like Belikov, people in our town have begun to be
afraid of everything." Ivan Ivanych, to whom Burkin tells
Belikov's story, adds:

"Yes, decent, thoughtful people, they read Shchedrin and
Turgenev and Buckle and the rest, but they had to submit and
put up with it. . . . That's what it's like."

Depth is achieved through the participations of the narrator and his listener. The narrator sometimes adds an ironic
touch through what purports to be an objective view of
Belikov. The comments of the listener Ivan Ivanych serve
as emphasis.

The ending of the story provides further commentary on
the theme and connects it with the next story. We are in the
lyrical atmosphere of a peaceful moonlit night. The vast
fields contrast to the constricted life of the town under
Belikov's thumb. Burkin's attitude is one of resignation
and he expresses pessimistic views ("how many such men
remain in shells . . . and how many more there will be").
But the same story leads Ivan Ivanych to general protest.

Our crowded lives in stifling towns, our writing of unnecessary
documents, our whist playing—is all that not a shell? And the
fact that we lead all our lives among idlers, pettifoggers, stupid
and empty women—speak and listen to all kinds of nonsense,
is that not a shell?

To see and hear how they all lie . . . and call you a fool for
suffering the lie; to bear insults, humiliations; not to dare to
declare openly that you are on the side of honest, free people;
to lie and to smile, and all that for a piece of bread, for a roof
over your head, for a rotten little rank which is not worth a
penny. No, one cannot go on living like that.

But Burkin quickly silences him and goes to sleep; Ivan,
however, is sleepless because of what he has heard.

The second part of the allegoric trilogy, "Gooseberries," is told by Ivan Ivanych, who bears the grotesque surname Chimsha-Gimalayski. It is the story of his brother, Nikolay Ivanych, who, obsessed with the desire for a little estate upon which to retire, scrimps and saves, and, like Akaki in Gogol's "The Overcoat," denies himself all the pleasures of life and even food. He had entered into a *mariage de convenance* with a rich old widow and had contributed to her death by forcing her also to stint on food. The idyllic life of retirement was symbolized for him by a gooseberry bush from which he could eat his own gooseberries. When Nikolay finally realizes his dream, Ivan Ivanych visits him and he finds Nikolay, the landowner, old and fat. The first homegrown gooseberries are served; but they taste sour. Nikolay has achieved what he had dreamed of, but Ivan realizes its futility and is appalled at the price at which it had to be bought.

This story can be explained, as many critics have done, as a comment on Tolstoy's late moral philosophy, and specifically on his didactic exemplary tale, "How Much Land Does Man Need?" (*Mnogo li čeloveku zemli nužno?*) in which Tolstoy advocates refusal of wordly goods. In Tolstoy's parable the peasant Pakhom, greedy for land, is told that he can buy cheaply as much land as he can walk around in one day. His avarice forces him to overstrain himself. He dies at the moment when he acquires a huge plot of land and is buried in six feet of earth. Tolstoy's answer to the question posed in the title of his *exemplum* is thus that man needs only enough earth to be buried in.

"Gooseberries" has many parallels with Tolstoy's story. The heroes of both stories lust for material possessions and both die as their desire is to be realized, although Chekhov's protagonist dies only spiritually having lost his humanity in his quest for property. But while externally the stories are similar, the treatment and implications of the theme are very different.

The import of Chekhov's story is more complex than that of Tolstoy's, as is implied by the remarks of the narrator, who seems to comment on the moral of Tolstoy's story.

It is a common saying that man needs only six feet of earth. But six feet is what is needed by a corpse, not by a man. It is also asserted that if our educated class is drawn to the land and seeks to settle on farms, then that is good. But then these little farms represent the same six feet of land. To leave the city, to leave the struggle and the noise, to escape, and to hide in one's own little homestead—that is not life, that is only egotism, laziness, a special kind of monasticism, but a monasticism without great deeds. Man needs not six feet of soil ... but the whole earth, all of nature, where unhindered he can display all his capabilities and the properties of his free spirit.

How closely "Gooseberries" is related not only to Tolstoy's parable, but also to Tolstoy's *The Death of Ivan Ilich,* can be gleaned from earlier versions of the story. In all but the final version, Nikolay truly dies; before death, like Ivan Ilich, he becomes conscious of the futility of his life. We read in Chekhov's notebook:

When he has cancer of the stomach and death is near, he is given a plate of his own gooseberries. He looks indifferently. ... Looking at the plate with gooseberries: this is the final achievement of my life.[2]

In a later entry we read:

The gooseberries were sour. "How stupid," said the official and died.[3]

But in the final version there is neither death nor awareness. Awareness, in the reversal of the story, is transferred to the narrator Ivan Ivanych and, in a scene heavy with irony, Nikolay, sentimental over his gooseberries, can hardly speak from agitation, and eats the sour berries greedily, exclaiming over and over again: "how tasty, how tasty!"

The emptiness of Nikolay's quest is implied, then, by the contrast between his sentimentalized dream of rural life and its reality, while in Tolstoy's works the quest ends more obviously in death ("How Much Land Does Man Need?") or in disillusionment and death (*The Death of Ivan Ilich*). Of Nikolay's dreams of idyllic country life Ivan Ivanych says:

> My brother Nikolay . . . dreamed of eating his own cabbage soup, which would fill the whole farmyard with its delicious smell, of eating on the green grass, of sleeping in the sun, of sitting for hours on a bench behind the gate, gazing at the fields and forests. Agricultural books . . . were his pleasure, beloved nourishment for his soul.

Expressions common in the language of the sentimental novel, as "nourishment for the soul" and "beloved," used with prosaic terms like agricultural books, set the note of the absurdity of Nikolay's aims. When he finally achieves his dream, the estate has none of the sentimental accouterments which he had imagined: there is no orchard, no gooseberry patch, no duck pond. "Country life has its advantages," Nikolay had said in his youth, "you sit on the porch drinking tea, your ducks swim in the pond, and everything smells so good and—and the gooseberries are growing." But reality brings a stream, on the banks of which there are a brick and a glue factory, which turn the water to the color of coffee. Even the gooseberries are not there and have to be planted.

The reality of the dream is clear in the narrator's description of his first view of his brother's estate, grotesquely called "Chumbaroklov" or "Himalayan Waste," which is strongly reminiscent of the description of Sobakevich's estate in Gogol's *Dead Souls*:

. . . It was hot. Everywhere there were ditches, fences, hedges, rows of fir trees. . . . I made my way to the house and was met by a reddish dog, so fat it looked like a pig. It wanted to bark, but was too lazy. The cook, a fat, barelegged woman, who also looked like a pig, came out of the kitchen and said that the master was resting after dinner.[4]

Nikolay, who had hoped to free himself from the banal life of the civil servant, finds only the *pošlost'* which he had sought to escape. In his *retour à la nature* he has become a typical landowner who cures his peasants with castor oil. While he used to be afraid to voice an opinion, he now speaks only in platitudes masked as "incontrovertible truths" and does so "in the tone of a minister of state": "Education is necessary, but the masses are not yet ready for it; corporal punishment is generally harmful, but under certain circumstances it is useful"; "I know the common people . . . they love me and will do anything I want." And twenty times over, he would repeat "we of the gentry."

The theme, stated as "man needs not six feet of soil but the entire earth," is poetically implied in the introduction to the story, which paints a limitless nature, a picture which also ended the preceding story; both pictures present a contrast to the constricted lives of Belikov and Nikolay Ivanych. The deliberate slowing of the action makes this introduction more impressive. Burkin is reminded that Ivan Ivanych had promised him a story. But before Ivan Ivanych begins his tale, the weather and the countryside are described; there follows a delaying episode in which the two huntsmen are seen on the estate of Alekhin where idyllically all three swim in the millstream (Alekhin will later tell his own story in "About Love"). This little prologue then introduces the allegory of the gooseberries.

In the conclusion Ivan Ivanych, who had already evinced impatience with the implications of "The Man in a Shell," says that he is old, too old to carry into effect his dreams of

action, but turns to Alekhin and begs him never to forget
the aims of life. As the next story indicates, however, this is
ironic, for Alekhin's life is also limited; it is essentially a
vie manquée as were Belikov's and Nikolay Ivanych's.

In "About Love," Alekhin tells of his love for Anna, the
beautiful wife of the judge of the district town. He feels
that his life of rural provincialism is unworthy of Anna.
"Where could I take her?" he says.

... It would be different if I led a beautiful interesting life; if,
for instance, I fought for the liberation of my country, or if I
were a well known scholar, musician or an artist. But as it is
I would just have taken her from one dull, ordinary life to
another one.

While Belkin's life is destroyed by fear and Nikolay
Ivanych's by the pettiness of his aims, Alekhin's limitations
are more elusive. Unlike the earlier protagonists of the
trilogy, Alekhin vaguely realizes his own failure, but he is
prevented from action by a lack of élan, by a feeling of
inertia. As he bids farewell to Anna for the last time, the
strength of their mutual feelings forces both into a declaration of love. But it is too late. Life and love have passed them
both by. Alekhin understands this, as he reasons:

I understood that if you love you must, in your thinking about
that love, begin from the highest kind of feeling, from feelings
which are more important than happiness or unhappiness, sin
or virtue in their common meaning. Or you must not think at
all.

"About Love" is united to the preceding story by the
figure of Alekhin who had appeared as so sensuously enjoying life in the introductory scene to "Gooseberries." The
contrast of that picture to the one of Alekhin as the story
ends is strong. But Alekhin's experience leaves only nostalgic feelings, and his life is unchanged. He continues "rush-

ing around his huge estate like a squirrel in a cage." His approach to life is only a sweet memory.

Chekhov never continued the larger work of which the little trilogy was to have been a part. But one story, "Ionych," written during the same year as the trilogy, is related to this cycle, though it lacks both the allegoric tones and the extremes of caricature in the first two stories of the trilogy. In this story the themes of *pošlost'*, of materialism and crassness and their effect on the individual are again dominant.

"Ionych" pictures the psychological decline of a man who succumbs to the banalities of society. But in this story Chekhov returns to his more familiar technique in which irony and satire are implied, with little use of direct comment by the author.

The chief protagonist of the story, the district physician Dmitry Ionych Startsev, falls in love with Katerina, nicknamed Kitten (*Kotik*) the daughter of the Turkins, a prominent family of the district town who are pretentious poseurs of culture. Kitten rejects the love of the doctor, who with increasing material success only succumbs to the general *pošlost'* of the town. In the end he becomes a rich, unkind, and unfeeling doctor who seeks only bodily comforts and distraction from a life which no longer interests him.

As in "A Teacher of Literature," the main protagonist succumbs to the smallness of his milieu, but while Nikitin, the hero of "A Teacher of Literature," is partly a victim of a conniving family, the Turkins in "Ionych" are more gently portrayed. They do not attempt to entrap the young doctor into a marriage proposal. On the other hand, Startsev becomes a more negative character than Nikitin, whose shortcomings are only mildly suggested. While Nikitin is unhappy and critical of his own weaknesses, Startsev grows even more cruel to his patients in his greedy search for riches.

The change in Startsev, from a naïve young man to the crude doctor in his later years, is indicated almost entirely by subtexts, details, and changes in the style of narration. The story is composed of five brief chapters, each presenting a different stage in Startsev's evolution, while the last chapter is like an epilogue. Throughout the story Dr. Startsev is juxtaposed to the static family of the Turkins who, with the exception of Kitten, represent a fixed point of reference. Only Startsev changes and, correspondingly, so does his attitude toward the Turkin family. The story begins and ends with a picture of the Turkins.

When newcomers to the district town of S. complained of boredom and of the monotony of life, the local inhabitants would, by way of justification, say that, on the contrary, life in S. is very pleasant, that there is a library, a theater, a club, that there are balls and that there are intelligent, interesting, agreeable families with whom one could become acquainted. And they would point to the Turkins as the most educated and talented of all.

The irony of this evaluation becomes apparent in the depiction of the Turkins as dilettantes. It is reinforced by the striking accumulation of laudatory epithets: intelligent, interesting, agreeable, educated, talented. It is sharpened by the stress on the "talent" of the family, which is depicted as so lacking in genuine talents, although not in human kindness.

. . . In one word, every member of the family had some kind of talent. The Turkins received their guests affably and showed them their talents happily, with a cordial simplicity.

The father, Ivan Petrovich Turkin, is an organizer of local amateur plays; he takes the parts of old generals and knows "how to cough very amusingly." "His facial expression does not reveal whether he is joking or in earnest." He loves to tell pointless anecdotes. But what delights him most are his puns and his affected word plays, which so often in Chekhov's canon point to the ridiculous. He says "How do you do please" (*zdravstvujte požalujsta*), "hugeous" (*bol'šinskij*), "not badsome" (*ne durstvenno*), "goodbye please" (*proščajte požalujsta*); he puns with the word *pravo* (which in Russian means both "right" and "law") and tells his guests that they do not have the "Roman right (law) to leave so early." Some of his puns that are more difficult to translate are *bonžurte,* a combination of the French *bon jour* and the Russian imperative verbal ending *-te;* and the "conjugation" of the Russian phrase "I walk on the rug" (*ja idu po kovru*), which by altering the word boundaries becomes "I walk while I speak lies" (*ja idu poka vru*). This phrase is then conjugated: *ty ideš poka vreš', on idet poka vret,* and so forth (you walk while you speak lies, he walks while he speaks lies). His wife, who considers herself a writer, playfully flirts with Startsev in front of her husband, whom she mincingly calls, to his face, a jealous Othello.

When Startsev meets the Turkins he is young and poor. He has no horses and he walks to the Turkins' house humming a romantic tune. He is comforted by the atmosphere of culture and charm, although suspicions of its superficiality disturb his visit. But the subtext provides commentary on the Turkin family. All three Turkins perform. Mrs. Turkin reads from her newest novel, on a sentimental subject. The novel is set in winter. It begins with the cliché, "the frost was intense." It was "about that which never happens in life. And yet it was pleasant and comfortable to hear it, and it brought such good quiet thoughts to mind. . . ." As Mrs. Turkin reads, the windows are open. First kitchen noises and smells waft through, but then Ionych notes the summery fragrance of lilac, the sound of laughing voices from the street and the folk song sung by the town choir, all incongruous to Mrs. Turkin's story which began "the frost was intense." These two contrasting motifs, the domestic smells and sounds of the kitchen, and on the other hand the sounds of music and the fragrance of nature from afar, denote the familiar conflict between beauty and banality which dominates many of the later works.

In the ensuing grotesque scene, which again contrasts with the charm of the summer night, Katerina plays the piano. Her noisy performance shatters the impression of tenderness and childishness which she gave to Startsev when he first saw her in the Turkins' salon.

... Ekaterina Ivanovna sat down and struck the keys with both hands; then she struck again with all her might, and again and again; her shoulders and bosom trembled, she struck obstinately always on the same keys, and it seemed as if she would not stop until she had hammered the keys into the inside of the piano. The living room was filled with thunder; everything reverberated, the floor, the ceiling, the furniture. ... Ekaterina Ivanovna played a difficult passage, interesting only because of its difficulty, long and monotonous, and Startsev, while listening, imagined that rocks were rolling down from a high mountain, more and more, and he hoped that they would soon cease to roll down. ...

Yet Startsev is drawn to the vitality and the charm of young Kitten and the atmosphere of pseudo-culture makes him feel comfortable:

... at the same time Ekaterina Ivanovna, rosy from the violent exercise, strong and vigorous, with a lock of hair falling over her forehead, attracted him. After the winter spent in Djalizh among patients and peasants, to sit in a drawing room, to watch this young, elegant, and, in all probability, pure creature, to listen to these noisy, tedious but still cultured sounds, was so pleasant, so novel. ...[5]

Two details complete the initial picture of the Turkin household. The Turkin's houseboy, Pava, is commanded by his master to strike a dramatic pose in the hall; "Well Pava, show them," he "raised his hand and spoke in a tragic tone: 'Die, unhappy woman!' " This silly gesture pleases Startsev. Finally, the kitchen smells of frying onions, mixed with the atmosphere of family culture, lull Startsev into the comforts of provincial life.

Throughout the chapter the poetry of life and the prose of *pošlost'* form a disturbing mixture. The cheerful street noises, the smell of lilac, the folk song sung by the town choir, Startsev's songs which he sings on his way to and from the Turkins', and his vague feeling of attraction to Kitten, are in disharmony with the Turkins' banality, the stupid jokes, unartistic novels, bad music, and the kitchen smells.

Similar discord prevails as Startsev declares his love for Kitten. In the setting of the old garden of the Turkins, Startsev's elevated speech is characterized by romantic expressions as "passionately," "I thirst for your voice," "Oh, if only you knew my suffering!" In contrast is the unresponsive note of Kitten, who speaks "dryly," in "a businesslike tone of voice," just as unmovingly as she plays the piano. Certain details already hint at Startsev's further development. While he formerly had to walk, he now has a pair of horses and a coachman, and he is beginning to get fat.

The third chapter, in which Startsev proposes marriage and is rejected, represents the turning point of the story. Startsev shows himself as increasingly calculating. He thinks fleetingly of the dowry he might receive with Kitten, and no longer entertains poetic and lyrical thoughts.

Startsev becomes a successful doctor. He now drives a *troika,* he and his coachman have grown fat, and every evening he likes to smooth out the bank notes received during the day from his patients. But the story deviates from the expected line. When, after four years, Startsev returns again to the Turkins', he meets Kitten, the only one of the Turkins who has changed. Disillusioned by her realization that she lacks musical talent and now more mature, Kitten is no longer so cold, but she has also lost her pride and charm. Instead of the high spirits of youth, she shows only nervous agitation. For a moment Startsev's love flickers, but it lasts only an instant. In a reversal reminiscent of that in "Three Years," it is now Kitten who pleads with Startsev to come into the garden and to hear her out; and it is Kitten who talks in a heightened emotional style. "What happiness to be a district doctor, to help sufferers, to serve the people. What happiness!" But this remark of Kitten's stills Startsev's last feeling of nostalgia, as he thinks uneasily of his bank notes. Again we see the unchanging play-acting in the salon of the Turkins, which serves as a background to the new Startsev and the wiser Kitten. The father puns, the mother reads another new novel "about that which never happens in life," Kitten plays the piano no better than before; the lackey Pava, now no longer a child, strikes his pose and shrieks "Die, unhappy woman!" All this, which had earlier attracked Startsev, now only irritates him as he thinks how fortunate it is that he did not marry Kitten. The dry tone of this chapter, in which lyrical passages are quite absent, further defines Startsev's now so prosaic character.

In the last chapter, we see all that is left of Startsev. He is even more greedy, and is rude and cruel to his patients. His isolation is complete and his only contact with others is that of hostile gestures, or empty card games which he does not really enjoy. When he drives through the city in his showy *troika* "it seems as if not a human being were driving, but some pagan god." He speaks only in command form and in curt, rude phrases. People no longer call him by his last name, Startsev, but by his patronymic, Ionych, a form of address which in Russian may indicate contempt. He has so forgotten his earlier life that he no longer acknowledges his erstwhile friendships with the Turkins. His contact with the foolish, but good-hearted Turkin family had been the only pleasure of his life; yet when he hears people talk of the Turkins, he cannot help but interrupt them with the curt question, "What Turkins are you talking about. Those whose daughter plays the piano?"

The story ends as it had begun, with the comedy of the Turkin family, who continue their empty lives, but now without Startsev-Ionych. The last word belongs to them, as we hear Turkin's senseless "Goodbye, please."

Chapter 13 / A New Mood

"The Darling," "The Lady with the Pet Dog," "The Betrothed"

> When one loves, then one opens up such inner riches in oneself, so much tenderness and affection, that it seems almost incredible that one can love so much.
>
> —from Chekhov's Notebook

During the last years of Chekhov's life a certain change in his viewpoint can be noted. After the trilogy and "Ionych," which represent the fullest expression of Chekhov's concern with man's destruction by *pošlost'*, we find a somewhat more optimistic tone in some stories written after 1898, as well as in the major plays, which were all written after 1896.

The three stories which express most clearly the mood of Chekhov's later years are "The Darling" (*Dušečka*, 1898), "The Lady with the Pet Dog" (*Dama s sobačkoj*, 1899), and the last of Chekhov's stories, "The Betrothed," (*Nevesta*, 1903). While all three stories are concerned with man's isolation, a qualified hope is expressed concerning man's ability

to find a certain happiness. Yet, lest we be tempted to over-
simplify trends in Chekhov's final years, it should be remembered that during this period Chekhov also wrote the
last of his milieu stories, "In the Ravine" (1900), which
although it ended with an assertion of humaneness, also provided a strong picture of man's brutality.

In January of 1899, Chekhov wrote to Suvorin concerning "The Darling": "I have recently written a humoristic
tale . . . and I am told that L. N. Tolstoy is reading this story
aloud. . . ."[1] We also know, from other sources, of Tolstoy's
enthusiasm for this story,[2] which he praised in a critique
published later in his *Readings for Every Day of the Year*.[3]
Tolstoy admired the wit in "The Darling," and also what
he called an involuntary switch in the story which caused
the heroine to become "not ridiculous, but a wonderfully
holy being."[4]

"The Darling" is the story of a young woman, Olenka,
who must find a person whom she can love with submission
and abandonment. Her first love is the manager of an open-
air theater, Ivan Kukin, a man who is neither young nor
handsome and who always complains that the rain ruins his
business. After their marriage, Olenka becomes so much a
part of Kukin's life, that she also can only talk of the rain
and the lack of culture of the audience. She repeats with
conviction all that her husband says. When, after Kukin's
death, Olenka marries Pustovalov, the manager of the local
lumber yard, she only interests herself in the price of lumber
and the taxes which threaten to ruin her husband. The
second husband also dies and Olenka soon unites her life to
that of Vladimir Smirnin, an army veterinarian who is
separated from his wife. While they are not married, everyone knows what has happened when Olenka suddenly begins
to complain about the dangers of animal epidemics. But
Smirnin leaves her also when he is transferred, and Olenka
almost ceases to live.

Now she was quite alone. . . . She got thinner and lost her looks and passers-by in the street did not glance at her and smile as they used to. . . . She ate and drank as though involuntarily.

Above all, and worst of all, she no longer had any opinions whatever. She saw objects around her and understood what was going on, but she could not form an opinion about anything and did not know what to talk about. And how terrible it is not to have any opinions! You see, for instance, a bottle, or the rain, or a peasant driving a cart, but what the bottle is for, or the rain, or the peasant, what is the meaning of them, you can't tell, and you couldn't even if they paid you a thousand rubles. When Kukin was about, or Pustovalov or, later, the veterinary, Olenka could explain it all and give her opinions about anything you like, but now there was the same emptiness in her head and in her heart as in her courtyard.[5]

But in the end Olenka finds a new love in Smirnin's schoolboy son, Sasha, who becomes her boarder, and whom she mothers. Now Olenka has opinions again, but this time they are about the difficulties of school work, about teachers and textbooks.

The picture of Olenka, devoid of a personality of her own, lacking inner resources and entirely dependent on others, on whom she thrusts her love, is partly a satirical one. But "The Darling" is not only the story of an empty human being; and whether or not one agrees with all the implications of the Tolstoyan view that Olenka is, in the end, not ridiculous but even "holy," this interpretation cannot be overlooked. While it appears at first that Olenka may become one of Chekhov's typical figures of emptiness and hypocrisy, the fact that she is capable of love, even though it is submissive and possessive, distinguishes her from many Chekhovian lonely protagonists. Tolstoy's position, however, that in the elevation of the submissive Olenka, Chekhov was rejecting, although not consciously, his earlier ideas of woman's emancipation,[6] is hard to justify. For Olenka's absurdity cannot be overlooked. Her naïve identification with anyone willing to accept her love, and her immature personality, which is only a reflection of others', contribute to ridicule, rather than to an idealization of woman's maternal role. Olenka's idealization of those she loves, when contrasted to an objective depiction of these persons, is also comic.

To Olenka "it seems that . . . Kukin is struggling with fate and takes his main enemy—the indifferent public—by frontal attack." But Kukin, her first husband, is described as a small, thin man, with a yellowish complexion and a reedy voice, who cannot speak without screwing up his mouth. Many oblique remarks contribute to a more realistic picture of Olenka and Kukin. Statements which seem to imply contentment may conclude with contradictory information thereby providing, in sudden glimpses, contrasts to Olenka's childish dreams. Thus, about the wedding day it is noted: "He [Kukin] was happy, but as it rained on their wedding day and the night that followed, the expression of despair did not leave his face."[7] And later on we read that "Olenka was gaining weight and beamed with happiness, but Kukin was getting thinner and more sallow and complained of terrible losses. . . ."[8]

Even the announcement of Kukin's death becomes a mock tragedy, because of a double meaning. Introduced by what appear at first to be traditional tragic notes, the announcement is rapidly modified by absurd details:

. . . there was a sudden ominous knock at the gate; someone was banging at the wicket as though it were a barrel—boom, boom, boom! The sleepy cook, her bare feet splashing through the puddles, ran to open the gate.
"Open, please!" someone on the other side of the gate was saying in a deep voice. "There is a telegram for you."[9]

While an "ominous knock" in the night and the "deep voice" augur a tragic sequence, phrases like, "as though it were a barrel," "bare feet splashing through puddles" and the onomatopoetic repetition of "boom, boom, boom!" alter the tragic. The text of the telegram itself, which follows, provides the *coup de grace*:

"Ivan Petrovich died suddenly today awaiting dode instructions funnyral Tuesday"

That is exactly how the telegram had it: "funnyral," and there was also the incomprehensible word "dode"; the signature was that of the director of the comic opera company.

The original Russian provides a clearer picture of the ludicrous. For the misspelled word for funeral, which might be rendered as "funnyral," is, *xoxorony* instead of *poxorony*, a misspelling which suggests an association with the Russian verb *xoxotat'* (to guffaw).

Pustovalov, the manager of the local lumber yard, whom Olenka marries after only briefly mourning Kukin's death, is portrayed by a few details. He is introduced by a brief description remarkable in its succintness even for the usually economical Chekhovian style.

. . . He was wearing a straw hat and a white waistcoat with a gold watch chain, and he looked more like a landowner than a businessman.

"There is order in all things, Olga Semyonovna," he was saying sedately, with a note of sympathy in his voice; "and if one of our dear ones passes on, then it means that this was the will of God, and in that case we must keep ourselves in hand and bear it submissively."[10]

This brief passage suggests not only Pustovalov's pompous character, but also Olenka's limitations. For the statement, "he looked more like a landowner than a businessman" does not represent a comment by the author, but rather suggests Olenka's own thoughts, revealing her pettiness. This characterization is reinforced later with this description of Olenka: "all the rest of the day she heard his sedate voice, and as soon as she closed her eyes she had a vision of his dark beard."

Four episodes provide the skeleton of the story: Olenka's two marriages, then her role as mistress of the veterinary, and finally the maternal Olenka. The four events are interrupted by three intervals in which Olenka appears to cease to live. After the first husband dies, we learn that Olenka cries. But "three months later" we see her walking with the man who is soon to become her second husband. After the departure of her third love, the army veterinarian, we note that life seems to have been drained from Olenka's body as well as from her soul, and the image is echoed by her house:

. . . Olenka's house had become dark with age, its roof was rusty, the shed was standing awry and her whole yard was over-grown with burdock and stinging nettles. Olenka herself had aged; and she was no longer pretty. In the summer she sat on the porch and her soul was empty as before, dreary and bitter as wormwood. And in the winter she sat by the window and looked out on the snow.

Olenka, in her emptiness, is not the idealized figure Tolstoy held her to be. Even her love is not selfless. The stereotyped exclamations of grief which follow the deaths of her two husbands, in elements of the traditional Russian folk lament, stress this trait.

"My darling!" sobbed Olenka, "Vanichka my precious, my darling. Why did I ever meet you! Why did I know you and love you! For whom have you forsaken your poor Olenka, your poor unhappy Olenka!"

Here the traditional Russian epic formulas, "why did I ever meet you" and "for whom have you forsaken . . ."

(*začem ja s toboj povstrečalasja, na kogo ty pokinul . . .*),
are joined, as they are in the folk-lament formulas, with
endearments such as *golubčik moj* ("my darling").

And after the lumberman's death she again recites the
traditional peasant lament:

"For whom have you forsaken me my dearest? . . . How will I
live now without you, oh my bitter and unhappy fate? Have
pity on me dear people, on the poor orphan. . . ."

Olenka's love for the child seems selfless, yet it is also
possessive. There is final irony in the suggestion that this
love, too, will abandon her when the child which is not hers
will be taken back by its mother, or when he grows older
and forsakes her himself. We know what Olenka's fate will
be then. It was the selfless aspect of Olenka's love for the
child which so pleased Tolstoy, although he exaggerated its
positive content.

We note again in this story the implication of literary or
mythological allusions. The relationship of "The Darling"
to the myth of Eros and Psyche has been discussed by Renato
Poggioli,[11] who sees Chekhov's story as a modern version of
the myth, "as a furtive hint that even in the profane prose
of life there may lie hidden poetry's sacred spark."[12] The
ironic implications of the parallel with the myth are, however, not noted by Poggioli. It will be recalled that Apuleius,
recounts the story of Psyche, loved by the god Eros who
appears only at night and forbids her to look upon him.
When Psyche breaks the command of Eros and secretly gazes
upon her sleeping lover, the god immediately vanishes. Poggioli noted that Chekhov's heroine, Olenka, is called
dušečka, an endearing expression similar to "darling,"
which is also the diminutive form for the Russian word
duša, soul. Psyche, the heroine of the myth, is also named
for the Greek word for soul. Thus the pet name of Che-

khov's heroine, which is the title of his story, hints at the ancient myth.

Like Psyche, Olenka loves blindly. Unlike Psyche, however, she is not forced by curiosity to inspect those she loves. Poggioli, in the spirit of Tolstoy's criticism, writes that Olenka realized unconsciously what Psyche failed to understand: that love is blind and must remain so.[13] But is Olenka a wiser version of Psyche, as Poggioli implies, or an ironic reflection? Those whom Olenka loves successively are but absurd shadows of the god of love. Had Chekhov's Olenka held a light to her lovers, as did Psyche to Eros, Olenka's lovers might also have vanished. It was, however, their prosaic attributes, not their godlike qualities, which could not bear close inspection. Thus Olenka and her lovers are again examples of lowered versions of a myth. The echo of the myth in the characterization of Olenka provides more than a romantic suggestion of the artless wisdom of Olenka's unquestioning love. For it also suggests that Chekhov's Olenka, who must retain her illusions, is too naïve to see or doubt.

In "The Lady with the Pet Dog," written the year following the publication of "The Darling," the note of gentler sympathy becomes more pronounced, and we find a more hopeful mood. In a Black Sea resort town Dmitri Gurov, a cynical ladies' man, becomes acquainted with a young married woman, Anna Sergeevna, with whom he hopes to find diversion. But when Anna becomes his mistress, Gurov changes, influenced by a love which transcends an insignificant summer affair.

Chekhov's treatment of the traditional adultery theme is, again, different from the expected. There are no dramatic turns of action, nor is there a tragic denouement. Parallels to Tolstoy's *Anna Karenina* again emphasize this contrast. While both are stories of an Anna who, unhappily married to a prosaic bureaucrat, finds a lover, Chekhov's Anna does not think of suicide. Rather, her love affair brings her contentment and some happiness.

Romantic love in "The Lady with the Pet Dog" is presented more hopefully than it is in other of Chekhov's stories. In a few stories, love was fleeting and unreal. In "A Little Joke" (*Šutočka*, 1884), the heroine hears the whisper "Nadya I love you," as she rushes down a hill on a sled. And she never learns whether it was a real whisper or an illusion created by the sound of the onrushing wind. In "The Kiss," a shy officer is kissed in the dark by a girl who has apparently mistaken him for someone else. He never learns the identity of the girl whose kiss has fleetingly changed his life. In most of Chekhov's stories about love, written in the 1880's and 1890's, emotion is destroyed by *pošlost'* or simply by the absence of human communication. Such important stories as "The Teacher of Literature," "Three Years," "The Grasshopper," "A Woman's Kingdom," "The House with the Mezannine," "My Life," "Rothschild's Fiddle," "Anna on the Neck," "Ariadne," "The Man in a Shell," all express some aspects of the theme of the destruction of love by a milieu of banality and vulgarity. "The Lady with the Pet Dog" is the only story by Chekhov in which this process is reversed.

The story progresses with a minimum of expository writing. A lyrical subtext is more important in this work than in any of those which preceded it. The abrupt opening sentence, "It was rumored that a new face had appeared on the embankment: a lady with a little dog," summons a resort-town atmosphere of boredom, where any newcomer gives rise to comment and to speculation. The story moves rapidly to its complication, as Gurov initiates an acquaintance with Anna, the lady with the dog. Gurov's contemptuous attitude to women and to love affairs, and the frequently very poetic atmosphere of nature begin to define the Che-

khovian conflict in the story, but it provides as yet no hint
of the surprising "curve" with which the story deviates from
the expected. Gurov refers to women as "a lower race of
man," but "he cannot live two days" without them. His
first thought when he sees Anna shows him to be a roué:
"If she is here without husband and friends, it wouldn't be
bad at all to get acquainted"; and with little difficulty he
makes her acquaintance with the pretext of a remark about
the little dog. More than the beginning of a superficial summer affair is hinted by the description of Anna's innocence
which evokes a feeling of pity even in the cynical Gurov.
The sensuous description of the ocean, which grows in intensity as the story progresses, also implies a more complex
mood. "They walked and talked about the strange color of
the sea; the water was of a lilac color, so soft and warm, and
over it there was a golden strip of moonlight."

    In the second of the five brief chapters there are the be-
ginnings of the dramatic conflict, as Anna becomes Gurov's
mistress. Details make clear Gurov's cynicism. When he
kisses Anna for the first time, he smells the moist aroma of
flowers which emanates from her, but he does not succumb
to her poetry. He immediately looks anxiously around to
assure himself that no one has witnessed the clandestine
kiss. He compares his previous conquests to Anna. The alternation between cynicism, sincerity, and lyricism becomes
almost rhythmical. It emerges in the contrasting description
of Anna's and Gurov's different reactions to their first night
together. Anna is remorseful, and thinks of what had happened as "her downfall."

. . . Her features drooped and faded, and her long hair hung
down sadly on either side of her face; she grew pensive and her
dejected pose was that of a Magdalene in a picture by an old
master.[14]

But when she expresses her feeling of remorse and shame to
Gurov, the latter calmly cuts himself a piece of watermelon

and eats it. Again food evokes a feeling of vulgarity and crudeness. When, after a long silence he answers her, it is in a tone of contempt and irritation. He even calls her by the familiar form of address, using the pronoun *ty*, while she continues addressing him by the polite form *vy*. "Gurov was already bored with her utterances, he was irritated by her naïve tone, by her remorse."

Gurov lacks the warmth and passion of Anna. Poetic nature descriptions again reflect the inner beauty of Anna. The poetic element has now grown in intensity; it begins even to affect Gurov's consciousness:

... Sitting next to the young woman, who in the dawn appeared so beautiful, Gurov, soothed and enraptured by the magical surroundings—the sea, the mountains, clouds, the broad sky—thought how, in the final analysis, everything is beautiful in this world, everything except that which we think or do when we forget about the higher goals of life, about our human dignity.

But this is a fleeting reflection, and the old cynicism returns when Gurov again nervously looks back after kissing Anna. The chapter ends with Anna's departure, in a wistfully lyrical scene, an ending which might well have been the unresolved finale to many of Chekhov's earlier stories.

The train moved off rapidly, its lights soon vanished, and a minute later there was no sound of it, as though everything had conspired to end as quickly as possibly that sweet trance, that madness. Left alone on the platform, Gurov listened to the twang of the grasshoppers and the hum of the telegraph wires, feeling as though he had just wakened. And he reflected, musing, that there had now been another episode or adventure in his life, and it, too, was at an end, and nothing was left of it but a memory. . . .
Here at the station there was already a scent of autumn in the air; it was a chilly evening.
"It is high time for me to go north, too," said Gurov, as he left the platform. "High time!"[15]

This passage, expressing only nostalgia for a passing affair, does not end the story, but leads instead to the next chapter in which we observe a psychological and moral change in Gurov after his return to Moscow. Gurov expects that with the return to his real life the memory of Anna will disappear. Instead, a conflict takes place within Gurov as his customary outlook seems to be at war with his dreams of the magic of Anna's personality. While earlier the poetic strain expressed in Anna found little response in Gurov's cynical nature, now Gurov's memories of Anna are contrasted with the world which *was* Gurov's and which cannot be reconciled to his new feelings. When Gurov attempts to talk about Anna with a fellow card player, the latter's discordant gastronomical retort causes Gurov to leave his former life in search of Anna.

One evening, as he was leaving the physicians' club with his partner, an official, he could not contain himself and said, "If you only knew with what a charming woman I became acquainted in Yalta!"

The official seated himself in his sleigh and started, but suddenly he turned and called, "Dmitri Dmitrich!"

"What?"

"You were right, the sturgeon was a bit strong!"

As Gurov arrives in S., Anna's town, he sees again a world of *pošlost'*, denoted by the predominating gray color: the rug in his hotel room is of a cheap gray military cloth, the inkwell on the desk is gray with dust. The bed is covered also with gray cloth. Anna's house is surrounded by a long gray fence. Anna also looks prosaic as Gurov finds her in the local theater, but this only arouses his love and pity for her.

. . . This little undistinguished woman, lost in the provincial crowd, with a vulgar lorgnette in her hands, now filled his whole life, was his sorrow, his joy, the only happiness which he now desired.

In the scene describing their reunion in the theater the tone of the narrative changes to one of dramatic tension. Anna is frightened by the encounter and Gurov is deserted by his former calm. Both speak in almost hysterical, short, exclamatory phrases; their thoughts are expressed by equally brief sentences, "Oh Lord! What are these people doing here, and this orchestra," thinks Gurov. "How you frightened me . . . oh how you frightened me! I am hardly alive. Why did you come? Why?" asks Anna.

"But do understand Anna, do understand," [Gurov] said hurriedly and quietly, "I beg of you do understand me". . . .
"I suffer so," she continued without listening to him.

Many other details further support the picture of the change in Gurov. He now respects Anna and he stands before her, while she sits; he addresses her with the polite pronoun *vy*, whereas in their earlier meeting he had addressed her in the familiar form. He no longer looks over his shoulder as he kisses Anna. Now, as Gurov and Anna stand on a narrow gloomy staircase of the theater, "two high-school boys stood on the landing above them, they were smoking and looking down; but Gurov did not care, he drew Anna Sergeevna to him and began to kiss her face, her cheeks, her hands. . . ."

The last chapter finds both Anna and Gurov together in a Moscow hotel room. They have found a pathetic marginal happiness together. In many respects the scene in this chapter is contrasted to the scene in the second chapter in which Gurov conquered Anna in another hotel room. Again Anna cries, as she had in the previous scene. But now Gurov is gentle and loving.

. . . [Gurov] felt deep compassion, he wanted to be sincere and tender.
"Please stop, my dearest," he said, "you have had your cry and that's enough. Let's talk, we'll think of something."

An unqualified happiness is not the final note even of this more optimistic treatment by Chekhov of human relationships. It ends on a lyrical note, but one mixed with gentle sadness. Gurov loves unselfishly for the first time and his love is returned. But both Gurov and Anna are growing older and their lives seem hopelessly complicated. The concluding mood is a gentle melancholia, expressed in the final words which represent the wistful hopes of the two lovers:

And it seemed as though in a little while the solution would be found, and then a new and glorious life would begin, and it was clear to both of them that the end was still far off, and that what was to be most complicated and difficult for them was just beginning.

"The Lady with the Pet Dog" bears all the features of the style and composition of Chekhov's late stories. The problems are internal, but they are indicated, as always, by means of external description, by metonymic devices: a gesture, a fleeting phrase or remark with an implied larger meaning. After Gurov has seduced Anna, she is crestfallen and blames herself for what she considers an immoral act. Gurov answers her without compassion, but Anna is soon comforted. In the ensuing scene, Gurov and Anna sit by the seashore until the morning breaks. Both silently submit to the mysterious stillness of the approaching dawn. The first words are Anna's:

"The dew is on the grass," said Anna Sergeevna, breaking the silence.
"Yes, it's time to go home." [Answered Gurov.]

On the surface this is a simple remark with a simple meaning. The dew is a sign of the break of day and of a poetic mood, and that is all. But this simple remark, coming as it does after the scene in which Anna had accused herself

of sinning, also expresses her new acquiescence to her love
affair which had recently caused her much inner turmoil.

Chekhov's development of the adultery theme, without
dramatic collision and tragic endings, is a typical avowal
of independence from traditional treatments. Stylistic and
structural devices also reveal Chekhov's antipathy to conventional forms. Thus frequently mounting tension is
broken with an unexpectedly prosaic remark, or by a surprising absence of the elevated picture which the reader expects. In the third chapter, for instance, Gurov sits in the
provincial theater, hoping that Anna will make her appearance. He has come to her town, unable to bear the separation
from Anna. Now he sits and waits, "greedily seeking her
with his eyes." And Anna does appear. But her entrance is
not dramatic. It is presented with anticlimactic simplicity:
"And Anna Sergeevna also entered." Gurov does not see
her in the clichés of a lover's vision. On the contrary, he
sees her as a little woman, in no way remarkable, with a
vulgar lorgnette. Gurov's thoughts of his love for her are
accompanied by the unpolished sounds of the theater, "of
the inferior orchestra, of the wretched provincial violins."

In the last chapter, Gurov visits Anna in her Moscow
hotel room. The lovers have not seen each other for a long
time.

. . . Anna Sergeevna was wearing his favorite grey dress; she
was tired from her journey and from having waited for him
since the evening before; she was pale, gazed at him without a
smile, and he had hardly entered when she fell on his neck.
Their kiss was prolonged, as though they had not seen each
other for years.

As they speak their first words, there is no further rise in
the intensity which has grown in the passage just cited. Instead Chekhov skirts the expected, and the ensuing words,
spoken by Gurov, are commonplace, though they are also

tender: " 'Well, how are you getting on there?' he asked, 'What's new?' "

We have already noted in passing that "The Lady with the Pet Dog," like "Anna on the Neck," is a variant of the theme of *Anna Karenina*. Anna in "The Lady with the Pet Dog," like Anna Karenina, takes a fateful trip during which a love affair begins. Chekhov's Anna had quickly become aware of the true nature of her husband as had Anna Karenina. The famous scene in which Anna Karenina recognizes the pettiness of her husband is paralleled in Chekhov's story by a statement of "the lady with the pet dog" to her new lover: "My husband is perhaps an honest and decent man. But he is a lackey. I don't know what he does there in his office. I only know that he is a lackey."

Gurov's behavior recalls Vronski, Anna Karenina's lover. He anxiously looks around each time he kisses Anna, as Vronski wished to do in similar circumstances. In the scene before the races, when Anna informs Vronski of her pregnancy, we read: "He wanted to run up to her; but remembering that others might be present, he glanced at the terrace door and blushed as he blushed always, feeling that he ought to be afraid and that he ought to glance around." Later in the same chapter, the gesture is used by Anna herself: "She heard the voice of her son who was returning and, casting her glance rapidly over the terrace, she rose rapidly."

The clearest parallels between the two works are in the seduction scenes in which both Annas react in grief. The obvious similarities between the characters of Vronski and Gurov point up some contrasts. Unlike Vronski, Gurov appears cynical. When faced with Anna's shame, he takes her unhappiness lightly and eats a watermelon while she weeps. Similarly, unlike Tolstoy's Anna, Chekhov's heroine becomes quickly reconciled to her new position; her gaiety soon returns and she joins Gurov in laughter.

Chekhov's people lack the glitter and elegance, as well

as the extravagancies of feeling, of Tolstoy's protagonists.
Gurov is a cynical roué, and later a sincere, but sentimental,
lover, whereas Vronski's feeling for Anna are those of passion. Chekhov's Anna is a simple woman, whose room is
cluttered and smells of cheap perfume. Just as Chekhov's
two lovers are of a lowered intensity, so is the denouement
of the story. Rather than tragedy, the final note is of pathos.
Muted and transient happiness is the fate which, as the
concluding passage suggests, awaits Chekhov's lovers.

In December 1903, only seven months before Chekhov's
death, there appeared in the journal *Žurnal dlja vsex* (*Journal for All*) Chekhov's last story, "The Betrothed" (*Nevesta*),
a work pervaded by the tone of melancholy optimism we
have noted in the late works of Chekhov. The story concerns
a young girl, Nadya, who is engaged to the handsome and
dull Andrey, the son of the local priest. Nadya, whose provincial childhood was spent with her widowed mother in
her grandmother's house, is awakened to the emptiness of
her life by a series of events and by her friendship with
Sasha, an artist and protégé of her grandmother. Unlike
earlier stories by Chekhov, which might have concluded
with a sad note of realization, in "The Betrothed" Nadya
forsakes the vulgar milieu of her youth and asserts her right
to a new life.

The themes of Nadya's revolt and that of the struggle of
the two worlds are both revealed by Nadya's changing per-
ceptions through which we observe the setting and personalities of her world. The Shumin household in which Nadya
lives is composed of her domineering grandmother, her
defeated mother who has intellectual pretenses, the priest
who is characterized by his ubiquitous jokes and puns reminiscent of Mr. Turkin in "Ionych," and the priest's prosaic
son Andrey, whom Nadya is to marry. In opposition is the
intellectual and intense Sasha, who makes explicit to Nadya

the inner conflict which strangely depresses her, and sym-
bolically there is also the image of the beautiful garden and
the poetry of nature.

The structural principle of the story might be likened
to a musical discourse in which rhythmic interplay between
the motifs of *pošlost'* and beauty develops with increasing
intensity.

"The Betrothed" is constructed of three parts, each ad-
vancing a phase of Nadya's development. The opening section, the first and second of the six brief chapters of the story,
places Nadya in her environment and suggests her growing
antipathy to it. Sasha, the young idealist, encourages Nadya's
nascent dissatisfaction by his sharp remarks about her surroundings.

In the second part, the third and fourth chapters, the
climax of the story is reached. Nadya rejects her world and
decides to escape and to follow Sasha's pleas to study. The
catalyst for her open rebellion is the new house prepared
for Nadya and Andrey after their marriage, the vulgar osten-
tation of which forces Nadya to flee.

In the third part, chapters five and six, Nadya escapes;
and when she returns to visit her provincial town, it is with
an attitude of distance and detachment. She has grown so
far away from her childhood that even Sasha, whose rebellious romanticism had stirred her once, seems now to be a
part of the past. When he dies, Nadya is sad, but she wonders that she can not feel more strongly.

The story serves to elucidate the inner world of one personality, that of Nadya. Other characters form only the
background. With one exception, when we gain insight into
Sasha's thoughts, the story is told from Nadya's point of view.
A familiar Chekhovian device, the holding of a number of
elements as static points against which a character changes,
is illustrated by Nadya's change which is contrasted to the

unchanging Shumin's house, the provincial town, to Sasha and even to the recurrent tapping of the night watchman.

In the first of the three parts of the story, Nadya is a young girl who only vaguely senses the inadequacy of her world. A peaceful if deceptive equilibrium between the conflicting themes of beauty and *pošlost'* is suggested by a rhythmic counterposing of the two themes. In the abrupt beginning we see the Shumin household from the distance of the garden into which Nadya has walked, in an act prophetic of her later escape. The world of the Shumins emerges through an atmosphere of beauty which blurs the outlines of the house and its inhabitants. The first words are of beauty. "It was ten o'clock in the evening and a full moon was shining over the garden." There follows a description of the Shumins' household, of which Nadya—we begin to sense—is not wholeheartedly a part.

In the Shumin house an evening service celebrated at the request of the grandmother, Marfa Mikhaylovna, was just over, and now Nadya—she had gone into the garden for a minute—could see the table being laid for supper in the dining room, and her grandmother, bustling about in her luxurious silk dress; father Andrey, the chief priest of the cathedral, was talking to Nadya's mother, Nina Ivanovna. . . . Andrey Andreich, Father Andrey's son, was standing by listening attentively.[16]

The first picture of the family, which is the kindest one we are to see, is nevertheless connected with food. ". . . the table [was] being laid for supper." As Nadya sees her mother through the window, the mother appears to her as beautiful. However, Nadya's later disenchantment is already anticipated by a number of modifiers:

. . . and now in the evening light through the window her mother for some reason seemed very young. . . . *i teper' mat' pri vecernem osveščenii skvoz' okno počemu-to kazalas'. . . .*

The simple phrase, "her mother seemed very young," is here modified four times ("now," "in the evening light," "through the window," "for some reason," "seemed").

A lyrical passage follows the first view of the Shumin household.

It was still and cool in the garden, and dark peaceful shadows lay on the ground. There was a sound of frogs croaking, somewhere far away, very far away, probably beyond the town. There was a feeling of May, dear May! One breathed deeply and wanted to imagine that not here, but somewhere under the sky, above the trees, far beyond the city, in the fields and forests a vernal life was unfolding, mysterious, beautiful, rich and sacred, beyond the understanding of weak, sinful man. And somehow one felt like crying.

Here the suggestion of beauty and poetry which is seen not as close, but as far beyond the town, again implies doubt about Nadya's present life.

The final phrase, "and somehow one felt like crying," leads to a new passage, to Nadya's faint thoughts about her forthcoming marriage to Andrey. He was only mentioned briefly as "listening attentively," among those composing the tableau which Nadya had seen through the window. Now, as Nadya thinks about him, there are suggestions of her disquiet. The passage, which follows the lyrical statements about nature, is cast in an abruptly changed dry, neutral tone. The short sentences are almost staccato; the mere statements of fact are devoid of emotional coloration. "Nadya was already twenty-three." When she thinks of Andrey, we learn only that "she liked him" (*"on ej nravilsja"*). Now the motif of food, which was noted earlier, is repeated more forcefully.

. . . From the basement where the kitchen was, one could hear through the open window the hurrying, the clattering of knifes, the banging of the swinging door; there was a smell of roast turkey and marinated cherries.

This passage, which suggests, by its hints of *pošlost'* the disharmony within Nadya, echoes in its conclusion the poetic passage which preceded it. "And somehow one felt like crying" is now cast as "and somehow it seemed that it would be thus as long as one might live, without change, without end!"

The depiction of Sasha which follows implies a new variation of the positive theme. While he is an idealist, his bohemianism and impracticality appear to hide a lack of vitality which is suggested by his thin, almost dead-looking fingers, his "apperance of lacking freshness" (*nesvežij vid*), his general illness, and his constant cough. The earlier hints concerning the Shumin world are now set forth in exaggerated tone by Sasha. He condemns Andrey and the Shumins as living in a world of social exploitation and filth, hidden only by the thin veneer of a *comme-il-faut* exterior. But Sasha's extreme remarks cause Nadya to protest in annoyance.

As if to reinforce Sasha's words, the world of the Shumins is now seen at closer range, as Nadya and Sasha leave the garden and enter the house. The house, which from the garden had seemed to Nadya "somehow" attractive, now becomes prosaic. The grandmother is "very fat, ugly, with bushy brows and a little moustache. She spoke loudly and from her voice it was apparent that she was the oldest in the house." Nadya's mother's lack of taste is stressed by her pince-nez and by her diamonds, which she wears on every finger of her hand. Father Andrey lacks dignity because his facial expression constantly seems to indicate that he has something very funny to tell. Finally Nadya's fiancé is "corpulent and beautiful with curly hair." And in a satiric twist, these shallow materialists speak in dilettante fashion of hypnotism.

At the end of the first chapter a subtext indicates Nadya's growing conflict. As she lies in bed, unable to sleep, she hears the sounds of Sasha and of the household, but at last she hears only Sasha.

... For a long time Nadya ... heard the servants cleaning up downstairs and Grannie's angry voice. Finally, everything became quiet and only from time to time she heard Sasha's bass cough from his room.

The next chapter opens at night as Nadya's gloomy thoughts are sustained by harmonizing nature imagery and by the lazy but ominous sound of the night watchman's tapping, which is heard through the window. Nadya awakens in the middle of the night in her "very soft and comfortable bed," suggesting her comfortable, but stagnant life. Earlier Nadya had mused that, instead of loving Andrey, she "had liked him" (*on ej nravilsja*). She now remembers, to the accompaniment of the tapping sound of the watchman, that she had only "gradually come to appreciate this good-hearted intelligent man" (*... malo-pomalu ocenila ètogo dobrogo, umnogo čeloveka*). But now that the wedding approaches, she is overcome by a feeling of dread and uneasiness.

However, the mood of gloom, evoked by Nadya's thoughts, is "answered" by the contrapuntal motif which immediately follows it, in the passage beginning significantly, "the watchman had long since ceased tapping," which suggests a possible escape from her surroundings. This phrase introduces another nature picture which suggests hope. It is morning and the garden is clear, warm, and beautiful.

The watchman had long ceased tapping. Outside the window, in the garden, birds were beginning to stir; the mist had left, everything was illuminated by a spring light as by a smile. Soon the entire garden, warmed by the sun and caressed, came to life; and dewdrops, like diamonds, glistened on the leaves; and the old, long neglected garden seemed so young and gay on this morning.

As Nina Ivanovna, Nadya's mother, appears, we return to the world of *pošlost'*. Nina Ivanovna is stupidly sentimental, talks about spiritism and homeopathy and about the deep doubts which disturb her. The close relationship of the two themes of beauty and *pošlost'* is suggested by the varying of one image. The sparkling dewdrops which had glistened on the leaves become Nina's tear-stained face and the glass of mineral water from which she sips as she speaks of her sentimental tears. Her mother's affected remarks had once seemed to Nadya "to contain some deep mysterious meaning," but now they only separate her from her mother. Nina Ivanovna answers Nadya's plea for understanding ("I have been so depressed lately. . . . Why is it I don't sleep at night!") with an egocentric lack of sympathy and with a vapid picture in which she identifies herself with Anna Karenina.

"I don't know my dear. When I can not sleep at night, I shut my eyes, tight, so tight, like this, and I picture to myself Anna Karenina, how she walks and speaks; or I picture to myself something historical from the ancient world."

Nadya realizes that her mother cannot understand her. Suddenly, what has hitherto been but faintly sensed by Nadya, becomes conscious:

. . . She felt this for the first time in her life, and it even frightened her, she wanted to hide. . . .

Briefly we return to the opposite theme, as Sasha implores Nadya to escape and to study. Details point again to the hypocrisy of the unchanging provincial life. Nadya accompanies Andrey to the door late in the evening.

At eleven o'clock, as he was leaving and already in his overcoat, he embraced Nadya and began to kiss her face, her shoulders, and her hands greedily.

"My dear, my darling, my beauty! . . ." he mumbled. "Oh, how happy I am. I am losing my mind from rapture."

Andrey, "already in his overcoat," mumbles his love in an artificially sentimental and elevated tone, while he "greedily" kisses her. The suggestion of Andrey's superficiality is increased by an abrupt switch of the narrative to Nadya's reflection:

And it seemed to her that she had heard this a long time ago, or had read it somewhere . . . in a novel, in an old tattered novel, long discarded.

As Nadya returns to her bedroom, her former doubts are conscious fears and realizations. She thinks unkindly of her mother, who had never loved her husband and "now had nothing and was totally dependent on her mother-in-law" and who appears to her as weak and ineffectual. The thought of a fate similar to her mother's makes Sasha's call to flight sound more imperative. She is still afraid: "better not think. . . . One must not think about this."

As the chapter ends, the sound of the tapping of the watchman is repeated. This motif, which earlier had marked Nadya's mood of vague depression, now accompanies the thoughts of a rebellious Nadya.

In the second part of the story, in which the conflict within Nadya comes to a climax and leads to the decisive turn in her life, evocations of vulgarity and banality are dominant. This is in contrast to the first section, in which the themes of *pošlost'* and beauty were played against each other in some form of balance, even though this balance gradually shifted toward the discords of *pošlost'*. Two episodes, each accompanied by the motif of a sympathetic nature, illustrate the intensification of Nadya's awareness and point to her final antipathy to the world of the Shumins. In the first of these episodes Sasha tells her grandmother that he cannot bear life in the town any longer; he does not wish to be present during Nadya's wedding. Here nature and sounds harmonize with Sasha's mood:

> The summer was damp and cold, the trees were wet, everything in the garden looked uninviting and dejected. . . . In the rooms downstairs and upstairs the sound of unfamiliar women's voices was heard and a sewing machine was rattling in Grandmother's room.

After this passage, Sasha's thoughts are indicated in a shift of focus, the only instance of direct insight into the psyche of someone other than Nadya: "The fuss irritated Sasha; he sat in his room and was angry . . . ."

In the second and more critical episode we again view the external world through Nadya as she and Andrey inspect the house in which they are to live after their wedding. The picture of the Shumin's house has already been noted as indicating empty vulgarity. Now, the new house, which cannot even be softened by the sentiment of Nadya's childhood life, appears unbearably harsh and vulgar. The house smells of fresh paint, the floor shines, and on the wall hangs a picture in a gold frame, representing a "naked lady and next to her a purple vase with a broken handle." Andrey's remarks and his posture indicate to Nadya a life of suffocation. " 'A magnificent picture,' said Andrey, sighing respectfully, 'the work of the artist Shishmachevski.' " Andrey's awe as well as the ridiculous name of the painter imply all too clearly the pretensions of their future life. A picture of Andrey's father, wearing his priest's hat, hangs in the drawing room, the furniture of which is harshly upholstered in bright blue. The sideboard is ready in the dining room. In contrast, the bedroom appears in half darkness, two beds stand side by side, and it seemed that "when they furnished the bedroom, it was with the idea that it should always be agreeable there and could not possibly be otherwise." The newly decorated house in the taste of bourgeois provincialism, which Nadya must admire, as Andrey's hand remained always around her waist—it felt to Nadya like an iron hoop—forces Nadya to thoughts of flight. ". . . Every minute she was on the point of running away, bursting into sobs, throwing herself out of the window."

But the inspection of the house continues. Andrey proudly shows Nadya the water spigot he has had installed in the bathroom, and boasts of the tank holding two hundred gallons in the attic. Outside an atmosphere of foreboding is suggested by other details: dust whirls about in the courtyard; it threatens to rain. But Andrey senses nothing and blithely voices his Tolstoyan aims to till the soil and live a simple life, just after he has boasted of the modern plumbing in the new house.

That night Nadya is haunted by gloomy sounds from the outside, as a storm grows and the wind sounds as if it were moaning "O-o-o-h my G-o-d!" To the accompaniment of these sounds, Nadya appeals again to her mother. Her mother cannot respond to Nadya's cry for help and only replies in banal and senseless statements concerning the "constant transmutation of matter." When Nadya accuses her of speaking only stupidities, her mother collapses and says in a pathetic echo of Nadya's own feelings, "You and your grandmother torture me! . . . I want to live! To live! . . . Let me be free! I am still young, I want to live and you have made me an old woman. . . ." Now she looked "small, pitiful, and foolish."

When in the morning, which is cold, gray and cheerless, the grandmother complains that "the wind had blown down all the apples in the garden and broken the old plum tree," this image of destruction also symbolizes the death of all Nadya's illusions. Nadya can only escape and she turns now to Sasha: "I can't . . . I don't understand how I ever could have lived here. I despise the man to whom I am engaged, I despise myself, I despise this whole empty, senseless life."

This is the first open word of dislike expressed by Nadya. She asks Sasha to take her away and she gazes at him "with adoring eyes, as though spellbound, expecting every minute that he would say something important, something infinitely significant." Sasha promises her "when you turn your life upside down, everything will be changed." She leaves with Sasha; and already as she drives away, the house and the town begin to lose their importance:

> . . . she suddenly thought of it all: Andrey and his father, the new house, and the naked lady with the vase; and all this no longer frightened her, nor weighed upon her, but seemed only naïve and shallow and retreated more and more into the past.

When Nadya returns after several months, she has achieved detachment, a sign of maturity and yet of sadness in the world of Chekhov. On her way she visits Sasha briefly. Her fondness for him is no longer colored by childish romanticism and she notes sadly how ill he is and how he is unable to arrange his own life successfully. As she returns to the little town, the distance which now separates her from her youth becomes evident. She sees her childhood surroundings without illusions in their smallness and insignificance. The houses seem little and squat and are covered with gray dust. The streets are wide and empty, giving an impression of lifelessness. Only an old man in a rust-colored overcoat is seen. Her grandmother appears old, ugly, and fat; her mother "looked much older and seemed shriveled up." Everything seems constricted and empty. The ceilings seem low, the house full of flies. Nina Ivanovna's inane remarks, "One must look at life as through a prism," no longer disquiet Nadja. The ubiquitous tapping of the night watchman that night does not rouse her to melancholy thoughts. Everything is now left behind, even Sasha, whose death disturbs Nadya's newly found equilibrium only briefly.

The story ends on the note of wistful optimism which is so characteristic of Chekhov's late plays. The decrepit town makes Nadya think of a vaguely optimistic future. . . . "It seemed to her that . . . everything was merely waiting— waiting not so much for the end, as for the beginning of something young and fresh."

But the wistful remarks which follow, "Oh, if only this new clear life would arrive more quickly, when one can look one's fate straight and boldly in the eyes . . ." and "such a life will come sooner or later," disturbs this hopeful note, as does the modification of the last phrase: "the next morning, lively and gay, she left the town—as she supposed, forever."

"The Betrothed" was completed in February 1903. In October of the same year Chekhov finished *The Cherry Orchard*, which was soon to be produced by the Moscow Art Theater. He was to write no more. On January 17, 1904 *The Cherry Orchard* had its premiere and at this occasion there was a surprise celebration of Chekhov's twenty-fifth anniversary as a writer. After the play, at a dinner in Chekhov's honor, the singer Chaliapin remarked in a short speech that man has a sixth sense, the sense of *pošlost'*, and that "nobody has uncovered this powerful sense so clearly as A. P. Chekhov. Nobody," he added, "has drawn this sense with greater sympathy for man than Chekhov."[17]

By the summer of 1904 Chekhov's deteriorating health forced him to abandon his work at the height of his artistic career and to leave with his wife for the German spa of Badenweiler. It was there that Chekhov died suddenly on July 2, 1904.

Appendix to Chapter 1

Page 7 Another parody of popular romantic fiction is "The Sinner from Toledo (A Translation from the Spanish)" (*Grešnik iz Toleda*) (*Perevod iz ispanskogo*) published in 1881 in the humor magazine, *The Spectator (Zritel')*. Events relating to the Spanish Inquisition are depicted in stylized form. The hero's wife is accused of witchcraft and, in order to avoid delivering her alive to the Inquisitor, he kills her and delivers her body instead. Throughout the story Chekhov employs exaggerated literary clichés, puns, and verbal clowning in the form of false etymologies, devices frequently utilized in Chekhov's later stories and plays. Thus a learned bishop derives the word *femina* from the two words *fe* and *minus* on the basis of the premise that woman has less faith than man. In presenting his parody as a translation from the Spanish, Chekhov was following a mid-century tradition in Russian literature of ridiculing the preference for Mediterranean local color which had been shown by the Russian Romantics. Many of such parodies were written in the two decades preceding Chekhov's writing by three authors, A. K. Tolstoy (1817-75), A. M. Zhemchuzhnikov (1821-1908), and V. M. Zhemchuzhnikov (1830-1884), who wrote under the joint pseudonym of Kozma Prutkov.

Another example of the presentation of a parody of a romantic fiction as a translation is the sketch "Aritists' Wives" (*Ženy artistov*), published at the end of 1881, which portends to be a translation from the Portuguese. A writer residing in a Lisbon Hotel composes novels whose titles suggest Russian cheap popular fiction of the day, such as *The Breaking on the Wheel of Forty-four Twenty-Wivers in Holy Muscovy* (*Kolesovanie v Sankt-Moskovske soroka četyrex dvadčatižencev*). In "Artists Wives" the hero outlines an absurdly melodramatic plot:

> Place of action is the entire world . . . Portugal, Spain, France, Russia, Brazil, etc. In Lisbon the hero learns from the papers of the heroine's accident in New York. He sets out for it. He is captured by pirates who are bribed by agents of Bismarck. The heroine is a French agent. There are hints in the newspapers. The English. A Polish sect in Austria and a gypsy sect in India. Intrigues. The hero in jail. Attempts to bribe him . . . Bismarck retires and our hero, no longer wishing to hide his name, calls himself Alfonso Zunzuga and dies under terrible torture. The Angel of Death carries his quiet soul into the blue sky.

The writer has a neighbor, a painter, who bemoans the fate which has bound him to a prosaic German wife who cannot appreciate his art. Parodistically, sudden stylistic shifts and inelegant imagery lower to comedy the tragic air:

> What a fool I was to chain a man who was free as the air, an eagle, a chamois, in one word an artist, to this piece of ice filled with prejudice and pettiness . . . Diabolo ! ! ! You piece of ice! You piece of stone, you wooden cow! You . . . you are a fool! Weep, you unhappy overdone German sausage! Your husband is an artist, not a trader! Weep, you beer bottle!

The story is filled with melodramatic situations which require fainting spells, marital quarrels, reconciliations and incredible events such as the visit to Portugal of the Russian writer Derzhavin in the company of the poet "Lermantoff."

Page 8 A second parody of the ghost story, the somewhat Gogolian "A Terrible Night," subtitled "A Christmas Story (dedicated to the Grave Digger M.P.F. . . .)," is marked by a surprise ending. The narrator has left a seance held at the deathbed of a friend. The night is dark, misty, and threatening; mysteriously the street lanterns have not been lit; thoughts of impending death fill the narrator with terror. Arriving at his apartment he strikes a match and is confronted with a coffin. He flees to a friend where another coffin awaits him. The event is repeated as he proceeds to yet another acquaintance. Still another friend tells him that he also has found a coffin in his rooms. The mystery, already parodied by repetition, is mockingly explained "realistically" as resulting from the contrivances of a coffin merchant who has hidden his inventory with friends in order to evade confiscation by creditors. Elements of burlesque are presented throughout the story by humorous details which include grotesque speaking names. The narrator himself is identified as Panixidin (fr. *panixida*—requiem) who lives on Demise-Cemetery Street (Uspensko-na-Mogil'cax). His landlord's name is Trupov (fr. *trup*—corpse). Names of other protagonists are: Upokoev (fr. *upokoj*—eternal rest), Čerepov (fr. *čerep*—skull), Kladbiščenko (fr. *kladbišče*—graveyard) and Čeljustin (fr. *čeljust'*—jaw).

Page 10 In the slight sketch "The Mask" (*Maska*, 1884) the surprise ending is more obvious. One of the guests at a masked ball behaves in a provocative fashion, insulting the town's dignitaries; but instead of the expected punishment he carries off victory when he proves to be the town's millionaire.

In the anecdote "It Was She" (*To byla ona*, 1886) we find a double surprise ending presented in a rather clumsy manner. An officer recounts his youthful amorous successes to a group of young ladies. Once a snowstorm brought him to a Polish estate where he noticed the beautiful wife of the steward. In the middle of the night the officer was awakened by a woman who entered his room but whom he could not see because of the dark. A passionate night ensued, and a second one. When the young ladies eagerly ask for the identity of the mysterious woman they are told, "It was my wife." Observing the disappointment of his listeners (who are too sophisticated to be satisfied with such a "happy ending"), the narrator changes the identity of the woman to the steward's wife and the audience is satisfied. Thus the second solution with its required emotional satisfaction becomes an added element of parody.

Three early stories illustrate the evolution of the zero ending. In "Examination for Advancement" (*Èkzamen na čin*, 1884) a petty post office clerk struggles with a civil service examination the outcome of which will determine his advancement in rank. As the questions of the examiners increasingly confuse and frighten the candidate, his answers deteriorate and he becomes convinced of his failure. We are reminded of the tragic fate of Gogol's petty clerk in "The Overcoat" who faces an incomprehensible world. But the unexpected conclusion, presented in understatement foreshadowing Chekhov's later style, shows the clerk to have been successful after all. The examining inspector remarks, "All right, you may go," and the story ends as the clerk is celebrating in the tavern. The deflation of tension terminating in a zero ending changes the proportion of the preceding events which had evoked our pity. The petty clerk now appears as only an absurd figure who unjustifiably lost his head.

The limited action of the anecdote "A Horsey Name" (*Lošadinaja familija*, 1885) is determined by the theme of a forgotten name. General Buldeev has a toothache which cannot be relieved. He is told of a man who can conjure away toothaches by spells. The main body of the story is concerned with the search for the forgotten name of the curer which someone recalls is vaguely related in meaning to horses. There is a deliberate slowing of the movement of the story as all possible combinations of "horsey" names are brought forth. The name is remembered, but too late, after the tooth has been pulled. Further, in a final twist, the forgotten name turned out to be

Ovsov from the Russian *oves* (oats) and is not really "horsey." Comic playing on names is also found in other early anecdotes such as "Forgotten" (*Zabyl*, 1882), a brief sketch about a man who is sent by his wife to buy some sheet music, but who cannot remember the name of the piece of music. Again the *fabula* of the story is limited to the search for the name. (Names are always a special source of interest to Chekhov, as they were to Gogol, but in Chekhov's later stories it is their subtle and sometimes lyrical symbolism which is significant.)

Page 13 One of the earliest works in which a more individualized speech pattern acts as a distinguishing feature is a little dramatic sketch, entitled "Fat and Thin" (*Tolstyj i tonkij*, 1883), which satirizes Russian rank-consciousness. The joyous reminiscences of two former schoolmates who accidentally meet are abruptly broken off when it becomes apparent that the "fat one" has attained high rank in the civil service while the "thin one" has not. Anticipating the technique of later stories, the change of outlook of the "thin one" is conveyed by the use of a few apparently disconnected remarks and details. The "thin one's" voice becomes a silly giggle as he speaks flattering words interspersed with the repeated "introduction" of his wife as "My wife Louise, née Wanzenbach . . . , a Lutheran." The repetition of an irrelevant detail ("a Lutheran") which conveys the speaker's lack of ease, continues to demark the "thin one."

Page 13 An early instance of such verbal clowning is to be found in the story "Forgotten" (*Zabyl*, 1882) whose hero intersperses his words with bastardized Germanisms rendered in the text in cyrillic transcription as *šprexenzi, gebenzi (sprechen Sie, geben Sie*). Playing with foreign languages is also a means of clowning in "Out of the Frying Pan into the Fire" (*Iz ognja da v polymja*, 1884). The hero says: *èto ja tak . . . naščet xapen zi gevezen*. In some instances Chekhov's characters appear to imitate French or other foreign languages. The foreign sound system may be simulated or nonsensical words may suggest the foreign language.

Že vu pri a lja trimontaž! (Maska, 1884)
Devica a lja komprene arevuar konsome. (Vorona, 1885)
Ona barišnja, delikates, konsume i vse takoe na blagorodnyj maner. (Otec, 1887)
"Bona sera, sen'ery, rigoletto-gugenoty-traviata!" skazal xudožnik [. . . said the artist]. *(Pripadok, 1888)*
Gavanna-tarakano-pistoletto" skazal medik [. . . said the medical student]. *(Pripadok, 1888)*

We may also note the pun on the Russian word *tarakan* (roach) which is part of the quasi-Italian language.

A foreign phrase may be placed in a context which renders it either meaningless or incongruous:

Spat' . . . ob"jatija Morfeja. Šprexen zi dejč. (To sleep . . . the embrace of Morpheus. *Sprechen Sie Deutsch.*) *(Nadležaščie mery, 1884)*
Nu, čto kasaetsja Prudonov i vsjakix tam Boklej, to ja tut švax. (Well, as far as all these Prudhons and Buckles are concerned, there I am *schwach.*) *(Imeniny)*

In Chekhov's later works verbal clowning most frequently takes the form of puns. At times the pun results from combining Russian and foreign morphemes to produce ludicrous words; *e.g.* Grigorianc (*i.e.* Grigorij with an Armenian ending), "A Nervous Breakdown" *(Pripadok, 1888);* Xoxlandija (fr. Russian *Xoxol'*, a derogatory term for Ukrainian, and the Russianized Latin ending—*ija*), "The Nameday" *(Imeniny, 1888); komil'fotnost'* (*comme il faut* plus the Russian ending—*nost'*) "A Trivial Incident" *(Pustoj slučaj, 1886); ploxissime* (Russian *ploxo*—bad—plus the Latin adverbial superlative ending—*issime* "Old Age" *(Starost', 1885).* This type of pun was popular among theology students and is not original with Chekhov.

Another frequent example of linguistic affectation is the embellishment of a colloquialism with a Latin or Greek morpheme. For example:

mordolizacija—Russian vulgar *morda:* mouth, mug; the verbal stem *-liza:* to lick, which provides a flavor of obsequiousness; plus the ending -*acija:* used in Russian with foreign abstract nouns which in the original end in -*atio.* "A Happy Man" (*Sčastlivcik,* 1886)

štukencija—Russian colloquial *štuka:* thing, trick; plus -*encija* (Latin -*entia.*) "Shrove Tuesday" (*Nakanune posta,* 1887)

Babencija—*baba:* old woman, hag; plus -*encija.* "The Father" (*Otec,* 1887)

fiziomordija—*physio-;* plus *morda;* plus -*ia.* (*Zinochka,* 1887)

Many of Chekhov's characters misquote literary citations, proverbs, or sayings, as for instance *aut mortuis nihil bene* (instead of *de mortuis nil nisi bene* "The Orator" (*Orator,* 1886), or *On axnut' ne uspel, kak na nego starost' pridet* (He did not have time to grunt before age was upon him.) "Boys" (*Mal'čiki,* 1887). The latter quotation, from I. A. Krylov's fable "The Peasant and the Worker," correctly cited is: *krestjanin axnut' ne uspel, kak na nego medved' nasel.* (The peasant did not have time to say "akh" before a bear was upon him.)

A stylistic feature which becomes rarer in Chekhov's later stories is the use of grotesque names or speaking names, employed simply for comic effect. Thus there are: *Svistickij* (fr. *svistet':* to whistle), *Merdjaev* (fr. French *merde*), *Kraterov* (fr. *krater:* crater), *Zakusin* (fr. *zakuska:* hors d'oeuvre), *Xamov* (fr. *xam:* cad, boor), *Razmaxajkin* (fr. *razmaxat':* to brandish, to wave one's arms), and *Lakeič* (fr. *lakej:* lackey), *Žmyxov* (fr. *žmyxi:* leftovers fed to pigs), *Axaxov* (fr. *axat':* to sigh, to say "ah"), *Zapupyrin* (fr. *pupyr':* a boil), and *Puzickij* (fr. *puza:* belly).

Notes

Introduction

1 For some recent studies concerning Chekhov's impact on literature outside of Russia, see Sofie Lafitte, "Čexov vo Francii" (Chekhov in France), *Literaturnoe Nasledstvo*, No. 68, Moscow, 1960, pp. 705-746; S. S. Bogatyrev, "Čexov v Čexoslovakii" (Chekhov in Czechoslovakia), *ibid.*, pp. 747-776; Thomas G. Winner, "Čexov v Soedinnenyx Štatax Ameriki" (Chekhov in the United States), *ibid.*, pp. 777-800; M. A. Šereševskaja, "Anglijskie pisateli i kritiki o Čexove" (English Writers and Critics on Chekhov), *ibid.*, pp. 801-834.

Chapter 1

1 N. I. Gitovič, *Leotopis' žizni i tvorčestva A. P. Čexova.* Moscow, 1955, pp. 31, 32.

2 Letter to A. S. Suvorin, October 23, 1899 in A. P. Čexov, *Polnoe sobranie sočinenij i pisem.* Moscow, 1944-51, XIV, 422 (henceforth all references to Chekhov's works and letters will be to this edition which will be indicated as PSS). In 1904 Chekhov refers again to this work as his literary beginnings, calling it "a trifle" (bezdeluška). Letter to F. D. Batjuškov, January 19,1904, PSS, XX, 210.

3 PSS, I, 536.

4 N. I. Gitovič, ed., "Iz dnevnika N. A. Lejkina," *Literaturnoe Nasledstvo.*

5 The complete letter, dated March 25, 1886 is cited in Gitovič, *Letopis . . .* pp. 128-130.

6 Letter of March 28, 1886, PSS, XIII, 191-194.

7 The term is Viktor Shklovsky's;

see his *Xod konja*. Moscow-Berlin, 1923, pp. 119-120.

8 Jurij Tynjanov, *Arxaisty i novatory*. Leningrad, 1929, p. 413.

9 "The Swedish Match" and *The Shooting Party*, as well as many other parodies are enlighteningly discussed by Ralph Matlaw, "Cechov and the Novel," in T. Eekman, ed., *Anton Čechov; Some Essays*. Leiden, 1960, pp. 148-158.

10 Letter to Alexander P. Chekhov, October 10-12, 1887, PSS, XXII, p. 372.

11 S. Ščukin "Iz vospominanii ob A. P. Čexove," *Russkaja Mysl'*, 1911, X, 44, cited in A. Derman, *O masterstve Čexova*. Moscow, 1959, p. 75.

12 D. S. Mirsky, *A History of Russian Literature*, edited and abridged by Frances J. Whitfield. New York, 1949, p. 361.

13 For a discussion of the use of ideolect in one of Chekhov's early plays, see Thomas Winner "Speech Characteristics in Čexov's *Ivanov* and Čapek's *Loupežnik*," *American Contributions to the Fifth Congress of Slavists*. The Hague, 1963, pp. 403-441. Also P. G. Strelkova, "O rečevyx stiljax v p'ese A. P. Čexova 'Višnevyj sad,'" *Isvestija Akademii Nauk, Otdelenie literatury i jazyka*, X, vyp. 2 (1951) p. 136-152.

Chapter 2

1 Cf. Bernard Pares, *A History of Russia*. London, University Paperbacks, 1962, pp. 405, 423 and *passim*.

2 Anton Chekhov, *St. Peter's Day and Other Tales*. New York, Capricorn Books, 1959, pp. 111-112. The translation is Frances Jones's, but I have taken the liberty of changing the translation where it seemed indicated.

3 Letter to V. V. Bilibin, January 18, 1886.

4 For the most distinguished discussion of this problem in English, see Victor Erlich, *Russian Formalism, History and Doctrine*. 's-Gravenhage, 1955, pp. 56-57, 150-151 and *passim*. The bibliography of Russian Formalist writings on this topic is too voluminous to be cited here. The reader is referred to the bibliography in Mr. Erlich's study.

5 For a discussion of this story see Gleb Struve, "On Chekhov's Craftsmanship; The Anatomy of a Story," *Slavic Review*, XX, 3 (1961), 465-476.

6 For a discussion of this relationship cf. P. Bicilli, *Tvorčestvo Čexova. Opyt stilističeskogo analiza*. Godišnik na universiteta sv. Kliment Oxridski; istoriko-filologičeski fakultet, tom. XXXVIII, 6, Sofia, 1942, pp. 15, 27. M. L. Semanova, *Turgenev i Čexov*. Učenye zapiski leningradskogo gosudarstvennogo pedagogičeskogo instituta, t. 134, kafedra russkoj literatury, 1957, pp. 208-209. G. A. Bjalyj, *Čexov i "Zapiski oxotnika,"* Učenye zapiski leningradskogo pedagogičeskogo instituta, t. 76, kafedra russkoj literatury, 1948, p. 186. G. Berdnikov, *A. P. Čexov. Idejnye*

i tvorčeskie iskanija. Moscow-Leningrad, 1961, pp. 60-71.

7 For a discussion of the relationship of this work to Turgenev's cycle, see Berdnikov, *op. cit.*, pp. 77-78.

8 Cf. also the comments on this story in Renato Poggioli, *The Phoenix and the Spider.* Harvard University Press, 1957, pp. 118-119.

9 "Misery" clearly served as a model for Katherine Mansfield's story "Ma Parker," in which the grandmother's sorrow at her grandchild's death also cannot be communicated to anyone. The relationship of these stories is perceptively discussed by Frank O'Connor (*The Lonely Voice,* Cleveland, New York, 1963, pp. 83-84).

10 Here I am indebted to Mr. O'Connor, *op. cit. passim.*

11 For a discussion of Chekhov's treatment of the clergy, see George Ivask, "Čechov and the Russian Clergy," in T. Eekman, ed., *op. cit.* Also Boris Zajcev, *Čexov, literaturnaja biografija.* New York, Chekhov Publishing House, 1954, *passim.*

12 A full, and witty, definition of this term is given by V. Nabokov in his *Nikolai Gogol.* London, 1947, pp. 67-74.

13 For a discussion of the renaissance archetype of the plot, see Bicilli, *op. cit.*, p. 126.

Chapter 3

1 Letter to D. V. Grigorovich, January 12, 1888.

2 See letters to V. Korolenko, Jan-

uary 12, 1888; to Ya. P. Polonski, January 18, 1888; to A. N. Pleshcheev, January 19, 1888.

3 Letter to A. Lazarev-Gruzinski, February 1, 1888.

4 Letter to Pleshcheev, February 3, 1888; to Grigorovich, February 5, 1888.

5 Letter of Pleshcheev to Chekhov, February 8, 1888.

6 Letter of Mikhailovski to Chekhov, February 15, 1888.

7 Cf. V. Šklovskij, *Zametki o proze russkix klassikov.* Moscow, 1955, pp. 428-29.

8 Letter to D. V. Grigorovich, February 5, 1888.

9 Šklovskij, *op. cit.*, pp. 428-29.

10 Cf. Ronald Hingley, *Chekhov; A Biographical and Critical Study.* London, 1950, p. 78.

11 Cf. Chekhov's letter to D. V. Grigorovich, January 12, 1888.

12 Letter to Grigorovich, February 5, 1888.

13 The term "alliteration" is used here in a broader sense to include not only consonant repetitions at the beginning of words, but also at the beginning of syllables. Cf. J. Marouzeau, *Lexique de la terminologie linguistique.* Paris, 1951, p. 14.

14 Note that no differentiation is here made between palatal and non-palatal *l*. In the ensuing remarks about systematic sound repetition, palatalized (soft) and non-palatalized (hard) variants of the same consonant will not be differentiated. I am following here Roman Jakobson's remarks concerning the possibility of intermixing such variant phonemes

in Russian rhymes (e.g. *osen'-sosen, den'-kolen, otnud'-trud*). (Cf. Roman Jakobson, "K lingvističeskomu analizu russkoj rifmy," *Michigan Slavic Materials* No. 1, Ann Arbor, Michigan, 1962, p. 11). Since sound repetition (alliteration, assonance, consonance) must be considered as internal rhyme, this appears to be justified.

Chapter 4

1 Nina A. Toumanova, *Anton Chekhov, The Voice of Twilight Russia*. New York, 1937. Ronald Hingley, *op. cit.* David Magarshak, *Chekhov, the Dramatist*. London, 1952; *Chekhov, A Life*. New York, 1953.
2 Letter to M. V. Kiseleva, January 14, 1887.
3 Letter to M. P. Chekhov, March 8, 1887.
4 Letter to I. L. Leontyev (Shcheglov), January 10, 1888.
5 Letter to A. N. Pleshcheev, February 15, 1890.
6 Letter to Suvorin, December 17, 1890.
7 Letter to V. G. Chertkov, October 30, 1901.
8 Letter to M. O. Menshikov, April 16, 1897.
9 Letter to A. N. Pleshcheev, October 4, 1888.
10 Margarshak, *Chekhov the Dramatist*, p. 121.
11 As early as March 17, 1890, he wrote to the poet Pleshcheev that he had strong doubts about the play. Nine years later he told his friend A. P. Urusov, a great admirer of *The Wood Demon*:

"I hate [*The Wood Demon*] and am attempting to forget about it." (Letter, October 16, 1899)
12 This has been noted by Hingley, *op. cit.*, p. 93.
13 Letter to Suvorin, March 27, 1894.
14 Letter to I. I. Gorbunov-Posadov, November 9, 1889.
15 Letter to M. O. Menshikov, January 28, 1900.
16 Letter to Suvorin, January 4, 1898.
17 Letter to M. Kiseleva, January 14, 1887.
18 *Ibid.*
19 Letter to Suvorin, October 27, 1888.
20 Letter to Suvorin, November 25, 1892.

Chapter 5

1 Letter to Suvorin, March 5, 1889.

Chapter 6

1 Letter to Suvorin, April 1, 1890.
2 Letter to Suvorin, June 16, 1891.
3 Letter by I. I. Gorbunov-Posadov to A. P. Chekhov, July 18, 1891. (The date of this letter is not established with exactitude. PSS, (VII,566) dates it July 18, whereas Gitovič (*op. cit.*, p. 294), who cites it directly from the original, which is in the manuscript division of the Lenin Library, dates it only as "first half of July."

Chapter 7

1 For a discussion of Chekhov's views on the theories of the Naturalist movement, see Leonid Grossman, "Naturalizm Čexova,"

Notes

49

Vestnik Evropy, 7, 1914, pp. 218-247.

2 The interesting question of the influence of Bernard's positivism on Chekhov's aesthetics is discussed by the late A. Roskin in "Zametki o realizme Čexova," in A. Roskin, *A. P. Čexov*. Moscow, 1959, 193-219.

3 Letter to Pleshcheev, September 3, 1889; letter to I. L. Ščeglov, September 18, 1889.

4 Letter to V. A. Tikhonov, September 13, 1889.

5 Letter to Pleshcheev, September 24, 1889.

6 Letter to A. M. Evreynikova, September 24, 1889.

7 A. Goldenvejzer, *Vblizi Tolstogo*. Moscow, 1922, Vol. 1, p. 71.

8 Letter to Chekhov, September 27, 1889.

9 Letter to Pleshcheev, September 14, 1889.

10 Cf. A. Derman, *Anton Pavlovič Čexov*. Moscow, 1939, pp. 91-92. M. Guščin, *Tvorčestvo A. P. Čexova*. Kharkov, 1954, pp. 58-59.

11 D. S. Merežkovskij, "O Čexove," *Vesy*. Moscow, 1905, No. 11, p. 13.

12 Letter to Pleshcheev, September 30, 1889.

13 This is perhaps nowhere so clearly developed as in *The Three Sisters*, especially in the first act, when the backstage remarks of Tuzenbakh, Soleny, and Chebutykin act as a commentary on the conversation among the three sisters, which is carried on in the front of the stage.

14 Letter to Suvorin, February 23, 1891.

Chapter 8

1 Cf. Guščin, *op. cit.*, pp. 119-131; Z. S. Papernyj, *A. P. Čexov, očerk tvorčestva*. Moscow 1954, pp. 67-77.

2 Guščin, *op. cit.*, p. 131.

3 Cf. Papernyj, *op cit.*, p. 78.

4 Guščin, *op. cit.*, pp. 119-131.

5 See T. G. Winner, "Chekhov's *Sea Gull* and Shakespeare's *Hamlet*: A Study of a Dramatic Device," *American Slavic and East European Review*, Vol. XV, February 1956, pp. 103-111.

Chapter 9

1 Letter to Suvorin, March 11, 1892.

2 Notebook I, p. 123, entry 3, PSS, XII, 268.

3 Edmund Wilson, "Preface," Anton Chekhov, *Peasants and Other Stories*. Anchor Books, New York, 1956, p. vii.

4 Letter to Suvorin, November 25, 1893.

5 Letter to Maria P. Chekhov, September 29, 1894.

6 Letter to A. S. Suvorin, December 5, 1894.

7 Guščin, *op. cit.*, pp. 137-144.

8 Notebook No. 1, p. 83, PSS. XII, 239.

Chapter 10

1 *Niva*, Nos. 10-12, October-December, 1896.

2 The same idea is expressed by Andrey Prozorov in *The Three Sisters* (1900-1901): "Our town exists already 200 years, it has a hundred thousand inhabitants, but not a single one who is not

like everybody else, not one zealot . . . not a single learned man or artist, never a single man who would evoke envy or a passionate desire to imitate him." (Act IV)

3 Constance Garnett's translation, slightly amended.

4 Garnett translation, slightly amended.

5 Chekhov, *Rasskazy:* 1. *Mužiki,* 2. *Moja Žizn'.* Sankt Peterburg, 1897.

6 Magazines were subject to preliminary censorship according to a regulation of 1871. (Pares, *op. cit.,* p. 421). Books were not subject to this regulation. For details concerning the objections of the censor, see PSS, IX, 578-580; Gitovič, *op. cit.,* pp. 462-463.

7 From the diary of V. S. Mirolyubov. In Gitovič, *op. cit.,* p. 821.

8 An English version of these two chapters, together with relevant entries from Chekhov's notebooks, can be found in Edmund Wilson's translation, in Anton Chekhov, *Peasants and Other Stories,* Edmund Wilson, ed. New York, Anchor Books, 1956, pp. 281-288.

9 Cf. Letter to Dr. G. I. Rossolimo, January 21, 1900, also S. N. Ščukin, "Vospominanija o Čexove," *Čexov v vospominanijax sovremennikov.* Moscow, 1954, p. 543.

10 Letter to O. L. Knipper, January 2, 1900.

11 Z. Papernyj, in his study of Chekhov, uses this saying as the title of one of the chapters. Papernyj, *op. cit.,* p. 78.

12 See Gitovič, *op. cit.,* p. 614; PSS, IX, p. 614.

Chapter 11

1 Letter to Suvorin, November 12, 1889.

2 A. Chekhov, *Povesti i rasskazy.* Moscow, 1894.

3 Notebook I, p. 47. PSS, XII, p. 220.

4 The decoration was worn both as a pendant and in the button hole, thus accounting for two "Annas" around the neck.

5 Cf. Winner, "Chekhov's *Seagull* and Shakespeare's *Hamlet.* . . ."

6 S. T. Semenov, "O vstrečax s A. P. Čexovym," *Put',* No. 2, February 1913, p. 38.

7 A. Derman, *Tvorčeskij portret Čexova.* Moscow, 1929, p. 266.

Chapter 12

1 Letter to A. F. Marx, September 28, 1899.

2 Notebook I, pp. 56-57, entry 5; PSS, XII, p. 224.

3 Notebook I, p. 62, entry 4; PPS, XII, p. 226.

4 Garnett translation, slightly amended.

5 Garnett translation, slightly amended.

Chapter 13

1 Letter to Suvorin, January 27, 1899, PSS, XVIII, p. 45.

2 E. g. letter by A. S. Buturlin to P. A. Stroev of September 15, 1902, cited in Gitovič, *Letopis',* p. 718.

3 *Krug čtenija* in L. N. Tolstoj, *Polnoe sobranie sochinenij,* Vol. 41. Moscow, 1957, pp. 374-377.

4 *Ibid.*, p. 375.
5 Quoted in Constance Garnett's translation, slightly amended.
6 Tolstoj, *Krug čtenija*, p. 377.
7 Quoted in Constance Garnett's translation.
8 Quoted in Constance Garnett's translation.
9 Quoted in Constance Garnett's translation.
10 Quoted in Constance Garnett's translation.

11 Poggioli, *op. cit.*, pp. 128-130.
12 *Ibid.*, p. 122.
13 *Ibid.*, p. 129.
14 Quoted in Constance Garnett's translation.
15 Quoted in Constance Garnett's translation.
16 Garnett translation, slightly amended.
17 *Russkoe slovo*, No. 185, 1904, quoted in Gitovič, *Letopis'*, p. 789.

Index

About the Author

Professor Winner was born in Czechoslovakia and attended the University of Prague. He came to America in 1939 after the German occupation of Czechoslovakia. He received his B.A. and M.A. from Harvard University, his Ph.D. from Columbia. The author of numerous articles and papers, he also wrote a book called *Kazakh Literature and Oral Art,* published in 1958. Now Professor of Slavic Languages at the University of Michigan, he lives in Ann Arbor with his wife and two daughters.

P

Fl
M